Self-direction in adult learning

A self-directed learner is one who takes responsibility for his or her own learning. The idea is not a new one, but has recently received renewed attention in education circles and has particular significance for the adult education sector. Self-direction represents a significant shift from traditional academic planning. It emphasizes autonomy and personal development and is now considered an important component of courses – not just in independent study or for external degrees, but in, for example, literacy training, continuing professional training, or computer and video technology.

The aim of this book is to provide the reader, whether academic or professional, with a comprehensive synthesis of developments, issues, and practices related to self-direction in learning. Suggesting that self-direction should be considered as a way of life, it presents strategies for facilitating self-directed learning as an instructional method and for enhancing learner self-direction as an aspect of adult personality. Together with an analysis of current research trends, the book has chapters on major issues for practice: institutional perspectives of self-direction, policy issues, international views, and ethical concerns.

Ralph G. Brockett is Associate Professor of Technological and Adult Education at the University of Tennessee, Knoxville. Roger Hiemstra is Professor of Adult Education, Administrative and Adult Studies, Syracuse University.

Routledge Series on Theory and Practice of Adult Education in North America
Edited by Peter Jarvis,
University of Surrey

Self-direction in adult learning

Perspectives on theory, research, and
practice

Ralph G. Brockett
and
Roger Hiemstra

First published 1991
by Routledge
11 New Fetter Lane, London EC4P 4EE

Simultaneously published in the USA and Canada
by Routledge
a division of Routledge, Chapman and Hall, Inc.
29 West 35th Street, New York, NY 10001

Typeset by Michael Mepham, Frome, Somerset
Printed in Great Britain by Biddles Ltd,
Guildford and King's Lynn

British Library Cataloguing in Publication Data
Brockett, Ralph G. 1954 –
    Self-direction in adult learning : perspectives on theory,
    research, and practice. – (Theory and practice of adult
    education in North America series).
    1. United States. Adult education
    I. Title   II. Hiemstra, Roger 1938 –   III. Series
    374.973

    ISBN 0–415–00562–0

Library of Congress Cataloging in Publication Data
Brockett, Ralph Grover.
    Self-direction in adult learning.
    (Theory and practice of adult education in North America Series)
    Includes bibliographical references (p.) and index
    1. Adult learning. I. Hiemstra, Roger.
    II. Title. III. Series.
    LC5225.L42B76   1991   374   90–9090
    ISBN 0–415–00562–0

Contents

Figures and tables

Series editor's note

The Routledge series of books on the Theory and Practice of Adult Education in North America provides practitioners, scholars and students with a collection of studies by eminent scholars of all aspects of adult education throughout the continent. The series already includes books on planning, history, and learning in the workplace. It is intended that others will be added to the list from all the sub-disciplines of adult education. They will cover both theoretical and practical considerations and each will constitute a major contribution to its own specific field of study. Some of these will be symposia while others will consist of single-authored treatises.

This series of books has been well received throughout the adult education world and the current volume is another relevant and significant study. One of the most predominant features of adult education over the past decade has been the study of self-direction, but there have been few books that have examined the theory and practice of self-directed learning. Many papers have been published on this subject and prominent among those authors have been Brockett and Hiemstra. Hence this book extends the debate and opens the discussion in some new and important ways.

Ralph Brockett is an Associate Professor at the University of Tennessee and has played a very active role in the American Association for Adult and Continuing Education in recent years. Roger Hiemstra is Professor of Adult Education at the Syracuse University, he is currently working with a Kellogg sponsored project in which the Syracuse adult education materials are being made more widely available through various technologies. In addition, Roger has been a past chair of the Commission of Professors of Adult Education in the United States and his previous writing is well known to the field.

Peter Jarvis

Preface

Few topics, if any, have received more attention in the field of adult education over the past two decades than self-directed learning. Ever since the 1971 publication of Allen Tough's seminal study, *The Adult's Learning Projects*, fascination with self-planned and self-directed learning has led to one of the most extensive and sustained research efforts in the history of the field. During the same time, a host of new programs and practices, such as external degree programs and computer and video technologies, have gained enthusiastic support from many segments of the field. The time seems appropriate for drawing some meaning from all of these theory, research, and practice developments.

Self-Direction in Adult Learning: Perspectives on Theory, Research, and Practice is our effort to make sense out of this body of knowledge and array of practices that have done so much to shape the current face of adult education in North America and, indeed, throughout much of the world. The purpose of the book is twofold. First, we have attempted to provide a comprehensive synthesis of major developments, trends, issues, and practices relative to self-direction and adult education. Second, we have offered an array of strategies that have direct application to practice. The ideas presented in this book represent over 25 years of combined commitment to better understanding the area of self-direction in adult learning.

In attempting to bridge theory and practice, the book was written with several audiences in mind. First, it was written for practitioners from a wide range of settings concerned with developing programs for adult learners where self-direction is an integral part of the program. Included here are practitioners involved in such areas as independent study/external degree programs, training and development activities, agricultural extension, health and human services, literacy efforts, and continuing professional education. We hope that the book will be of value not only to those who are currently employed in programs where self-direction is stressed, but also for those who may be considering adopting some of these approaches within existing programs. We also hope that the book will be helpful to those readers with a more general interest in learning about areas of current development relative to the education of adults.

Another major audience for which this book is intended is made up of those professors, graduate students, and researchers in adult education who have an interest in the area of self-direction in adult learning. We have tried to provide a comprehensive look at the "state of the art" of self-direction and, thus, believe that the book could be used effectively either as a primary text for courses on self-direction in adult learning or as a supplemental text for courses on adult learning or current issues in adult education. In addition, it is our hope that the book has generated many questions that are worthy of further investigation; thus, the book is also intended as a tool for researchers exploring the territory of self-direction.

The 13 chapters of the book are arranged into five sections, or parts. Part I, "Introduction," consists of two chapters. Chapter 1 sets the stage for the book by presenting scenarios for three types of learners, in order to illustrate that self-direction is a way of life. We also present and discuss a number of popular myths that have helped to create confusion about self-direction and its potential for adult learners. In the second chapter, we define self-direction and offer a model designed to help alleviate some of the confusion surrounding the many ways in which self-directed learning and related terms have been described. In this model, we suggest that self-direction can best be understood as both an instructional method and as a personality dimension.

Part II, "The Underlying Knowledge Base," consists of three chapters that critically examine the research literature on self-direction. Here, we look at the various ways in which self-direction has been studied and provide a critical analysis of this research.

The next two chapters, which comprise Part III, "Process and personal orientation", are intended to bridge theory and practice. These chapters present strategies for facilitating self-directed learning as an instructional method and for enhancing learner self-direction as an aspect of adult personality. Thus, each chapter emphasizes one of the dimensions presented in the model in Chapter 2.

In Part IV, "Fostering Opportunities for Self-Direction in Adult Learning," we present four chapters that address what we believe to be major issues for practice. Chapters in this section focus on self-direction in institutionally-based adult education programs, policy issues, international perspectives on self-direction, and ethical issues.

Part V, "A Glance at the Future," begins with a hypothetical scenario of what a family of the near future might look like if they embrace the ideals of self-direction. And the final chapter includes a number of recommendations that we believe are important in creating future growth of self-direction ideals.

Finally, it might help to put this book into perspective by knowing a little more about our own journey over the past several years in trying to better understand the idea of self-direction in adult learning. We both have carried out and supervised research studies where we have watched with amazement how alive people become when they begin to talk about their own learning and how they have been able to take control of these efforts. When they come to realize that it is "okay" to be the major planner of such learning, that enthusiasm generally jumps another notch. The enjoyment and thrill of seeing this self-discovery has led us to talk about self-direction at professional meetings, to conduct workshops on the topic, and to search continuously for new ways to enhance opportunities for self-direction within the university classes we teach. This book is an attempt to document our "odyssey" in the search for new and creative ways to embrace the ideals of self-direction in adult learning. If we have been able to stimulate awareness further, by conveying our enthusiasm for self-direction and our expectations for future promise, we are doubly gratified.

We would like to offer special thanks to Peter Jarvis, Series Editor for Routledge, for believing in our project, and to Sue Joshua, Editor for Routledge, for her advice and assistance. We are especially gratified for the editorial support and advice offered by our colleague Mary Beth Hinton. A special thanks is owed to Wanda Chasteen, who provided valuable assistance in preparing the final manuscript. We would also like to thank the many graduate student colleagues from five different universities with whom we have worked on research projects, in classes, and during workshops; our own ideas have been vastly refined over time as a result of these interactions. Finally, we wish to acknowledge the support given to us by our families: Patricia and Megan Brockett; and Janet, Nancy, and David Hiemstra. They have lived with us through the struggles and the joys of our work in self-direction, and this book is our way of saying "thanks."

Ralph G. Brockett
Knoxville, Tennessee

Roger Hiemstra
Syracuse, New York

Part I
Introduction

Self-direction has been one of the most exciting topics to emerge relative to adult learning in the past two decades. As a way of introducing the topic, it is stressed that self-direction is not a fad; rather it is a way of life for most adults. In the opening chapter, three hypothetical cases are presented in order to illustrate this point. Also, the chapter includes a look at self-direction throughout history and a discussion of several common myths that have often brought confusion to what self-direction means.

Chapter 2 presents a conceptual framework for better understanding the concept of self-direction. There has been much confusion over what is meant by self-direction. In this chapter, the Personal Responsibility Orientation (PRO) model is presented as a tool for better understanding this distinction. The PRO model is premised on the idea that individuals taking personal responsibility for their learning is central to understanding self-direction. From this, it is possible to recognize that self-direction can be seen as both an instructional method (self-directed learning) *and* a personality characteristic (learner self-direction). Also, the PRO model stresses the importance of understanding the social context in which learning takes place. This model serves as a framework for the remainder of the book.

1 A way of life

Mary's interest in genealogy grew slowly out of the enjoyment of hearing her grandparents talk about the "old country" and all the interesting characters on the family tree. However, high school, college, first job, more college, and marriage all took considerable energy. Then, soon after moving with her family for a college teaching position, she read about a course in genealogy offered through the local community college. Wanting some variety in her otherwise heavy schedule of juggling home and work responsibilities, Mary enrolled in the 8-week course.

Taking the course revealed to Mary a whole world of ideas, resources, and other people interested in tracing their family backgrounds. However, it was after the course ended that Mary's real learning about genealogy began. She started reading everything she could get her hands on about how to gather genealogical information. Her university library had an excellent genealogy section with experienced librarians eager to show people how to use the resources. Mary also filled out many forms requesting archival information and sent them to the Genealogical Society in Salt Lake City for their computer searches.

As her family information began to accumulate, she had the bonus of communicating with relatives not only in the United States, but in other countries as well. In addition, Mary had an opportunity to visit with a second cousin who was gathering genealogical information on one portion of the family tree. She also began to communicate with people she did not know, but who happened to share her family name, about possible connections with other families. Each exchange of information led to more clues. She believed, too, that she helped her second cousin gain some new searching skills.

Over the past 15 years Mary has continued gathering information about the family and about how to do genealogical work. She wrote a 40-page summary for her relatives, visited two of the countries where ancestors had lived, and even taught a non-credit genealogy class twice. Her visit to one of the countries was especially educational, resulting in some new and valuable information. She also stimulated a third newly met cousin to begin genealogy work on the family name. In short, her independent genealogical research has become a way of life.

Neal's approach to life and learning was quite different from Mary's, and it has changed dramatically in the past 15 years. When he retired at age 62 from an engineering position, Neal didn't really have a hobby, unless one counted the occasional golf game he played with colleagues. He had always worked very hard, and his wife's sudden death two years before he retired had only intensified his need to stay very busy with work. However, his son John often voiced concern about Neal's working too hard, and a growing disenchantment with his firm's emphasis on weapons development prompted Neal to jump at an offer for early retirement.

For the first few weeks Neal enjoyed rising late, working in the garden, cleaning out the long-neglected attic, and visiting his grandchildren. He woke one morning, though, and realized that he wanted something a little more challenging out of life. He visited a senior citizen center twice, but tired of the card playing so popular with many of the men there. Then one morning he drove to the local library hoping to find an interesting book. By accident he stopped in the magazine room and picked up a recent issue of a science periodical. His life suddenly took a large turn in direction.

The magazine featured several articles on alternative power development in the United States and throughout the world. As he read about various experiments, his mind wandered to the ranch house that his son and family occupied. They had a ranch house on a small hill in the country. There were about 10 acres of mostly weeds, scrub trees, and large rocks surrounding the house; a small trout stream draining from the nearby hills wound through the property. Musing to himself that some of the experiments might work at that site, he called his son that afternoon to talk about starting an alternative power project. John agreed enthusiastically, as he had complained for years about the high price of electricity that seemed a part of living in the country.

Neal then began reading everything he could find on alternative power. With his engineering background, he soon discovered the need for more technical information than the popular press could provide. He attended two conferences devoted to alternative power, toured some experimental homes, and began to correspond by letter with people in other states and countries about what they were doing.

The first project he tackled involved wind as an energy source. He had read about a new type of windmill design developed in The Netherlands that showed promise. There was a flat, open field behind the house, so Neal designed and installed a windmill there similar to The Netherlands' prototype. After Neal conquered some design and regulation problems, the windmill began generating enough electricity at peak wind conditions to meet about 20 percent of John's needs.

Neal then spent several months clearing brush around a portion of the stream where he installed a miniature water-driven turbine patterned after a Colorado experiment. The turbine generated enough electricity to pump water to the garden area, meeting another 10 percent of John's power requirements. Neal's next task was to install a solar panel on John's roof that now meets most of the family's hot water needs. Meanwhile, throughout these activities Neal has continued to read as much as he can about alternative power. He has actually become somewhat of an expert and a local celebrity. He has been interviewed on local television, taught a course on alternative energy sources, and is now writing a book about the topic.

Alice's independence as a learner was slow to develop as compared with Neal. Alice had been a home economics field-worker for a family planning organization in her native country, Nigeria, for eight years. Her college education in home economics education had consisted of a four-year program with grades that placed her in the top one-third of the class. Alice had earned the respect of her teachers as a hardworking student who would make an excellent professional in the home economics field.

Alice was quite ambitious, however, and by the end of 10 years she wished to leave field work and serve in some administrative capacity with the national headquarters in Lagos. She applied for federal support and was granted a fellowship for advanced education. She then applied to several universities in the United States and was accepted into a masters degree program in adult education in one of them.

Upon arriving at the university she began to experience several frustrations. Finding an affordable place to live within walking distance of the campus was confusing and difficult. The International Student Office eventually helped her find a place, but those first three days were nerve-racking. Then she met with her graduate advisor and had a difficult time understanding the program's philosophy: students were expected to take major responsibility in designing their graduate programs by choosing their own courses, final advisors, and even intensive examination questions. Although Alice understood the words of her advisor and the written materials, her past experience in a traditional academic program had not prepared her very well for what was being described.

Her biggest shock came when she met with the instructors for the three courses she was to take that semester. They also described a self-directed teaching and learning approach where she was expected to assess her own needs and complete a learning contract for each course. She had decided to come to the United States to study adult education because she believed that she would find the best professors there, and now they were asking her to select her own learning path. It simply did not make sense.

Alice was confused for the first two weeks of the semester, and after discussions with two of the instructors she met with her advisor who was also the instructor of the third course. Alice described how other students seemed comfortable with the teaching approach, and were even working together on learning activities; but she was concerned that she would not get from the courses what she had come to learn. After talking about the courses and the teaching approach, the advisor suggested that she go a little slower than she had originally planned in the first semester, and that the two of them should meet frequently during that time . Alice agreed to drop one of the courses, and her advisor agreed to work with her on needs assessment and to help her complete her learning contracts for the other courses.

The concept of learning contracts proved to be perhaps the most confusing aspect of the courses for Alice. However, discussion with her advisor and with the other course instructor helped her develop a plan for learning that followed quite closely some of the specific options described by the instructors in their course materials. By the time the courses were finished, and after Alice had heard other students describe their own initial frustrations with the teaching and learning process used by the faculty for the adult education program she had begun to understand how she could carry out learning activities by herself. She realized that she actually had learned a great deal in both courses and that those learnings had taken her well beyond her initial skill and knowledge levels.

During the two adult education courses that she took in the second semester, Alice felt much more comfortable filling out the learning contracts, although she still asked several questions of other students and her instructors. In fact, the third course she took that semester was not in adult education, and the teaching and learning philosophy was quite similar to what she had experienced in her previous formal education in Nigeria. To her surprise, she found herself feeling frustrated at having to fulfill many requirements with little relevance to what she would need professionally. This helped her to understand the value of a teaching approach that encourages learners to take more responsibility for decision-making.

During the last year of her degree program, she became quite comfortable with self-directed learning. She began to develop learning plans in adult education courses that deviated markedly from the more structured options suggested by the instructors. She also began to assert herself more in courses outside of the adult education program by talking with instructors about altering course requirements to better meet her professional needs. By the end of her graduate program Alice had become a successful self-directed learner. During her final intensive exams she described how she was going to take her new learning skills and apply them in her future job.

While the situations of Mary, Neal, and Alice are very different, they share some common threads. Each of them made a conscious choice to take responsibility for their own learning. For each of these individuals, self-direction in learning has become a way of life.

The field of adult education has long embraced such ideas as autonomy, independence, and personal development of adult learners. These ideas are implicit in such terms as lifelong learning, self-directed learning, self-planned learning, independent study, distance education, learning projects, andragogy, and self-directed learning readiness. All of these in some way stress the role of individual learners in the learning process.

Thus, the three examples chosen to begin this book illustrate some of the possible ways in which an individual comes to use self-directed learning approaches. There are in reality many possible routes. In fact, we have observed that no two learners approach self-directed learning in the same way. Perhaps this is why the concept of self-directed learning has become so popular in recent years among adult education scholars. This also is why the concept has existed in some form for hundreds of years. The purpose of this chapter will be to describe the phenomenon of self-direction in learning, which has become a way of life for a great many people.

A HISTORICAL LOOK

In North America, many adult education scholars trace the current interest in such topics as learning projects, andragogy, and self-directed learning to Houle's (1961) typology of goal, activity, and learning orientations among adult learners, or to Johnstone and Rivera's (1965) seminal work on adult education participation. However, the idea of self-direction, under the guise of numerous names, has existed from classical antiquity to the present. In fact, Kulich (1970) noted that, prior to the widespread development of schools, self-education was the primary way for individuals to deal with happenings going on about them.

Self-education, according to Kulich, played an important part in the lives of the Greek philosophers. Socrates described himself as a self-learner who capitalized on opportunities to learn from those around him. Plato believed that the ultimate goal of education for the young should be the development of an ability to function as a self-learner in adulthood. Aristotle emphasized the importance of self-realization, a potential wisdom that can be developed either with or without the guidance of a teacher.

Kulich (1970) illustrates numerous other examples of self-education throughout history. Alexander the Great was said to have carried the works of Homer with him when he travelled. Caesar set time aside daily for writing and study. Erasmus of Rotterdam's *Study of Christian Philosophy*, published in 1516, offered guidelines for self-education. In the seventeenth century, René Descartes, in his *Discourse on Mind*, described how he abandoned formal study at an early age and gained his education by experiencing and observing the world around him and by reflecting on these experiences. Newsom (1977) examined the role of "self-directed lifelong learning" in London between the years 1558–1640. He concluded that there were many opportunities for self-directed learning during this period through private tutors, lectures, books, libraries, and schools – for those persons who had the time and money to take advantage of these opportunities.

Self-direction is also clearly reflected throughout the history of the United States. Long (1976) addressed the history of adult education prior to the American Revolution. According to Long, the social conditions that existed in Colonial America, combined with a lack of formal educational institutions, led many persons to learn on their own during this period.

Self-directed learners in Colonial America had a wide range of learning resources from which to choose. They relied heavily on the "oral tradition", which was supplemented by the use of letters, diaries, and written records of the times that could be passed on orally to others. Societies and associations also provided a wide range of opportunities to self-directed adult learners. However, Long puts the main emphasis on available printed materials. Personal libraries were common among persons wealthy enough to afford a collection of books. Subscription libraries, whereby patrons paid a specified amount for the use of services, made libraries accessible to a greater number of people. Almanacs offered the self-directed learner in Colonial America a plethora of information, much as they do today. Newspapers helped mobilize political activities leading to the Revolution. Magazines also proved to be a valuable resource for the self-directed learner in Colonial America.

Benjamin Franklin was an important example of a self-directed learner, and some consider him to be the "patron saint" of adult education in the United States. He was involved in discussion clubs, library activities, and helping others with learning efforts. The Junto, a discussion club organized in Philadelphia in 1727 (Grattan, 1955), utilized reading and discussion as a means for intellectual development. Franklin's numerous contributions are, to a great extent, a result of various self-education efforts.

Serious thinking about self-directed learning took place some 150 years ago. For example, Craik's *Pursuit of Knowledge Under Difficulties* (1840) describes the self-directed learning behaviors of many people. As Six (1989a) notes, through a variety of examples Craik demonstrates:

(a) the practicability of self-directed learning, (b) the most effective methods for self-instruction, and (c) the potency of a determined self-directed learner in overcoming barriers to learning. Moreover, he [Craik] asserts that success or failure in an act of learning depends more upon the learner than upon any set of circumstances in which the learner may be placed.

(Six, 1987: 26)

Another early author was Hosmer, whose 1847 work entitled *Self-Education* makes a distinction between what he referred to as self-initiated learning acts and other educational forms. His definition of self-education is offered in Chapter 2.

More recently, in 1980, Gibbons and his colleagues demonstrated that self-directed education was foundational to the success of several past notables who had completed less formal education than the norm for their time. Using a content analysis of their biographies, Gibbons, *et al.* (1980) studied twenty people, including such individuals as Amelia Earhart, Harry Truman, Frank Lloyd Wright, Malcolm X, and Walt Disney. Each of these individuals made important contributions to their field of expertise despite a lack of formal training beyond the high school level.

Clearly, self-direction in learning has played an important, though sometimes easy to overlook, role in history. Today, the term and, more important, the basic ideals underlying the notion, have been embraced by educators and learners throughout the world. What are some of the reasons for this?

As we emphasize in the definition and conceptual framework that will be presented in the next chapter, we believe that self-direction in learning is a combination of forces both within and outside the individual that stress the learner accepting ever-increasing responsibility for decisions associated with the learning process. Rogers (1983) saw this as the personal process of learning how to learn, how to change, and how to adapt. Smith (1982) applied this concept of "learning how to learn" to the adult education field. Bruner's (1966) perspective was similar to Rogers, and to the point we are making in this book. He goes so far as to define teaching as "the provisional state that has as its object to make the learner ... self-sufficient" (Bruner, 1966: 53). Kidd suggested that "the purpose of adult education, or any kind of education, is to make the subject a continuing 'inner-directed', self-operating learner" (Kidd, 1973: 47).

Tough (1979) is another North American scholar associated with self-directed learning because of his seminal work on adults' learning projects. He found that learners prefer to assume considerable responsibility for planning and directing their learning activities if given the choice. This has since been substantiated by many researchers. Chapter 3 will provide much more detail about learning projects research and its foundational importance to our current understanding of self-direction in learning.

Knowles (1975) describes several reasons for advocating this development of "self-directed" skill. These include the following: (a) individuals who take initiative in learning are more likely to retain what is learned than the passive learner; (b) taking initiative in learning is more in tune with our natural processes of psychological development; and (c) many recent educational developments actually place the responsibility for learning right on the shoulders of learners. Knowles provides a long-term reason that cuts across various cultural boundaries and provides a rationale for why self-direction in learning applies to a wide variety of educational situations:

To sum up: the 'why' of self-directed learning is survival – your own survival as an individual, and also the survival of the human race. Clearly, we are not talking here about something that would be nice or desirable; neither are we talking about some new educational fad. We are talking about a basic human competence – the ability to learn on one's own – that has suddenly become a prerequisite for living in this new world.

(Knowles, 1975: 16–17)

We believe it is important to add that individuals will vary in their readiness for self-direction thereby requiring varying degrees of assistance by facilitators, especially as self-directed learning skills are developing. Another point is that self-directed learning will not always be the best way to learn for certain people. As we have noted elsewhere, "perhaps it is more appropriate to think of self-directed learning as an ideal mode of learning for certain individuals and for certain situations" (Brockett and Hiemstra, 1985: 33).

TEN MYTHS ASSOCIATED WITH SELF-DIRECTION IN LEARNING

As one looks at the literature of adult education that has accumulated over the past two decades, a number of what we believe are myths or misconceptions regarding self-direction in learning have emerged. These myths have often added to the confusion over the meaning of self-direction and its implications for adult education practice. At least ten such myths can readily be identified. The purpose of this section is to discuss these myths and to set the scene for dispelling them throughout the remainder of the book.

Myth 1: Self-directedness is an all or nothing concept

Some educators and some learners have come rushing to embrace self-directedness as though it were finally *the* answer to finding fulfillment in life.

It should be obvious that learning styles and approaches will vary with particular individuals and learning situations. In addition, as people face new learning challenges, they will find differing needs for outside assistance, personal initiative, and individual reflection in terms of their learning activities. Thus, as we have noted elsewhere (Brockett and Hiemstra, 1985), self-directedness is best viewed as a continuum rather than as some dichotomous model. Here, self-direction is viewed as a characteristic that exists, to a greater or lesser degree, in all persons and in all learning situations.

The complexity of this continuum view, however, can be illustrated when looking at some of the research on cognitive styles. Even (1982), for example, notes that people who exhibit field-independent learning styles are likely to benefit from a self-directed emphasis, since field-dependent learners who typically require a more social orientation, are not as likely to be successful with self-initiated learning activities. Yet, field-dependent learners also tend to prefer more structured, formal learning environments, which is inconsistent with much of what is typically associated with self-direction. Thus, the distinction is not as clear cut as it may appear at first.

The fact that learners will be at different places on the continuum has implications for facilitators and for learners, especially as learners plan and carry out their educational efforts or move toward higher levels of personal self-direction. In Chapters 6 and 7 we explore these implications.

Myth 2: Self-direction implies learning in isolation

For purposes of this book, and especially in light of the teaching and learning process detailed in Chapter 6, we are referring to learning based on a preference for taking individual responsibility. However, we do not necessarily equate self-direction with learning that is independent of a facilitator or of some outside resource. In other words, we believe it is a mistake to automatically associate self-directed learning with learning in isolation or learning on an independent basis (Hiemstra, 1985c). Moore (1973: 669) also argues that a self-directed learner is not "an intellectual Robinson Crusoe, castaway and shut off in self-sufficiency". Brookfield (1985c: 7) believes this, too, noting that "it is evident that no act of learning can be self-directed if we understand self-direction as meaning the absence of external sources of assistance".

An assumption often made by those looking at the concept of self-directedness for the first time is that learning takes place primarily in isolation or only through limited contact with others. Some instructors believe that this would mean sending a student away from a group or formal setting to do independent study. Another example is the stereotype of a person cloistered in the corner of a library reading a book, or at home using a package of individualized learning materials.

However, self-direction in learning does not necessarily mean learning in isolation. What it does mean is that the learner assumes primary responsibility for and control over decisions about planning, implementing, and evaluating the learning experience. This may happen in isolation – or in a large group, or when two or more learners share responsibilities for their learning. Hiemstra (1975) and Baghi (1979), for example, found that learners often go to others as resources for their self-directed efforts. Brookfield (1980) also found that learners working part of the time in isolation often come together in what he calls a "fellowship of learning" where competition among learners is balanced with a degree of cooperation and sharing.

Myth 3: Self-direction is just another adult education fad

The 1970s and 1980s in the United States, and to some extent throughout the world, have produced what some refer to as the "me" generation, known for hedonism and self-centeredness. Self-direction in learning may be tied to such notions in some people's minds. In addition, the adult education field has not been immune from fads or from short-lived movements. Competency-based adult learning efforts, group process methods, and even the "Great Books" movement are examples of the ebb and flow of adult learner involvement.

However, the notion of individuals taking personal responsibility for their learning and the ideal of a facilitator providing guidance for self-directed efforts have been around for some time. As we noted earlier in this chapter, the history of self-direction in learning is long and enduring. These notions have been strengthened by research during the past two decades, and it is our contention that such research will continue for some time. While terms such as "self-direction in learning" or "self-directed learning" may be replaced at some point in the future, the emphasis on personal responsibility and the belief in the never-ending potential of humans will survive and, indeed, thrive, because they lie at the heart of adult education as a field of practice and study.

Myth 4: Self-direction is not worth the time required to make it work

One myth frequently bandied about reflects beliefs that there are no special benefits to promoting self-directedness or individualization of the teaching and learning process. So why go to all the time and bother necessary for success? In fact, as is described in subsequent chapters, considerable "up-front" time is required by instructors and learners in organizing the learning activities. However, we believe that the benefits far outweigh the effort required by learners and facilitators.

For example, from our experience there appears to be a greater transfer of learning from one situation, or course, to another – of both knowledge obtained and self-direction skills. These skills enable learners to diagnose needs, secure resources, and carry out learning activities. Knowles (1975) believed this, too, and Skager (1979: 519) noted that an essential feature of self-directed learners appears to be "a willingness to initiate and maintain systematic learning on their own initiative". We also believe that other positive educational results come from self-direction in learning, such as increased retention, greater interest in continued learning, greater interest in the subject, and more positive attitudes toward the instructor, and we hope that this can be verified by future research.

Another benefit is enhanced self-concept (Brockett, 1983c; Sabbaghian, 1980). For example, some students who are not as strong or vocal as others because of shyness or a lower self-concept, in the self-directed setting can progress at their own rate and surpass what they might do when following the same path as everyone else, or a path set by an instructor. Thus, learning to develop personal patterns for approaching and solving problems will enhance one's confidence and concept of self as a learner.

Myth 5: Self-directed learning activities are limited primarily to reading and writing

We have actually found quite the opposite to be true. A wide variety of learning activities and approaches generally are used to encourage learners to take personal responsibility for their own learning. The following are only some of the activities used by those learners with whom we have associated that go beyond just readings, discussions, and writings related to a subject matter: (a) personal investigation of a topic using interviews as a basic information source; (b) self-guided reading, where the instructor or some other person in a mentoring role provides some guidance and evaluative support as needed or as required; (c) participation in a study group, where three or more people cooperate in finding information and compiling a report on a topic through reading, research, and discussion; (d) involvement in an agency visitation or study tour of some organization; (e) completion of a practicum or internship in an agency or with some expert; (f) studying a topic through correspondence with an instructor or some expert; and (g) engaging in a debate via on-line computer conferencing software. In addition, the literature contains descriptions of several other individualized study methods, such as learning packages/kits, programmed instruction, and computer or electronic assisted materials.

Myth 6: Facilitating self-direction is an easy way out for teachers

For some, self-direction implies that the facilitator sits back and takes a passive approach to teaching. The image of the instructor who says "go ahead and do whatever you want to do" comes to mind. Taken to an extreme, this means that self-direction can be a "cop-out" for instructors who, either deliberately or out of ignorance, misuse the concept for their own benefit or to manipulate learners, rather than as a way to better serve them. In reality, however, the successful facilitator of self-directed learning assumes a very active role that involves negotiation, exchange of views, securing needed resources, and validation of outcomes.

Effective facilitators establish a special relationship with learners that, while sometimes painful and frustrating (Brookfield, 1986), is most often rewarding for both learner and facilitator. Hiemstra (1988a) refers to this as a "learning partnership" that must develop between participants in the teaching-learning transaction. In order for this to happen, though, it is necessary to move beyond the view of the facilitator as a passive observer to one who actively works to ensure a high-quality learning experience and, as Brookfield (1987) notes, even the promotion of critical thinking by learners.

Myth 7: Self-directed learning is limited primarily to those settings where freedom and democracy prevail

In some circumstances learners experience external pressures to learn. Incarcerated people, Adult Basic Education students, and those involved in mandatory continuing education programs, for example, typically will think much differently, at least initially, about their involvement than a person voluntarily taking an evening course or participating in a graduate program of adult education. Those who are studying under some sort of duress or who have been used to a teacher directed and controlled experience may need much more time than others to accept that they can take personal responsibility for much of their learning. In addition, as we demonstrate in Chapter 10, self-direction in learning takes place in a variety of societal settings throughout the world.

There also are times in any person's life when the desire to be self-directed will be low or difficult to maintain. These are times when the learner wants an instructor or some expert to give the information directly, or to present it in a well-written booklet. However, we believe that the value of self-directed approaches in freeing learners far outweighs any problems from slower starts or heavier loads on instructors. In fact, we have observed that authority-based approaches frequently force individuals into learning modes that may not be conducive to maximum learning. Thus, we hope that one of the results of this book will be the inspiration of learners and facilitators to utilize self-directed approaches.

Myth 8: Self-direction in learning is limited primarily to white, middle-class adults

Brookfield (1984c, 1985b, 1988) contends that self-directed learning is limited primarily to white, middle-class adults. Although much of the research noted in Chapters 3, 4, and 5 focuses on white adults with considerable education and economic means, other research has demonstrated that various groups are capable of self-direction in learning. For example, Baghi (1979), Denys (1975), Field (1979), Guglielmino and Guglielmino (1983, 1988), Hassan (1982), Heisel (1985), Long and Agyekum (1983, 1984, 1988), Penland (1978), Ralston (1979, 1981), Shackelford (1983), and Umoren (1978) are only some of the researchers reporting results or conclusions based on self-directed learning research with black adults.

Brockett (1985c) also responds to Brookfield's criticism and suggests that most of the considerable research on hard-to-reach adults was not included in the evidence cited by Brookfield. Caffarella and O'Donnell also point out that the evidence goes well beyond white adults. They note (1988: 45) that various studies confirmed "that the majority of adults, from all walks of life, are actively involved in self-directed learning projects, though the number of projects involved and the amount of time spent on those projects were quite diverse." Chapter 10 provides some illustrations of self-directed activity in various locations around the world and with a variety of people.

Myth 9: Self-directed learning will erode the quality of institutional programs

It is true that many institutions do not support self-directed learning. In some instances this is a result of a lack of understanding about the potential of self-direction in learning. In other instances, this is because they embrace the traditional notion that teachers are experts and that learners should be willing receivers of that expert knowledge. However, as Brockett (1988a) notes, that traditional outlook is safe, but also static. Such a circumstance may make it difficult for teachers and learners to obtain full support for self-directed approaches, thereby potentially affecting quality.

Some learners will take advantage of a self-directed learning process and not work to their maximum. In addition, it will be difficult for some instructors to place full trust in the ability of learners to take responsibility for their own learning. Obviously, much of the responsibility for quality must reside with the learner in situations where individual initiative is expected.

Fortunately, our experience has been that when the trust is given, the vast majority of learners will work to their maximum and seek out high-quality learning experiences. Knowles and Associates (1984) are among the growing numbers demonstrating how excellent learning experiences are possible when self-directed attitudes prevail.

Myth 10: Self-directed learning is the best approach for adults

This myth may appear to support the book's main thrust. However, we believe it important to acknowledge potential problems in never questioning when to use self-directed learning approaches. Certainly we support the value of promoting self-direction in adult learning, but we recognize that there will be times when utilizing an individualized teaching approach (we describe how to individualize instruction in Chapter 6) may not be appropriate or expedient.

Collins also is concerned that the facilitation of self-directed learning, especially for individuals with restricted freedom (i.e. prison inmates), can become a vehicle for promoting accommodation, rather than promoting individual autonomy: "Thus, attention is diverted away from the need for a genuine emancipatory practice of adult education on behalf of those whose interests are most poorly served within existing power relations" (Collins, 1988: 107).

While Collins's philosophy regarding the expected or suspected use of self-directed approaches or management tools is different from ours, we believe it is important always to ask both practical and ethical questions regarding when it may not be prudent to utilize an individualizing approach. Chapter 11 provides more discussion on some of the ethical considerations that we believe should be made.

CONCLUSION

Self-direction in learning is a way of life. It is not merely a fad that fits in with the emphasis on self-development and self-help that have been popular over the last decade or so. Nor is it the latest in a series of current trends in adult education that will likely pass within a few years. The idea of self-education or taking responsibility for one's own learning is clearly rooted in history and, in our view, the current popularity of self-directed learning reflects the adult education field's *deliberate* effort to embrace these values and incorporate them into the mainstream of practice.

In this chapter, we have identified and attempted to dispel several myths relative to self-direction in learning. These myths have grown largely out of a misunderstanding of what self-direction in adult learning is about. The remainder of the book is intended to replace misconceptions with information and to raise questions that can guide us toward a future wherein self-direction is, in fact, clearly in the mainstream of adult education theory, research, and practice.

2 A conceptual framework for understanding self-direction in adult learning

Self-direction in learning is a way of life. This idea, which served as the backdrop for Chapter 1, may be self-evident to many readers. Yet much of what we do as educators of adults runs contrary to this basic idea. The myths presented in Chapter 1 illustrate some of the ways in which we, as educators, sometimes misunderstand or misuse our roles in a way that may run contrary to this "way of life." It is our view that much of this misunderstanding and misuse is due, in large part, to confusion that exists relative to what is meant by self-direction in adult learning.

In this chapter, we work to alleviate some of this confusion by providing a conceptual framework that can help to clarify the concept of self-direction relative to the process of adult learning. We begin by looking at various ways in which self-direction and related concepts have been defined. We then offer our own definition of self-direction in adult learning. Finally, we share a conceptual framework that emphasizes distinctions between self-directed learning as an instructional method and learner self-direction as a personality characteristic.

SELF-DIRECTION IN ADULT LEARNING: A MISUNDERSTOOD CONCEPT

As with so many of the ideas found within the study and practice of adult education, self-direction in learning is fraught with confusion. This confusion is compounded by the many related concepts that are often used either interchangeably or in a similar way. Examples include self-directed learning, self-planned learning, self-teaching, autonomous learning, independent study, and distance education. Yet these terms offer varied, though often subtly different, emphases. To illustrate these differences, several views of self-direction can be compared and contrasted.

An early view of self-education

In the nineteenth century, Hosmer (1847) described self-education in the following way:

> The common opinion seems to be that self-education is distinguished by nothing but the manner of its acquisition. It is thought to denote simply acquirements made without a teacher, or at all events without oral instruction – advantages always comprehended in the ordinary cause of education. But this merely negative circumstance, however important..., is only one of several particulars equally characteristic of self-education.... Besides the absence of many, or all of the usual facilities for learning, there are at least three things peculiar to this enterprise, namely: the longer time required, the wider range of studies, and the higher character of its object.
>
> (Hosmer, 1847: 42)

A lifelong learning perspective

It is important to think of self-direction in learning from a lifelong learning perspective. Lifelong learning, as will be noted in Chapter 8, is not the exclusive domain of adult educators; it refers to learning that takes place across the entire lifespan. This view is supported by Kidd in the following passage: "It has often been said that the purpose of adult education, or of any kind of education, is to make the subject a continuing, 'inner-directed' self-operating learner" (Kidd, 1973: 47).

Another way of looking at self-directed learning has been provided by Mocker and Spear (1982). Using a 2 x 2 matrix, based on learner vs. institution control over the objectives (purposes) and means (processes) of learning, Mocker and Spear identify four categories comprising lifelong learning: *formal*, where "learners have no control over the objectives or means of their learning"; *nonformal*, where "learners control the objectives but not the means"; *informal*, where "learners control the means but not the objectives"; and *self-directed*, where "learners control both the objectives and the means" (Mocker and Spear, 1982: 4).

Self-directed learning and schooling

Looking at self-direction as it relates to schooling for young people, Della-Dora and Blanchard offer the following view:

> Self-directed learning refers to characteristics of schooling which should

distinguish education in a democratic society from school in autocratic societies.

(Della-Dora and Blanchard, 1979: 1)

However, in describing the nature of self-education, Gibbons and Phillips offer a different view of self-education and schooling:

Self-education occurs outside of formal institutions, not inside them. The skills can be taught and practiced in schools, teachers can gradually transfer the authority and responsibility for self-direction to students, and self-educational acts can be simulated, but self-education can only truly occur when people are not compelled to learn and others are not compelled to teach them – especially not to teach them a particular subject-matter curriculum. While schools can prepare students for a life of self-education, true self-education can only occur when a person chooses to learn what he can also decide not to learn.

(Gibbons and Phillips, 1982: 69)

This second view reinforces the idea of learning as a lifelong process. Though the focus of this book is on self-direction in learning during adulthood, it is important to recognize that self-direction is not restricted solely to learning in the adult years.

A learning process perspective

Self-direction in adulthood has often been described as a learning process, with specific phases, in which the learner assumes primary control. Tough (1979), for instance, has emphasized the concept of self-*planned* learning. His research was concerned with a specific portion of the process: the "planning and deciding" aspects of learning.

Using the related concept of the "autonomous learner," Moore has described such an individual as one who can do the following:

identify his learning need when he finds a problem to be solved, a skill to be acquired, or information to be obtained. He is able to articulate his need in the form of a general goal, differentiate that goal into several specific objectives, and define fairly explicitly his criteria for successful achievement. In implementing his need, he gathers the information he desires, collects ideas, practices skills, works to resolve his problems, and achieves his goals. In evaluating, the learner judges the appropriateness of newly acquired skills, the adequacy of his solutions, and the quality of his new ideas and knowledge.

(Moore, 1980: 23)

Still another view of self-direction that stresses the phases of a learning process has been offered by Knowles. His view has been perhaps the most frequently used in the adult education literature to date:

> In its broadest meaning, 'self-directed learning' describes a process in which individuals take the initiative, with or without the help of others, in diagnosing their learning needs, formulating learning goals, identifying human and material resources for learning, choosing and implementing appropriate learning strategies, and evaluating learning outcomes.
>
> (Knowles, 1975: 18)

An evolving perspective

Not only do individuals differ in their views of self-direction in learning, but each individual's view is likely to change over time. Thus, when considering definitions, it is not only necessary to understand *who* has offered a particular definition, but *when* it was offered. This evolutionary process can be illustrated through the writings of Stephen Brookfield. For example, in 1980, Brookfield used the term "independent adult learning" to describe a process that takes place in situations "when the decisions about intermediate and terminal learning goals to be pursued, rate of student progress, evaluative procedures to be employed, and sources of material to be consulted are in the hands of the learner" (Brookfield, 1980: 3).

Subsequently, as Brookfield began to contribute his ideas about self-direction to the North American adult education literature, the term "self-directed learning" started to appear in his writing. In using this term, Brookfield (1984c) noted the need to recognize differences between "learning" and "education". Citing various authors who had addressed this distinction (e.g. Jensen, 1960; Verner, 1964; Little, 1979; and Boshier, 1983), Brookfield (1984c: 61) noted that learning has been used alternately to describe "an internal change in consciousness ... an alteration in the state of the central nervous system" as well as "a range of activities ... equivalent to the *act* of learning". In this view, the former is used interchangeably with learning while the latter is used in a way similar to education.

Most recently, Brookfield has expressed this concern about semantic ambiguity to the extent that, instead of using the term "self-directed learning," he is "reverting to talking about the complex phenomenon of *learning* (as an internal change of consciousness) and making a distinction between this phenomenon and the educational setting or mode in which such learning occurs" (Brookfield, 1988: 16). While some may disparage writers who make such drastic changes in stance over time, we applaud Brookfield's effort since, although we do not agree with his recent view that the adult education field should abandon its enthusiasm for the concept of self-directed learning, Brookfield demonstrates a willingness to accommodate new insights and information and to modify his position accordingly. Indeed, the conceptual framework presented later in this chapter reflects the evolution of our own thinking about self-direction over the past several years.

INSTRUCTIONAL METHOD OR PERSONALITY CHARACTERISTIC?

As has been noted earlier, most efforts to understand self-direction in learning to date have centered on the notion of an instructional process in which the learner assumes a primary role in planning, implementing, and evaluating the experience. Yet this view becomes weakened when considered in relation to semantic and conceptual concerns such as those raised by Brookfield. One of the first authors to address the confusion over the meaning of self-directed learning was Kasworm, who stated that self-directed learning can be viewed as a "set of generic, finite behaviors; as a belief system reflecting and evolving from a process of self-initiated learning activity; or as an ideal state of the mature self-actualized learner" (Kasworm, 1983: 1). At about the same time, Chene addressed the concept of autonomy, which she largely equated with self-directed learning. Chene distinguished between two meanings of autonomy, where one view is psychological and the other "is related to a methodology which either assumes that the learner is autonomous or aims at achieving autonomy through training" (Chene, 1983: 40).

Clearly, the concern over what is meant by self-directed learning is a relevant one. Take, for example, the researcher who is interested in studying self-directedness as an internal change process, but who operationalizes self-directed learning as an instructional process. While there are definite similarities between the two concepts, the ideas are *not* the same. In fact, as will be noted in Chapter 4, this has been a problem in much of the research on self-direction conducted to date.

During a period of about one year, three authors tried to clarify the meaning of self-directed learning. Brookfield (1984c), as was noted earlier, used an argument presented by Boshier (1983) to point out that ambiguity of the term self-directed learning might be linked to confusion between *learning* (an internal change process) and *education* (a process for managing external conditions that facilitate this internal change). In this view, the term "self-directed learning" might best be reserved for the former while the latter would actually be viewed as "self-directed education."

At about the same time, Fellenz made a distinction between self-direction as a learning process and as an aspect of personal development. According to Fellenz, self-direction can be viewed in one of two ways:

either as a role adopted during the *process* of learning or as a psychological state attained by an individual in personal development. Both factors can be viewed as developed abilities and, hence, analyzed both as to how they are learned and how they affect self-directed learning efforts.

(Fellenz, 1985: 164)

In building the link between self-direction and personal development, Fellenz draws from such concepts as inner-directedness (Riesman, 1950), self-actualization (Maslow, 1954), locus of control (Rotter, 1966), autonomy (Erikson, 1964), and field independence (Witkin, *et al.*1971).

A third effort to clarify the concept of self-direction was made by Oddi (1984, 1985), who reported the development of a new instrument designed to identify what she refers to as "self-directed continuing learners". The Oddi Continuing Learning Inventory (OCLI), a 24-item Likert scale, grew out of Oddi's concern over the lack of a theoretical foundation for understanding personality characteristics of self-directed continuing learners. The development of this instrument, which will be discussed more fully in Chapter 4, was an outgrowth of the need to distinguish between personality characteristics of self-directed learners and the notion of self-directed learning as "a process of self-instruction" (Oddi, 1985: 230). This distinction is not unlike the one made by Chene (1983) relative to the concept of autonomy.

In a subsequent article, Oddi (1987) distinguished between the "process perspective" and the "personality perspective" relative to self-directed learning, suggesting that the process perspective has been the most predominant in discussions of research and practice to date. As will be shown later in this chapter, this distinction between process and personality perspectives lies at the heart of the model we will present.

Finally, Candy (1988) has offered further support for a distinction between concepts. In a critical analysis of the term "self-direction" through a review of literature and synthesis of research findings, Candy concluded that self-direction has been used "(i) as a personal quality or attribute (personal autonomy); (ii) as the independent pursuit of learning outside formal instructional settings (autodidaxy); and (iii) as a way of organizing instruction (learner-control)" (Candy, 1988: 1033A). Thus, Candy is essentially taking the distinction even further by differentiating between the learning process taking place both within and outside of the institutional setting.

Clearly, the concept of self-directed learning has undergone close scrutiny over the past several years. What has emerged is an important distinction between the process of self-directed learning and the notion of self-direction as a personality construct. This distinction needs careful consideration if we are to move ahead with the study and practice of the phenomenon.

SELF-DIRECTION IN LEARNING AS AN UMBRELLA CONCEPT

As we have noted, the idea of self-directed learning has undergone considerable evolution over the past several years. Indeed, this evolution can sometimes be seen in the case of a single author, as has been the case with Brookfield. It can also be seen in the subtle changes resulting from the research of many individuals over several years. Like Brookfield's, our own notions of self-directed learning have evolved over time. The following two definitions are indicative of our earlier thinking about the concept:

> *Self-planned learning* – A learning activity that is self-directed, self-initiated, and frequently carried out alone.
>
> (Hiemstra, 1976a: 39)

and

> Broadly defined, self-directed learning refers to activities where primary responsibility for planning, carrying out, and evaluating a learning endeavor is assumed by the individual learner.
>
> (Brockett, 1983b: 16)

Unlike Brookfield, however, instead of advocating movement away from the concept, we embrace the view that what is needed is to *expand* the concept and to encourage its continued development as a central theme in the field of adult education. However, it is our belief that in doing this, we need to move away from overemphasis on the term "self-directed learning." Instead, given the confusion over self-directed learning as instructional method versus personality characteristic, we suggest that the term *self-direction in learning* can provide the breadth needed to reflect more fully the current understanding of the concept.

In our view, self-direction in learning refers to two distinct but related dimensions. The first of these dimensions is a process in which a learner assumes primary responsibility for planning, implementing, and evaluating the learning process. An education agent or resource often plays a facilitating role in this process. This is the notion of *self-directed learning* as it has generally been used in the professional literature. The second dimension, which we refer to as *learner self-direction*, centers on a learner's desire or preference for assuming responsibility for learning. This is the personality aspect discussed earlier. Thus, self-direction in learning refers to both the external characteristics of an instructional process and the internal characteristics of the learner, where the individual assumes primary responsibility for a learning experience. The remainder of this chapter will center on discussion of a model designed to clarify this definition further.

Figure 2.1 The "Personal Responsibility Orientation" (PRO) model

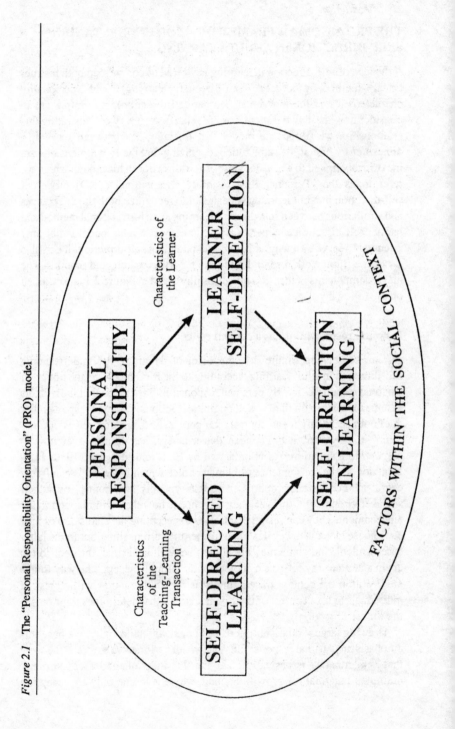

PERSONAL RESPONSIBILITY

Characteristics of the Learner

LEARNER SELF-DIRECTION

Characteristics of the Teaching-Learning Transaction

SELF-DIRECTED LEARNING

SELF-DIRECTION IN LEARNING

FACTORS WITHIN THE SOCIAL CONTEXT

THE PRO MODEL: A FRAMEWORK FOR UNDERSTANDING SELF-DIRECTION IN ADULT LEARNING

If the idea of self-direction in learning is viewed as comprising both instructional method processes (self-directed learning) and personality characteristics of the individual (learner self-direction), it is important to consider how these two dimensions are related. As a way of illustrating this relationship, we propose a model that distinguishes between these two dimensions while at the same time recognizing that the two dimensions are inextricably linked to a broader view of self-direction. This model, which we refer to as the "Personal Responsibility Orientation" (PRO) model of self-direction in adult learning is designed to recognize both the differences and similarities between self-directed learning as an instructional method and learner self-direction as a personality characteristic. The model is not only intended to serve as a way of better understanding self-direction, it can also serve as a framework for building future theory, research, and practice. The major components of the PRO model, as illustrated in Figure 2.1, are outlined on the following pages.

Personal responsibility as a central concept

As can be seen in Figure 2.1, the point of departure for understanding self-direction in adult learning, according to the PRO model, is the notion of personal responsibility. By personal responsibility we mean that individuals assume ownership for their own thoughts and actions. Personal responsibility does not necessarily mean control over personal life circumstances or environment. However, it *does* mean that a person has control over how to *respond* to a situation. As summarized by Elias and Merriam (1980: 118), behavior "is the consequence of human choice which individuals can freely exercise". For instance, oppressed people typically lack control over their social environment; however, they can choose how they will respond to the environment. They can resign themselves to accepting the status quo or they can choose to act in a way designed to alter the current situation. In the latter case, while the outcome may not always be what is desired, the decision to act in a certain way reflects a choice not to willingly accept "the way things are". Within the context of learning, it is the ability and/or willingness of individuals to take control of their own learning that determines their potential for self-direction.

Drawing largely on assumptions of humanistic philosophy, we base this emphasis on personal responsibility on two ideas. First, we embrace the view that human nature is basically good and that individuals possess virtually unlimited potential for growth. Second, we believe that only by accepting responsibility for one's own learning is it possible to take a proactive approach to the learning process. These assumptions imply a great deal of faith and trust in the learner and, thus, offer a foundation for the notion of personal responsibility relative to learning.

Perhaps another way of understanding what we mean by personal responsibility can be found in the idea of autonomy, as discussed by Chene, who provides the following perspective:

> Autonomy means that one can and does set one's own rules, and can choose for oneself the norms one will respect. In other words, autonomy refers to one's ability to choose what has value, that is to say, to make choices in harmony with self-realization.

(Chene, 1983: 39)

Autonomy, as defined above, assumes that one will take personal responsibility, because one is independent "from all exterior regulations and constraints" (Chene, 1983: 39).

While we envision personal responsibility as the cornerstone of self-direction in learning, it is important to stress three related points. First, while we emphasize our commitment to the view that human potential is unlimited, we believe that each individual assumes some degree of personal responsibility. It is not an either/or characteristic. Thus, adult learners will possess different degrees of willingness to accept responsibility for themselves as learners. As was noted in the last chapter, it is a misconception to assume that learners necessarily enter a learning experience with a high level of self-direction already intact. Self-direction is not a panacea for all problems associated with adult learning. Nor is it always necessary for one to be highly self-directed in order to be a successful learner. However, if being able to assume greater control for one's destiny is a desirable goal of adult education (and we believe it is!), then a role for educators of adults is to help learners become increasingly able to assume personal responsibility for their own learning.

Second, the emphasis on personal responsibility as the cornerstone of self-direction in learning implies that the primary focus of the learning process is on the individual, as opposed to the larger society. Yet, accepting responsibility for one's actions as a learner does not ignore the social context in which the learning takes place. Such a view would be extremely short-sighted. What personal responsibility *does* mean, however, is that the *point of departure* for understanding learning lies within the individual. Once this individual dimension is recognized, it is then important to examine the social dimensions that impact upon the learning process. And related to this point is a belief that someone who assumes personal responsibility as an individual is in a stronger position to also be more socially responsible.

Finally, it is important to point out that in taking responsibility for one's thoughts and actions, one also assumes responsibility for the *consequences* of those actions. As Rogers (1961: 171) has stated, to be "self-directing means that one chooses – and then learns from the consequences." Within the context of adult education, Day (1988) has used fictional literature to illustrate this point. Drawing from the works *Oedipus Rex*, *Martin Eden*, *Pygmalion*, and *Educating Rita*, Day argues that adults are "decision-making beings" who are "ultimately responsible" for the decisions they make, that the "results of our learning experiences may as likely lead to discontent as to a state of well-being", and that in general "learning produces consequences" (Day, 1988: 125).

In conclusion, the notion of personal responsibility, as we are using it in the PRO model, means that learners have choices about the directions they pursue as learners. Along with this goes a responsibility for accepting the consequences of one's thoughts and actions as a learner. The idea of personal responsibility will be further developed throughout the book, particularly in Chapter 7, where the theoretical underpinnings of learner self-direction are explored.

Self-directed learning: the process orientation

Self-directed learning, as we have come to view the term, refers to an instructional method. It is a process that centers on the activities of planning, implementing, and evaluating learning. Most of the writings and research on self-directed and self-planned learning from the early and mid-1970s were developed from this perspective (e.g., Knowles, 1975; Tough, 1979). Similarly, the definitions of self-directed learning that we have used previously (Hiemstra, 1976a; Brockett, 1983a) stress this process orientation. Further, one of us (Hiemstra, 1988a; Hiemstra and Sisco, 1990) has described this as individualizing the teaching and learning process.

The process orientation of self-direction in adult learning focuses on characteristics of the teaching–learning transaction. Thus, when considering this aspect of self-direction, concern revolves around factors external to the individual. Needs assessment, evaluation, learning resources, facilitator roles and skills, and independent study are a few of the concepts that fall within the domain of the self-directed learning process. The illustrations compiled in recent books by Knowles and Associates (1984) and Brookfield (1985a) exemplify this concept of self-directed learning as an instructional process in such areas as human resource development, continuing professional education, graduate and undergraduate study, and community education. Given the distinction between learning and education made earlier in the chapter, some readers may wish to think of this process orientation as "self-directed education". We do not disagree with this term, but choose to refer to the process as "self-directed learning" in order to stress the link to the foundation laid by Knowles. Chapter 6 offers a closer look at the process orientation of self-directed learning.

Learner self-direction: the personal orientation

While most of the work that has been seminal to the foundation of self-direction in learning has focused on the process orientation described above, the importance of understanding characteristics of successful self-directed learners has generally been stressed as well. For instance, Knowles (1970) identified several assumptions underlying the concept of andragogy as a model for helping adults learn. The first of these assumptions was that the self-concept of adult learners is characterized by self-direction, whereas dependence characterizes the self-concept of the child. Knowles (1980) later revised his view of pedagogy and andragogy from a dichotomy to a continuum. However, his emphasis on self-concept reflects the centrality of personality as an element of self-direction in learning. This emphasis on personality characteristics of the learner, or factors internal to the individual, is what we refer to as the "personal orientation" or learner self-direction.

Thus, in our view, learner self-direction refers to characteristics of an individual that predispose one toward taking primary responsibility for personal learning endeavors. Conceptually, the notion of learner self-direction grows largely from ideas addressed by Rogers (1961, 1983), Maslow (1970), and other writers from the area of humanistic psychology. Evidence of this personal orientation can be found in much of the research on self-direction in adult learning since the late 1970s. For instance, self-directedness has been studied in relation to such variables as creativity (Torrance and Mourad, 1978), self-concept (Sabbaghian, 1980), life satisfaction (Brockett, 1983c, 1985a), intellectual development (Shaw, 1987), and hemisphericity (Blackwood, 1989). Learner self-direction is discussed further in Chapter 7.

Self-direction in learning: the vital link

As we pointed out earlier, self-direction in learning is a term that we use as an umbrella concept to recognize both external factors that facilitate the learner taking primary responsibility for planning, implementing, and evaluating learning, and internal factors or personality characteristics that predispose one toward accepting responsibility for one's thoughts and actions as a learner. The PRO model illustrates this distinction between external and internal forces. At the same time it recognizes, through the notion of personal responsibility, that there is a strong connection between self-directed learning and learner self-direction. This connection provides a key to understanding the success of self-direction in a given learning context.

It was noted in Chapter 1 that one of the myths related to self-direction in learning is that it is an "all-or-nothing" characteristic. In our view, both the internal and external aspects of self-direction can be viewed on a continuum. Thus, a given learning situation will fit somewhere within a *range* relative to opportunity for self-directed learning and, similarly, an individual's level of self-directedness will fall somewhere within a *range* of possible levels. Related to this view of self-direction as a continuum is our belief that it is a mistake to consider high self-direction as ideal in *all* learning situations. As we have noted previously, because of "the great diversity that exists both in learning styles and in reasons for learning, it is extremely short-sighted to advance" the view that self-direction is the best way to learn and that instead, it is more desirable to think of self-direction as "an ideal mode of learning for certain individuals and for certain situations" (Brockett and Hiemstra, 1985: 33). It is this point that serves to link the concepts of self-directed learning and learner self-direction.

We suggest that optimal conditions for learning result when there is a balance, or congruence, between the learner's level of self-direction and the extent to which opportunity for self-directed learning is possible in a given situation. If, for example, one is predisposed toward a high level of self-directedness and is engaged in a learning experience where self-direction is actively facilitated, chances for success are high. Similarly, the learner who is not as high in self-directedness is likely to find comfort and, in all likelihood, a greater chance of success in a situation where the instructor assumes a more directive role. In both instances, the chances for success are relatively high, since the learner's expectations are congruent with the conditions of the learning situation.

Where difficulties and frustrations arise is when the balance between internal characteristics of the learner are not in harmony with external characteristics of the teaching–learning transaction. Individuals who enter a learning situation with a clear idea of how and what they wish to learn are likely to become frustrated and disenchanted if not given the freedom to pursue these directions. In the same vein, the learner who seeks a high level of guidance and direction will probably have similar feelings in a situation where the facilitator emphasizes an active leadership role by the learners. For individuals in either situation, the problem is that the teaching–learning situation is not in harmony with the needs and desires which the learner brought to the situation. This does not mean that the learner was "unsuccessful", nor that the facilitator was "ineffective". Rather, it suggests that success and effectiveness are relative terms that depend on clear communication of needs and expectations among all parties engaged in the teaching–learning transaction.

The notion of learner self-direction, as an element of the PRO model, suggests a general tendency that exists to a greater or lesser degree in all learners. However, it is important to recognize that situational factors are often likely to impact on the type of instructional method a learner will seek. An adult who seeks to learn about current trends in real estate, for example, may be willing to relinquish control over the learning situation to the session leader for reasons of expedience or because of a personal lack of knowledge and experience in the real estate area. This does not diminish the learner's level of self-direction; indeed, the decision to relinquish a degree of control was consciously made by the learner.

Several years ago, the first author attended a research conference where participants met to exchange information and ideas based on current research. The format for this conference, as is often the case for research conferences, was a series of paper sessions and symposia consisting of formal presentations followed by questions and discussions from the audience. In one symposium, the first presenter began by discussing some of the research trends in the topical area under consideration. However, about 20 minutes later, the second presenter began his portion of the symposium by asking participants to move their chairs into a circle so that it would be easier to "share ideas." At least half of the group exercised a degree of self-direction by immediately leaving the room.

The above examples have been presented to illustrate two points. First, self-directed learning – the method that the second presenter was trying to implement – is not inherently the *best* method for adult learning. Although we believe that self-directed learning situations will most often be compatible with the needs, desires, and capabilities of adult learners, there *are* times when a highly teacher-directed approach will prove most effective and, indeed, will be expected and even demanded.

Second, when considering the fit between self-directed learning and learner self-direction, it is important to keep in mind that the congruence between these dimensions may at times be mitigated by factors such as the expectations of the learners. That symposium presenter must certainly have felt a degree of frustration and perhaps hurt as half of the audience walked out on his efforts to create a climate that most likely had served him very well in other settings. However, it is likely that the lack of congruence between his approach and the *context* in which the learning situation was taking place is what led to the exodus of so many participants. This brings us to a final element of the PRO model, which is a consideration of the social context in which self-direction in learning exists.

The social context for self-direction in learning

The final element of the PRO model is represented by the circle encompassing the other elements. One of the most frequent criticisms of self-direction in learning has been an overemphasis on the individual, which is usually accompanied by a failure to consider the social context in which learning takes place. Brookfield, for example, has suggested that by "concentrating attention on the features of individual learner control over the planning, conduct and evaluation of learning, the importance of learning networks and informal learning exchanges has been forgotten" (Brookfield, 1984c: 67). In the PRO model, the individual learner is, in fact, *central* to the idea of self-direction. However, such learning activities *cannot* be divorced from the social context in which they occur. This point is further reinforced through discussions on the role of institutions in Chapter 8 and policy issues in Chapter 9. We agree with Brookfield that social context is vital to understanding self-direction and that, to date, this concern has largely been overlooked. Brookfield's (1981b) own research, in which he found that "independent adult learners" often function as a "fellowship of learning" is a noteworthy exception to this gap in knowledge. One of the myths of self-direction identified in Chapter 1 is that such learning takes place in isolation. In order to truly understand the impact of self-direction, both as an instructional method and as a personality characteristic, it is crucial to recognize the social milieu in which such activity transpires.

Related to the social context are the political implications of self-direction in learning. Again, Brookfield (1984c) has helped to raise consciousness about the politics of self-direction. This, in turn, triggered the following response:

> Brookfield's comments are most insightful, for they force us to ponder the *real* consequences of situations where learners are *truly* in control of their learning .... many individuals, especially those who can be considered "hard-to-reach", may believe that formal educational settings can reinforce conformity while stifling creativity. For such persons, institutions may be perceived as antithetical to the self-directed learning process. On a larger scale, these issues are amplified in situations where individuals view themselves as powerless in determining the direction of their lives. What are the potential consequences ... of promoting self-direction in societies where individual human rights may be in question? Clearly, the issue of control is a crucial one because, ultimately, it must move beyond the individual dimension into the social and political arenas.
>
> (Brockett, 1985c: 58)

Thus, while the individual is the "starting point" for understanding self-direction in adult learning, the social context provides the arena in which the activity of self-direction is played out. In order for us to truly understand the phenomenon of self-direction in adult learning, it will be crucial to recognize and deal with the interface between these individual and social dimensions. Chapters 8 and 10 address the social context from institutional and cross-cultural perspectives, respectively.

CONCLUSION

In this chapter, we have attempted to alleviate some of the confusion surrounding the meaning of self-direction and related concepts. By proposing the PRO model, we are suggesting that in order to understand the complexity of self-direction in adult learning, it is essential to recognize differences between self-directed learning as an instructional method and learner self-direction as a personality characteristic. These two dimensions are linked through the recognition that each emphasizes the importance of learners assuming personal responsibility for their thoughts and actions. Finally, the PRO model is designed to advance understanding of self-direction by recognizing the vital role played by the social context in which learning takes place. Moving to a critical examination of research on self-direction in the next two chapters, the remainder of the book is designed to further illuminate the ideas expressed in the PRO model.

Part II

The underlying knowledge base

Since the early 1970s, few if any topics have been the focus of more study in adult education than self-direction in learning. In looking at the knowledge base of self-direction, this part is divided into three chapters, each of which examines a different stream of research. In Chapter 3, studies growing out of Allen Tough's seminal work on adult's learning projects are presented. Through this research, it became clear that self-planning is the most frequent approach adults take in their learning efforts.

As researchers became more enthusiastic about the potential of studying self-direction, efforts were undertaken to find ways to measure levels of self-directedness among learners. To date, two instruments have been the primary vehicles for such studies. These are reviewed in Chapter 4.

The next chapter, 5, considers studies on self-direction based on naturalistic research and qualitative data. These studies have added considerably to how the process of self-directed learning is undertaken and to the social context in which such learning takes place.

Together, the studies presented in the three chapters of Part II fill in many pieces of the puzzle that is self-direction in adult learning. But, more important, they help to provide an understanding of where holes still exist in the knowledge base.

3 Adult learning as an iceberg: establishing the knowledge base on self-direction

As was stressed in Chapter 1, self-direction in learning is not a new idea. Yet, while self-direction or self-education has been held as an ideal for adult education by various authors over the past several decades (e.g., Lindeman, 1926; Bryson, 1936; Snedden, 1930), only since the early 1970s have adult education researchers actively and systematically directed their efforts toward this area. This may be due, in part, to the relative newness of adult education as a field of study in North America. While some authors (e.g., Boshier and Pickard, 1979; Boyd and Apps, 1980) have described adult education as a "discipline," the idea of adult education as an area of academic inquiry is nonetheless quite recent. In fact, much of the seminal thinking about the study of the adult education field can be traced to the publication of *Adult Education: Outlines of an Emerging Field of University Study* (Jensen, *et al*., 1964). Further, a content analysis of *Adult Education* (Dickinson and Rusnell, 1971) revealed that during the mid-to-late 1960s, the number of descriptive/opinion-oriented articles declined while the number of original research articles increased. We suggest that self-direction in learning, therefore, has actually been one of the first major areas within the field to undergo systematic and sustained inquiry. Indeed, Beder (1985) supported this view by suggesting that, along with the area of participation, self-direction has been the only other research area to be extensively examined within adult education.

Another possible reason for the relatively recent emphasis on self-direction as a research area is the inherent difficulty of studying learners outside of educational institutions. Since so many self-directed learning efforts take place outside of institutions, it can be quite difficult to examine self-directedness in a holistic way that considers social, cultural, political, and psychological dimensions of the concept. As will be demonstrated in this chapter, the knowledge base of self-direction in adult learning has evolved largely through the efforts of researchers to identify numerous, often creative, strategies for answering questions about the frequency and nature of-self-directed learning.

While efforts to study self-direction in learning have escalated since the early 1970s, one individual who seems to have played a key role in laying the groundwork for this research as far back as the early 1960s is Cyril Houle. In addition to serving as major professor for Malcolm Knowles and Allen Tough, two of the seminal contributors to current thought on self-direction in learning, Houle is author of *The Inquiring Mind*, first published in 1961. For this study, sometimes credited with sparking the current interest in self-direction, Houle interviewed twenty-two adult learning participants in Milwaukee, Wisconsin, during 1960. Using an informal interview schedule, he concluded that these individuals fell within three subgroups with regard to their reasons for engaging in a continuing education activity. The first group, which Houle called *goal-oriented*, consisted of individuals who viewed their participation as a means to some other end, such as career advancement or change. A second group, the *activity-oriented*, chose to participate in continuing education primarily for fellowship, or the opportunity to meet new people. Finally, a group that Houle referred to as the *learning-oriented*, was comprised of individuals who participated for the sake of personal enjoyment; these individuals viewed learning as an end in and of itself. As will be discussed later in the chapter, it is this latter orientation that led Tough to pursue an interest in what he initially referred to as "adult self-teachers."

The focus of this and the following two chapters will be a review and critical analysis of existing research related to self-direction in learning. In this chapter, we will introduce what we believe to be the three major directions that research in this area has taken to date. We will then highlight the first of these areas. In the following two chapters, we will look at each of the other two major research directions and will offer an assessment of the current state of this research area. Subsequent chapters will apply this knowledge to examine ways in which adult educators can utilize these findings in order to improve practice.

THREE STREAMS OF INQUIRY

Despite the relatively recent emergence of self-direction in learning as a research direction for adult education, the picture resulting from this body of knowledge seems rather bright. Unlike many of the researchable areas within the field that have been largely unexplored, deliberate efforts have been made to bridge theory, research, and practice in self-direction. As a result, it has been possible to apply information gained from research both to improve practice and to further expand research and theory-building efforts. For example, in the twenty issues of *Adult Education Quarterly* appearing during the 5-year period between Fall, 1984 and Summer 1989, a total of sixteen articles dealt directly with self-direction in learning, while several other articles were related in a secondary way. Also, during the 1985 Adult Education Research Conference, over 11 percent of the paper sessions were on the topic of self-direction.

Nonetheless, while we are encouraged by the picture presented in this and the following two chapters, we believe that the future of adult education research in general depends on continuing research efforts. To this end, self-direction in learning can serve as a "miner's canary," something of a gauge for measuring the ability of adult education to develop, sustain, and utilize a substantial knowledge base. Beder (1985) has suggested that while self-directed learning is one of the two relatively well developed research areas in adult education, it is doubtful whether this knowledge has been utilized to guide practice in a major way. While, as we have stated above, research *has* often been used to improve practice, Beder's point is well taken, and should be kept in mind when implementing self-directed learning in the future.

In trying to make sense of the research base on self-direction in learning, it may be helpful to classify the various types of studies that have contributed to the development of this research base. Caffarella and O'Donnell (1988: 40) have offered one such scheme. According to this view, research can be classified along five categories:

1 *Nature of the philosophical position* – conceptual perspectives on the process of self-directed learning;
2 *Verification studies* – descriptive investigations of adults learning projects;
3 *Nature of the method of self-directed learning* – questions of "how" people plan and implement learning projects;
4 *Nature of the individual learner* – questions of who participates in self-directed learning and for what purposes; and
5 *Policy questions* – pertaining to the educator, institutions, and society.

This classification is based on the *content* of research studies. Further, it emphasizes both empirical research "as well as serious conceptual articles" (Caffarella and O'Donnell, 1988: 39).

An alternative classification scheme is based on the type of research paradigm under which an investigation falls. Several years ago, we presented a classification scheme consisting of three major categories or "streams" of inquiry: descriptive learning projects investigations, research involving measurement of self-directed learning levels, and qualitative studies (Brockett *et al.*, 1982). In our view, this "three-streams" model still serves as an appropriate classification scheme, for the vast majority of studies on self-direction still fit within one of these categories.

The first major branch of inquiry grew out of the methodology utilized initially by Tough in his work, *The Adult's Learning Projects* (1971, 1979). This line of research, since replicated by numerous researchers with a wide range of adult populations, provides convincing descriptive evidence of the *frequency* of self-planning by adult learners.

A second major branch of research has essentially defined self-directedness as a personological, or personality-related variable. In this approach, written instruments are used to determine the extent to which individuals possess qualities associated with self-directedness. This branch of inquiry has led to a number of studies linking self-directedness with such concepts as creativity (Torrance and Mourad, 1978), self-concept (Sabbaghian, 1980), motivational orientation (Reynolds, 1986), life satisfaction (Brockett, 1985a), and intellectual development (Shaw, 1987). Also, several researchers have used instruments designed to measure self-directedness in a diagnostic capacity within the classroom setting (e.g., Caffarella, 1983b; Kasworm, 1983; Savoie, 1980; Six, 1987; Six and Hiemstra, 1989a). This branch of inquiry has been responsible for moving our understanding of self-direction in learning from basic description toward greater understanding of how such variables may be related to one another and, to a lesser degree, where changes in one variable may cause a change in the other. Chapter 4 will highlight this branch of research.

A third approach to studying self-direction in learning has employed qualitative methods such as observation and interviewing in order to develop models that can help to explain the meanings and contexts of self-direction in learning during adulthood (e.g., Brookfield, 1981b; Gibbons *et al.*, 1980; Spear and Mocker, 1984). This branch of research (which will serve as the focus for Chapter 5) has helped adult educators in theory-building, which, in turn, has influenced the ways in which researchers and practitioners now understand self-direction in adult learning.

It is important to bear in mind that while these three streams of research have evolved in a somewhat sequential manner, they are not distinct stages of research. In other words, newer methodologies have not replaced previous approaches. Rather, each stream of inquiry continues to serve an important role in addressing specific types of research questions relative to self-direction in adult learning. The remainder of this chapter will offer a closer look at the first major stream of research by focusing on selected studies that reflect the learning projects paradigm.

LEARNING PROJECTS RESEARCH

The work of Allen Tough

In 1965, Allen Tough completed his doctoral dissertation at the University of Chicago on teaching tasks performed by "adult self-teachers." He found that, while self-teaching implies a degree of independence or autonomy, the learning that occurs through self-teaching does not generally take place in isolation (Tough, 1966). Those individuals who engage in self-teaching are highly likely to seek the assistance of others, such as close friends and relatives, librarians, subject-matter experts, and fellow learners.

Tough, in this study, focused on individuals engaged in a self-teaching project. As an outgrowth of this work, he began to raise questions about the extent to which self-teaching is a part of the total range of an individual's learning activities. Subsequently, during 1970, Tough and several colleagues at the Ontario Institute for Studies in Education (Toronto) interviewed 66 adults in an attempt to examine "the highly deliberate learning efforts" of adults. Particular emphasis was placed on the "planning and deciding" aspects of the learning project.

Tough defined a learning project as "a series of related episodes, adding up to at least seven hours" where "more than half of the person's total motivation is to gain and retain certain fairly clear knowledge and skill, or to produce some other lasting change in himself" (Tough, 1971: 7). Similarly, an episode was defined as "a period of time devoted to a cluster or sequence of similar or related activities, which are not interrupted much by other activities" (Tough, 1971: 7). Examples of episodes might include reading a newspaper or a chapter of a book, visiting a museum, or attending a class. An episode had a definite beginning and concluding time, and, to be classified as an episode, the information had to be retained for at least 2 days after the learning activity took place. This qualification excluded activities in which learning was intended to serve an immediate purpose, such as being able to assemble a piece of household furniture – an ability quickly forgotten. A learning project, then, was considered to be the total of all episodes that a person had undertaken in order to gain (and retain) some specific knowledge or skill.

Tough was very specific in stating that a learning project must encompass a minimum of seven hours. There were two major reasons for setting this seven hour minimum. First, this period of time is approximately equivalent to a traditional working day (excluding breaks and "down time"), which Tough thought a considerable investment of time for a single learning project. Second, seven hours was found to work well in interviews with subjects because it eliminated very brief activities but not major learning efforts. Additionally, this seven hours must have taken place within a six-month period. It is important to emphasize that the "seven hours within a six-month period" qualification was intended as a *minimum* expenditure of time. In reality, Tough found that the majority of learning projects uncovered by his survey team far exceeded this minimum.

Thus, the 66 subjects were interviewed about their involvement in learning projects over the previous year. These individuals were drawn from the following seven sections of the population:

1 Blue-collar workers;
2 Women in lower-level white-collar positions;
3 Men in lower-level white-collar positions;
4 Beginning elementary school teachers;
5 Municipal politicians;
6 Social science professors; and
7 Upper-middle-class women with pre-school children.

To obtain data, a highly structured interview process was employed. Interviewers were trained in how to use the interview format and in how to identify learning projects. Thus, interviewees could uncover many different kinds of efforts while eliminating "borderline learning," such as brief episodes and activities in which learning was not the major reason for undertaking the effort. While the interview procedure was generally structured, there were certain points in the process where interviewers would share with subjects various "probe sheets" that prompted a recall of learning projects from a wide range of areas (e.g., child-rearing, gardening, music, collecting, and job-related knowledge and skills).

It was found that the "typical" adult had been involved in about eight different learning projects during the year prior to the interviews. The mean number of projects was 8.3; the median was 8. Of the sixty-six persons interviewed, all but one reported having been involved in at least one learning project. The highest median number of projects were completed by the social science professors (11.5) and elementary school teachers (9.0), while blue collar workers and municipal politicians had the lowest mean number of projects (5.5 and 7.0 projects, respectively). The mean number of hours spent on an individual learning project was 104 while the median was 81, a figure well above the minimum criterion set by Tough. Further, less than 1 percent of all learning projects were undertaken in order to gain credit. Why do adults make the choice to undertake deliberate learning projects? According to the individuals interviewed in the Tough survey, the major reasons included preparation for a job and maintenance of job skills, solving a specific problem or task on the job, gaining knowledge and skill about some aspect of one's personal development or responsibilities within the home, and learning out of curiosity or interest in a topic or as a leisure pursuit. Tough stressed that most learning projects are motivated by "some anticipated use or application" of what has been learned. This finding is quite consistent with other surveys of reasons for adult learning participation (e.g., Aslanian and Brickell, 1980; Cross, 1981; Boshier and Collins, 1985).

Probably the most important finding to emerge from Tough's study – certainly with regard to our current discussion – pertains to the question of *who* assumes responsibility for planning learning projects. By far the majority of projects identified in the Tough study (68 percent) were planned primarily by the individual learners themselves. Another 12 percent were planned by a group or its leader/instructor (e.g., formal classes), 8 percent were planned primarily by another person in a one-to-one situation (e.g., tutorial), and a non-human resource (e.g., a programmed instruction manual) served as the planner in only 3 percent of the projects. In the remainder of projects, no single type of planner could be clearly identified.

It is this finding about individual planning preferences that lies at the heart of the current emphasis on self-direction research. While self-direction has long been assumed to be a major goal of adult education, it was not until Tough's investigation that the impact of this preference for individual responsibility in planning was made apparent. In fact, Tough used the analogy of an iceberg to describe adult learning. Only a very small portion of each (i.e., an iceberg and learning) is clearly visible, while the rest lies beneath the surface. The point here is that the vast majority of what adults learn is not easily observed as through rates of participation in formal adult education programs.

More recently, Tough (1982) has expanded his focus from the notion of adults learning projects to the broader concept of intentional changes. Here, Tough looked at the ways people undertake major personal change in various aspects of their lives. Using a format similar to the learning projects interview protocol and via a team of interviewers, Tough found that 75 percent of the changes reported by interviewees fell into four areas: job, career, and training; human relationships, emotions, and self-perception; enjoyable activities; and changes in residence location. With regard to taking responsibility for intentional changes, Tough (1982: 52) observed that, on average, "the person assumes about 70 percent of the responsibility for all the subtasks involved in choosing the change, planning the strategy, and implementing the change".

While the intentional changes approach does not seem to have been embraced as widely as the learning projects paradigm (e.g., Caffarella, 1983a; Sisco, 1983), there have been a few efforts to build on Tough's initial study. Moore (1986), for example, found that most of the prison inmates in his survey undertook several important changes in a year, with self-directed learning serving as an important foundational aspect of the change. Lundgren

(1988) interviewed 46 Type II diabetics in Montana, and found that at least 85 percent had made at least one health-related change in the previous five years. Self-planned learning projects were an important part of the change process for many of the individuals interviewed by Lundgren, and reading was viewed as the primary learning activity. From these studies, it can be seen that while the thrust of the intentional changes paradigm is different from Tough's earlier work, the link to self-planned learning nonetheless remains.

With the publication of *The Adults' Learning Projects* in 1971, numerous researchers began to adopt the methodology used by Tough in conducting additional studies with different segments of the adult population. In the following sections, we discuss several of these replication studies. Our intent in these sections is to provide a feel for the diversity and flavor that have characterized the follow-up work to Tough's study. In reviewing these replications, it should be noted that despite considerable variation in both the total number of learning projects and in the total percentage of self-planned projects, the findings from the original Tough investigation are largely substantiated.

Mothers with pre-school children

Johnstone and Rivera (1965), in their study of participation in adult education, found that mothers with young children had especially low rates of participation in institutional adult education programs. Of the seven groups studied by Tough, mothers with children of pre-school age completed the third smallest number of projects during the study period. In one of the earliest learning projects replications, conducted by someone other than one of Tough's associates, Coolican (1975) explored the total range of learning activities (institutional as well as non-institutional) of a sample of 48 mothers in Syracuse, New York, whose oldest child had not yet entered school.

Data were obtained through the use of a two-part survey instrument. One part of the instrument was a questionnaire designed to obtain demographic information about the interviewee. The other instrument was an interview schedule adapted from the one used by Tough. All interviews were conducted by the researcher and took place in the subjects' homes. Each interview began with the researcher striving to develop a relaxed tone. After rapport was established, the structured interview began. On the average, interviews lasted 85 minutes.

Coolican found that the subjects in her sample had conducted an average of 5.8 projects per year with a mean length of 43 hours for each project. It was found that 66 percent of these projects were self-planned, a figure very similar to that of Tough. Nearly half of the projects were concerned with home and family issues. Other major areas of interest included hobbies and recreation (18 percent) and personal development (11 percent). With the demands of caring for small children and running a household, Coolican found that these women typically were only able to spend short amounts of time on subjects in which they were interested.

Several possible limitations of the study identified by Coolican serve to point out some of the potential constraints of the learning projects methodology. First, since the data were obtained from a rather homogeneous sample, results cannot be generalized to a more heterogeneous population. Second, there may be limitations in using the interview approach, especially with regard to the recollection of learning projects that had taken place several months prior to the interview. Third, because of an unwillingness of subjects to reveal certain kinds of information or an inability to verbalize responses, there may be instances where the responses of subjects do not accurately reflect their actual experience. Fourth, no attempts were made to verify the accuracy of interviewees' statements. Fifth, the sample was based entirely on willing participants and, thus, there is a possibility that those who chose to respond were more oriented to or interested in learning than those who did not participate in the study. These limiting factors do not detract from the importance of Coolican's findings. Rather, they serve to articulate some of the very real concerns that need to be taken into account when interpreting the findings of studies using the learning projects methodology.

Rural and urban adults

In the earliest large-scale study comparing the learning projects of adults within a particular geographical area, Peters and Gordon (1974) interviewed a total of 475 persons residing in Knoxville, Tennessee and a nearby rural county. At the outset, fifteen interviewers received 9 hours of formal training and were involved in several days of related activities such as readings, role playing, and practice interviews. The interviews consisted of the basic structure developed by Tough and lasted an average of 1 hour.

The 475 persons who were interviewed for the study ranged in age from 18 to 90, with a mean age of 41; the majority (61 percent) were male; 54 percent reported having less than a high school education; 17 percent were high school graduates while the remaining 29 percent held either undergraduate or graduate degrees.

Peters and Gordon found that their subjects had conducted an average of 3.7 learning projects in the year prior to the study. This figure was higher for the urban subjects (4.1 projects) than for the rural interviewees (3.1 projects). Half of the subjects reported four or more learning projects during the study period; however, nearly 12 percent conducted no projects during this time.

The number of projects for females and single people was slightly higher than for men and those who were married. Looking at age groups, persons in the 35–39 age group conducted the largest number of projects (4.8) while those in the 55+ age group conducted the fewest projects (3.7). It is interesting to note the difference between urban and rural subjects in the older group. While interviewees in the 55+ age group who lived in the city averaged 5.4 projects – somewhat higher than the average for the total sample – those who lived in rural areas averaged only three projects.

Consistent with the findings of Tough (1979) and Coolican (1975), learning projects conducted by persons in the Peters and Gordon sample were overwhelmingly self-planned. In fact, of these projects 66 percent were planned by the individual learner. Unlike Tough's findings, however, 12.6 percent of the Peters and Gordon sample were enrolled in formal courses, a finding attributed by the authors to the relatively high number of college graduates found within the sample. This figure is consistent with data from the National Center for Education Statistics, which found that, in 1981, 12.8 percent of all adults participated in an adult education course of some type (Kay, 1982). Other findings reported by Peters and Gordon dealt with utilization of resources, obstacles to participation, and content areas studied by learners in the sample. Resources most frequently used included books, magazines, tools and raw materials, and other individuals. The obstacles most often perceived by learners were lack of time, money, motivation, or education, plus family conflicts. The content of the majority of projects focused on topics related to employment or recreational pursuits.

In a follow-up analysis of the Peters and Gordon data, Brasfield (1974) focused specifically on the link between learning projects activity and educational attainment. In this analysis, Brasfield found that those adults with more formal education reported a greater number of learning projects than those with less formal education. However, she also found that the highest proportion of *self-planned* projects were found among those with fewer years of formal education. While the figures for self-planning among those with high school diplomas, or those with high school diplomas and some college experience but no college diploma, and those with at least a bachelor's degree were 72 percent and 74 percent respectively, the self-planning figure for those with 0–12 years of education was 86 percent. This is a major departure from previous and subsequent research supporting a link between self-direction and educational attainment. We believe that the findings lend empirical support to the idea, which will be stressed further in the next chapter, that self-direction holds much potential for serving learners traditionally considered to be "hard-to-reach."

Older adults

For the most part, learning projects research has been based on general adult samples, not focusing upon any specific age group within the population. Yet, in studies of formal adult education participation (e.g., Kay 1982), an almost universally consistent finding has been that participation declines drastically among those persons age 55 and above. However, at least four studies employing the learning projects methodology have painted a somewhat more optimistic picture of the older adult as a potential learning participant.

The first study in North America to focus on the learning projects of older adults was Hiemstra's 1975 study in Nebraska. He examined 256 adults, at least 55 years of age, selected randomly from the voter registration cards in two communities and 18 rural townships, and from the membership list of a Hispanic community center. The sample for this study was predominantly white (88.7 percent) and middle-class blue or white collar (87.8 percent). Slightly more than three-quarters of the subjects (75.4 percent) lived in their own homes, and 63.3 percent were married while 25.4 percent were widowed. In terms of previous education, 66.3 percent were at least high school graduates and nearly 20 percent had graduated from college. The mean age of the sample was 68.1 years of age (Hiemstra, 1975, 1976a).

Using the learning projects interview schedule, seven trained interviewers spent between 1 and 2 hours with each of the interviewees. Hiemstra found that of the 256 individuals interviewed, 214 or 83.5 percent reported conducting one or more learning projects in the previous year. An average of 325 hours per year was spent on a mean of 3.3 projects. And, as with other learning projects studies, it was also found that the majority of projects (55 percent) were self-planned. The primary planner used by subjects in this study is shown in Table 3.1.

With regard to various sub-groupings, there were some important differences. For example, a higher proportion of people 65 and older reported no learning projects in the year before the interview than did younger

Table 3.1 Different types of primary planner in learning projects

Type of primary planner	%
A group or its leader/instructor	20.45
One person in a one-to-one situation	10.30
Material/non-human resource	3.95
The learner him- or herself	55.15
Mixed (no dominant type of planner)	10.16

Source: Hiemstra (1975)

individuals. However, there were no significant differences across age groups between those who participated in more *self-planned* projects and those participating in fewer projects of this type. Finally, when asked to name the primary subject matter of their learning projects, there were no significant differences among the two age groups (i.e., those over and under age 65) in terms of preferences for self-fulfillment subjects (Hiemstra, 1985b).

From this study, we believe there is evidence that older adults often *are* active learners and that most of this activity is reflected through the self-planned learning projects in which such individuals are engaged. This study suggests that "educators must learn how to remove their institutional blinders and recognize all the self-directed, independent learning going on and needed outside institutional structures" (Hiemstra, 1976b: 337). Such research on older adults is important in terms of understanding how to facilitate daily learning efforts (Hiemstra, 1987c).

A second study using the learning projects approach with older subjects was reported by Ralston (1981), who was interested in comparing black and non-black groups. Ralston interviewed 110 randomly selected persons age 65 or older in Champaign-Urbana, Illinois. Among the findings of this study, Ralston found that her interviewees conducted a mean of 2.45 projects. She noted that "respondents who were white, white-collar, and had higher educational levels were involved in significantly more learning projects than other subgroups" (Ralston, 1981: 1237). She did not seek to identify the primary planner of projects, so it is not possible to determine the extent to which these projects were self-planned.

Hassan (1982) studied self-directed learning among a sample of 77 adults residing in Ames, Iowa. Of this sample, more than 37 percent were over 55 years of age. The 29 people in this older age group conducted a mean of 9.7 projects per year, a figure that was not significantly different from that of the 48 younger people. The Hassan study is discussed further in Chapter 4.

In a fourth study involving older adults, Estrin (1986) examined the relationship between life satisfaction and learning participation among older women living in two subsidized senior housing developments in southern Rhode Island. Of the 87 women in this study, 54 were widowed, the mean age was 72.5, and the mean educational level was 10.3 years. Estrin found a significant positive relationship between life satisfaction and learning activity, both in terms of number of projects and number of hours spent engaged in learning. She concluded that participation in learning can be viewed as a strategy for enhancing life satisfaction in the later years. This conclusion is further supported through research (Brockett, 1985a) that will be addressed in the next chapter.

A U.S. national sample

Probably the most comprehensive learning projects study to date was conducted by Penland (1977, 1978, 1979). For the most part, learning projects studies have focused on self-planned activities within specific groups; thus, the findings have not been generalizable to a larger population. By obtaining data from a U.S. national-probability sample, Penland attempted to overcome this limiting factor by conducting a study that would address what he felt to be a "lack of a systematic behavioral foundation for a professional helping relationship" (Penland, 1978: 1).

The study sample was drawn from the total U.S. population of persons aged 18 or older, in a manner similar to the way in which public opinion polls are conducted. Since the study was conducted under different circumstances than other learning projects studies, the interview format was modified somewhat from the structured interview schedule developed by Tough (Penland, 1979). The instrument used by Penland was developed so that interviews could be completed in 1 hour, and so those subjects not involved in learning could be accommodated "more efficiently" (Penland, 1978). For purposes of the study, Penland defined a continuing self-learner as "an individual (usually adult) who plans and designs an independent learning project", and independent self-designed learning was defined as "the overt behavioral evidence of a sequence of information processing episodes" (Penland, 1978: 3).

The interview schedule used by Penland looked at three different sets of questions. The first set sought information about the "patterns and purposes" of adult learning activities. These questions explored the frequency and nature of learning projects. A second group of questions explored the use of resources as a part of the learning process. In addition, several questions focused on obtaining demographic information about the subjects.

Penland found that 78.9 percent of the sample perceived themselves to be "continuing learners" and that 76.1 percent had conducted at least one self-planned learning project in the year prior to the study. The average number of projects per person was 3.3 with a range of from 1 to 18. A mean of 155.8 hours was spent on each project. Penland attributed much of this figure to the involvement of the learner in planning aspects of activities that might otherwise be assumed by someone or something else.

The three reasons cited by subjects for preferring self-planned learning include the desire to learn what they choose and at their own pace, to maintain flexibility in their learning activities, and to structure their own project. According to Penland, the widespread emphasis on self-planned learning can be viewed as evidence to support the centrality of individualism in United States society.

An important component of the Penland survey was the use of resources, particularly the library, in conjunction with self-planned learning projects. It was found that 73.2 percent of those persons who considered themselves to be continuing learners had deliberately looked up some piece of information during the 7 days prior to the interview. However, only 14 percent of the sample stated that they used the library on a regular basis, while another 60 percent never used the library for self-planned learning. Penland concluded that those persons who participate in lifelong learning activities need "shopping center" access to resources. This, he feels, requires the cooperation of adult educators, information brokers, and community development personnel. In Chapter 9, we suggest some policies related to this need.

Low levels of self-planning

The studies described above indicate a high degree of self-planning among learners from a variety of settings. Indeed, most learning projects studies have shown that a clear majority of projects are self-planned. However, some studies have found half or less of all projects to be planned primarily by the learners themselves.

Johnson (1973) interviewed forty adults in Fort Lauderdale, Florida, who had recently completed senior high school examinations. This group conducted an average of 14.4 learning projects, 50 percent of which were self-planned.

Miller and Botsman (1975), using a modified case study approach, examined the learning projects of nine Cooperative Extension agents in New York State. Subjects conducted an average of twelve projects; of these, 40 percent were self-planned, while more than half of the projects consisted of workshops planned by others.

Umoren (1978) studied 50 individuals from two socioeconomic groups in Lincoln, Nebraska. In this sample, the 38 low income adults and 22 middle or high income individuals conducted an average of 4.7 learning projects, and about 40 percent of these projects were self-planned.

Field (1979) examined the learning activities of 86 low-literacy attainment adults in the Brownstown, Jamaica, area. Of the 4.2 average number of projects conducted by these subjects, about 20 percent were self-planned and more than 50 percent were planned by group leaders. Field attributed these figures to a prevalence of literacy training and projects pertaining to religious activities, both of which tended to rely on group leaders.

Baghi (1979) looked at the learning project activity of 46 participants in adult basic education classes and learning centers near Des Moines, Iowa. These individuals reported an average of 6.6 projects per year, 57 percent of which were self-planned. In this sample black respondents reported a higher mean number of learning projects and of hours spent on learning projects activity than white interviewees, although the differences were not statistically significant.

While studies reporting low figures for self-planning are a clear minority of learning projects research, they make an important contribution to this research area in at least three ways. First, the findings indicate that such groups are, indeed, much more actively involved in adult learning activities than studies focusing on more "formal" participation typically indicate. This has clear implications for how educators of adults might work to reach traditionally "hard-to-reach" groups of adults (Brockett, 1983b). Second, these studies accentuate the need to use caution when espousing the value of self-planning for all adult learners. This concern is related to some of the myths presented in Chapter 1. Finally, these findings can serve as an impetus for encouraging a critical look at both the contributions and potential limitations of the learning projects methodology.

Contributions and limitations of learning projects research

Has the learning projects methodology had a major impact on efforts to understand self-direction in adult learning? To address this question, it is necessary to assess both the contributions and limitations of this approach. Looking first at contributions, there are at least three ways in which learning projects research has benefited the field of adult education. First, it has offered a method for studying the learning efforts of countless individuals who prefer to engage in learning activities outside of the formal, educational institution setting. Because the methodology emphasizes learning that takes place both within and outside of institutions, it has provided a way of studying learning among individuals, such as older adults and those persons with little or no formal education, who have traditionally been considered "hard-to-reach."

A second, related contribution is that the learning projects methodology has served to redefine the meaning of adult education participation (Brockett, 1983b). For the most part, surveys of participation in adult education, such as those conducted by the National Center for Education Statistics (e.g., Kay, 1982) are based only on involvement in adult education courses. However, as the Tough study and subsequent replications indicate, courses comprise only a very small portion of all adult learning activity. The learning projects approach can provide data that are much more inclusive – and, as such, representative of the actual nature of adult learning – than data reported in most survey studies to date.

Still another contribution of learning projects research is that the approach has represented the first effort by adult education researchers to study systematically the concept of self-direction in learning. The learning projects approach seems to have served a "consciousness-raising" function for the adult education field, providing data to confirm that which was known intuitively for many years. If the extent to which the research approach has been replicated by other researchers can serve as testimonial, Tough's initial study would have to be considered one of the most significant pieces of research in all of North American adult education.

It is clear that the contributions of the learning projects methodology are quite substantial. At the same time, as with any other research approach, the paradigm has certain constraints that define and delimit the ways in which learning projects data may be interpreted. Brookfield (1981a), for example, has reviewed Tough's research and identified three limitations with the approach.

First, there are limitations in using the structured interview. While the structured interview format has the advantage that it can be replicated, Brookfield (1981a: 115) points out that the methodology can "run the risk of forcing the researcher's notion of what are admissible and appropriate substantive concerns" upon subjects without taking into consideration what they believe to be relevant. In other words, the interview questions and the biases of the interviewer might prompt subjects to respond in a specific way.

Second, most of the subjects in Tough's 1971 survey were highly educated. Using the popular notion that education begets education, it could be argued that, since self-planning was clearly the predominant mode of learning in this study, it is not surprising for these learners to express a preference for this mode. Since then, however, several studies have investigated the learning projects conducted by adults of lower educational attainment than those in Tough's sample and have often found high degrees of self-planning (e.g. Brockett, 1983b, 1985c). Yet, as noted earlier, in the studies where the figures for self-planning were low, the samples tended to have a large number of "undereducated" adults. Thus, one could believe that a preference for self-planned learning will tend to be higher among those who have completed more formal schooling. But the relationship between self-directedness and previous education is not entirely clear and might, in fact, be related to other factors. In any case, this potential limitation is certainly a relevant concern when assessing the impact of self-directed learning research, and is therefore addressed further in Chapter 5.

Third, one might question the appropriateness of studying self-planned learning. Brookfield summarized this argument by stating that:

> extended investigations into the nature of noninstitutionalized adult learning, while interesting, are inappropriate in the current economic climate.

Instead of studying those adults who choose to ignore formal adult education provision and to devise their own learning schemes, we should be concentrating our efforts on retaining the loyalty and continuing participation of existing students as well as working to increase overall student numbers.

(Brookfield, 1981a: 117).

However, Brookfield is quick to negate this argument by stating that if, in fact, self-planning is as prevalent as the learning projects research suggests, adult education faces the challenge of identifying ways to support such efforts. It is this emphasis on supporting self-directed learners and their efforts that comprises the major focus of subsequent chapters in this book.

There are at least two other considerations that we believe are important when reviewing learning projects research. These have less to do with the methodology, *per se*, than with the way in which results could potentially be misinterpreted. When interpreting the results of learning projects studies, it is important to bear in mind that, while most researchers have used the Tough interview schedule as a point of departure, there is often considerable variation in the specific questions asked, the actual interview process, and the data analysis procedures. For example, most studies report figures for self-planning as a percentage of the *total* projects conducted by all subjects in the sample. However, Penland (1979) based his finding relative to self-planning on the percentage of the sample who completed *at least one* self-planned project, rather than the total percentage of projects that were planned by the learners themselves. This kind of variation is not a limitation in and of itself; however, those who utilize the findings need to be aware of these variations when interpreting data from these studies.

Another way in which learning projects data can be misinterpreted is that the approach is sometimes described as a qualitative research method. In reality, it is a quantitative descriptive survey approach. While interviewing is frequently associated with qualitative research, it is the way in which learning projects data are analyzed that places the method into a descriptive category. Fingeret (1982) points out that qualitative data are presented as quotations that have been taken from an interview or observation. She states that data are not the numbers of responses given to a particular question but, rather, are the actual words of the subjects themselves. In learning projects studies data are treated primarily through descriptive statistics.

Finally, Caffarella and O'Donnell have raised the concern that learning projects studies have "reached the point of dullness." They go on to offer the following suggestion:

We may need to put the element of surprise into future verification studies. If we know the answer in advance, do we really need to ask the question?

The greater the surprise or astonishment with the findings of our self-directed learning research, the greater the new knowledge about the concept will be.

(Caffarella and O'Donnell, 1988: 47)

The implication here is that while learning projects research has been vital to our understanding of self-direction in adult learning, we have pretty much reached a point of saturation with this approach. The kinds of studies that will be reported in the next two chapters are indicative of a healthy evolution in the development of research on self-direction in adult learning.

CONCLUSION

In summary, we believe that the learning projects approach has made a landmark contribution to the adult education literature and has, both directly and indirectly, served as a major source of impetus for the development of a systematic body of knowledge in the area of self-directed adult learning. At the same time, we believe that it is important to interpret learning projects findings with a degree of caution, and to recognize that the approach was designed to address the *frequency* and *nature* of learning projects activity, not to assess the quality of or reasons for such activities. These kinds of issues have begun to be addressed through other methodologies and will be explored in the next two chapters.

4 Measuring the iceberg: quantitative approaches to studying self-direction

In the previous chapter, we suggested that research on self-direction in adult learning has followed three different, though related, streams of inquiry. As was noted in Chapter 3, the first stream consists of descriptive research studies using the learning projects methodology. While this line of inquiry laid a foundation for our present understanding of self-direction by illustrating the widespread emphasis on such learning efforts, it became clear during the late 1970s and early 1980s that the "iceberg" concept, as outlined by Tough (1979) was itself only the tip of an iceberg. Thus, researchers began to search out new ways to gain a broader understanding of the self-direction phenomenon that would stretch beyond merely describing the frequency and nature of such activities.

As a result, two additional streams of research have evolved: the quantitative measurement of self-direction through written instruments and the use of qualitative methods such as observation and interviewing. This chapter will offer an examination of efforts to expand the knowledge base of self-direction by reviewing the first of these research directions. The third stream of research will be considered in Chapter 5.

QUANTITATIVE MEASURES OF SELF-DIRECTION

As was pointed out above, learning projects investigations provided greater understanding of the frequency and nature of participation in self-directed learning by many segments of the adult population. However, many questions remained unanswered. After several years of extensive replication of the Tough methodology by various researchers, it became clear that there was a need for research that would go beneath the surface explored by learning projects studies. For instance, little was known about personological variables, like self-concept and creativity, that might enhance or limit the urge toward self-direction. Similarly, questions remained about the nature and extent to which self-direction can influence the teaching-learning process in institutional settings. Thus, it was only possible to make indirect links to self-direction through measures such as the Internal–External Scale (Rotter, 1966), a scale designed to assess one's locus of control (the amount of personal control one perceives oneself to have), or the Personal Orientation Inventory (Shostrom, 1964, 1974) (a scale that measures the extent to which one believes oneself to possess characteristics associated with self-actualiz-ation) as conceptualized by Maslow (1970). An exception was the Autonomous Learner Index (ALI), a twenty-item self-administered Likert scale designed to measure attitudes toward dependence and independence in learning (Ferrell, 1978). However, this scale does not seem to have been used in research on self-direction beyond its initial reporting.

During the late 1970s, it became clear that, in order to advance the knowledge base of self-direction, it would be necessary to move beyond description toward prediction and comparison of self-direction *vis-à-vis* other characteristics. To this end, Guglielmino (1977) developed the Self-Directed Learning Readiness Scale. A few years later, the Oddi Conti-nuing Learning Inventory was developed (Oddi, 1986). Together, these two instruments have played a major role in making self-direction one of the most extensively researched areas in adult education during the decade of the 1980s.

THE SELF-DIRECTED LEARNING READINESS SCALE

One of the first efforts to move beyond Tough's learning projects methodo-logy was the development of the Self-Directed Learning Readiness Scale (SDLRS). Developed in 1977 by Lucy M. Guglielmino, for a doctoral dissertation at the University of Georgia, the SDLRS was designed to assess the extent to which individuals perceive themselves to possess skills and attitudes frequently associated with self-directedness in learning. The instru-ment was designed through a three-round Delphi survey process involving 14 individuals considered to be experts on self-directed learning. Upon revision, the instrument was administered to 307 persons in Georgia, Ver-mont, and Canada. From this administration, additional revisions were made and a reliability coefficient of 0.87 was estimated.

The SDLRS is a 58-item, 5-point Likert scale that yields a total score for self-directed readiness. In addition, a factor analysis of the instrument by Guglielmino (1977) identified the following eight factors:

1 Love of learning;
2 Self-concept as an effective, independent learner;
3 Tolerance of risk, ambiguity, and complexity in learning;
4 Creativity;

5 View of learning as a lifelong, beneficial process;
6 Initiative in learning;
7 Self-understanding; and
8 Acceptance of responsibility for one's own learning.

Although Guglielmino (1977) urged caution in utilizing this factor structure, it is nevertheless possible to recognize from these factors some of the attitudinal and personality factors that may be related to a tendency toward self-directedness.

At present, the SDLRS has been used in two major ways. First, it has been utilized to explore relationships between self-directed readiness and other personological variables through experimental, quasi-experimental, and correlational research designs. Second, it has been used as a diagnostic tool for assessing learners' perceptions of readiness for self-directed learning. A steadily growing number of studies have employed the SDLRS to date. In order to present a review of these investigations, the remainder of this section will be broken down into the following subsections: early studies using the SDLRS, studies examining psychosocial correlates of self-directed readiness, diagnostic studies, and investigations of self-directed readiness among a specific professional group (nurses). Finally, the section will conclude with an overall assessment/critique of the instrument.

Early studies

The first study to use the SDLRS with adults, other than Guglielmino's initial investigation, was reported by Torrance and Mourad (1978) and provided support for the construct validity of the instrument. Forty-one graduate students who were enrolled in a course on creative thinking completed the SDLRS and eight other instruments that produced eleven measures. Significant positive correlations were found between self-directed learning readiness and the following: three measures of originality, the ability to develop analogies in the description of photographs, creative personality, creative achievements, and right hemisphere style of learning. A significant negative correlation was found between SDLRS scores and the left hemisphere style of learning. The authors thus concluded that a link exists between creativity and the tendency toward self-directedness.

An especially interesting finding of this study was the positive relationship between self-directed readiness and right hemisphere style of learning. Among the functions of the right hemisphere of the brain are "preferences for subjectively processing information, dealing simultaneously with several problems at a time, grasping at new and uncertain truths, intuitive problem solving, playfulness in solving problems, using metaphors and analogies, and improvising" (Torrance and Mourad, 1978; 1170). Thus, by reporting a relationship between the SDLRS and several learning-related factors, this study has contributed to the way in which self-directed learning might be defined. It should be noted, however, that a more recent study (Blackwood, 1989) reported very different findings relative to the link between self-direction and hemisphericity; this study will be discussed later in the chapter.

In another study, Mourad (1979) examined the validity of the SDLRS, comparing SDLRS scores with selected creativity measures, and considering grade level and gender differences on SDLRS scores. The SDLRS was administered to 684 gifted elementary, junior, and senior high school students and to 185 members of the University of Georgia's School of Education faculty. In addition, the gifted students completed several tasks of the Torrance Tests of Creative Thinking and 569 students were rated on their self-directedness by their teachers using a Teachers Rating Scale.

With regard to the professors, Mourad found that SDLRS scores were not significantly related to faculty rank, research production during a three-year period, nor to the number of citations over two years. When SDLRS scores were compared with those of gifted students, however, a significant difference was found. Mourad suggested that the SDLRS thus discriminates between these two samples. Among the gifted students, significant relationships were noted between teacher ratings and seven of the eight factor scores on the SDLRS; also, there were statistically significant differences on SDLRS scores among the three levels of students (elementary, junior, and senior high) and between males and females.

One of the factors identified by Guglielmino as a component of self-directed readiness is self-concept as an effective learner. Sabbaghian (1980), therefore, took a closer look at the importance of self-concept relative to self-directedness. She mailed copies of the SDLRS and the Tennessee Self-Concept Scale (Fitts, 1965) to 80 randomly-selected adult undergraduate students at Iowa State University. A total of 77 individuals responded.

At least five major findings emerged from the Sabbaghian study and can be summarized as follows:

1 There was a significant positive correlation between self-directed readiness and self-concept;
2 Self-concept was found to be related to all factors of the SDLRS except for "acceptance of responsibility for one's own learning;"
3 A positive relationship was found to exist between self-image and self-directed readiness;
4 Individuals who had completed more years of formal education tended to demonstrate higher self-directed readiness and scored significantly

higher on four of the eight factors (love of learning, creativity, initiative in learning, and self-understanding); and

5 Age and gender, by themselves, were not significantly related to either self-directed readiness nor self-concept; however, the interactions between class rank were significantly related to SDLRS scores.

Based on these findings, Sabbaghian was able to conclude the following:

> There is a strong positive relationship between the self-image of adult students and their self-directedness in learning. As adults gain the ability to direct and organize their own learning, they consider themselves more and more as worthy persons in every aspect of life. Adult students with higher self-concepts appear to be ... more likely to be able to plan and direct the majority of their learning projects themselves than adult students with lower self-concepts.
>
> (Sabbaghian, 1980: 114–15)

When examining self-directed learning readiness, it is crucial to bear in mind that the SDLRS is a measure of the degree to which individuals *perceive* themselves to possess skills and attitudes associated with self-directed learning. It is *not* a measure of actual behavior. In an attempt to compare individuals' perceptions of self-directedness with their actual participation in learning projects, Hassan (1982) studied 77 adults selected at random from the population of Ames, Iowa. Each subject was interviewed using the Tough interview format and, at the close of the interview, was asked to complete the SDLRS.

Participants reported completing a mean of 9.8 learning projects in the year prior to the interview, 78 percent of which were self-planned. Less than 11 percent of the projects were undertaken for credit. As for the relationship between SDLRS scores and learning projects involvement, Hassan found significant positive correlations between number of learning projects and scores on the total SDLRS, and seven of the eight factor scores of the instrument. In other words, adults who were higher in self-directed readiness tended to be involved in a greater number of learning projects.

However, when Hassan compared high, average, and low self-directed readiness with the various types of primary planner that were identified by participants, she did not find a significant relationship. Self-planning was found to be the predominant approach to learning, regardless of the learners' degree of self-directed readiness. Individuals who are higher in readiness for self-direction are likely to be involved in more learning projects than adults whose self-directed readiness is lower. However, highly self-directed learners are not significantly more likely to choose self-planning of their projects than those who are average or low in self-directed readiness. Still, this study is an important one in that it builds a link between the descriptive-oriented learning projects approach and the prediction-oriented perspective of the SDLRS.

A more recent study (Hall-Johnsen, 1986) found further evidence for the link between self-directed readiness and actual learning involvement. Based on a sample of 65 professional staff from the Iowa State University Cooperative Extension Service, it was found that there was "a positive, predictive relationship between readiness and the number of self-planned projects conducted, as well as the amount of time spent on them" (Hall-Johnsen, 1986: 2522A).

Skaggs (1981) was also interested in the relationship between self-directedness and self-directed learning activity. The SDLRS and three other measures, including a biographical data form, a measure of locus of control, and a survey designed to assess self-directed learning involvement, were administered to a sample of registered nurses in Texas. She found that there was a relationship between SDLRS scores and number of hours devoted by respondents to self-directed learning. In addition, Skaggs found self-directedness to be related to internal locus of control and negatively related to influence by powerful others such as supervisors. Based on her findings, Skaggs suggested that the SDLRS is an effective tool for identifying nurses with a tendency toward self-directedness in learning and, thus, can be useful in providing educational opportunities for registered nurses.

Psychosocial correlates

Into the early 1980s, the SDLRS was being used by an increasing number of researchers as a way of linking self-directed readiness to a wide range of psychosocial factors. The studies by Torrance and Mourad (1978), Mourad (1979), and Sabbaghian (1980) paved the way for this research focus. Numerous studies have followed over the years.

For instance, the first author of this book looked at the link between self-directedness and perceived life satisfaction among a sample of older adults from a public housing building and an adult home (Brockett, 1983c, 1985a). Sixty-four persons, age 60 and older, were administered the SDLRS and the Salamon-Conte Life Satisfaction in the Elderly Scale (since renamed the Life Satisfaction in the Elderly Scale) (Salamon and Conte, 1981). A weak but statistically significant positive relationship was found between the two variables, suggesting that a relationship may exist between one's perception of self-directedness as a learner and such concepts as independence and quality of life during the later years. In addition, however, several concerns were raised about the appropriateness of the SDLRS for certain populations, particularly those with relatively little formal education. This issue is addressed in greater detail later in the chapter.

While the link between self-directed readiness and life satisfaction was statistically weak in the Brockett (1983c, 1985a) study, further support for this link was provided in a study by East (1987). This study was based on 103 older adults drawn from a retirement village in South Central Florida. Results of this study lend further support to the self-directedness–life-satisfaction link. Further, East noted that two SDLRS factors – "acceptance of responsibility for one's own learning" and "love of learning" were "mostly responsible for the effect on life satisfaction" (East 1987: 2848A).

In another study involving older adults, Curry (1983) looked at the self-directed readiness of 300 participants involved in formal adult education programs. Using a descriptive-comparative *ex post facto* design, she found significant differences in SDLRS scores based on gender, marital status, educational background, and self-reported measures of intellectual functioning, learning and health, self-help groups and health, and current life satisfaction. In addition, when comparing the SDLRS scores of this group with those of the sample on which Guglielmino's norms were based, Curry found that the older group "excelled" on SDLRS scores. Taken together, these studies provide reasonably strong support for a link between life satisfaction and self-directedness among older adults.

Leeb examined the relationship between self-directed readiness and the tendency to practice a health-conducive lifestyle. In a study involving thirty-five adults between the ages of 21 and 55, Leeb (1985: 159) found that "the people who demonstrate positive health behaviors can be described as highly self-directed" Also, in this study, Leeb looked at the notion of cognitive and ethical development as proposed by Perry (1970). According to the Perry scheme, as individuals mature, they move from thinking about knowledge and values in a dualistic way (i.e., right/wrong, good/bad) toward affirmation that there are multiple views of reality based largely on the context through which situations are perceived. As an exploratory hypothesis, then, Leeb predicted that as individuals move away from dualist thinking, there would be an increase in readiness for self-direction. While this finding was not confirmed, she suggested that this potential linkage should not necessarily be abandoned, given the limited size of her sample and the exploratory nature of the hypothesis in this particular investigation.

Long and Agyekum (1983) employed a multitrait-multimethod approach in order to test thirty-seven hypotheses related to the validation of the SDLRS. Using a sample of 136 college students, slightly less than half of whom were black, they compared SDLRS scores with age, educational achievement level, dogmatism, and agreement response set (i.e., the extent to which subjects' responses on a given scale are determined by personal beliefs and knowledge or by a tendency to respond consistently regardless of the content of various items). Also, they asked college instructors to rate students on "self-direction in learning based on the same characteristics Guglielmino identified in her original work" (Long and Agyekum, 1983: 79). Among the findings of this study were the following:

1 Increasing age was significantly related to a higher SDLRS score;
2 Black students scored significantly higher on the SDLRS than white students;
3 Those individuals who scored higher on the SDLRS were significantly more likely to receive lower scores on dogmatism and agreement response set;
4 Instructor ratings were not significantly related to scores on the SDLRS; and
5 Instructors rated white students significantly higher on self-directedness than black students.

The finding pertaining to race and SDLRS score would seem to be a most important one, given the notion that self-directed learning is frequently described as a middle-class, white phenomenon. With regard to this finding, however, Long and Agyekum offer the following caution:

> Any effort to explain differences in performance between two cultural or racial groups is fraught with danger. Such explanations are often interpreted as an effort to use "race" as the causal factor .... Important differences that seem to favor the black students seem to be associated with the psychological variables that are influenced by performance on the dogmatism and agreement response set instruments.
>
> (Long and Agyekum, 1983: 85)

While the cautions raised here are certainly in order, we believe that the findings nevertheless offer at least tentative empirical support for taking a closer look at the potential for self-directed learning among groups that have traditionally been less involved in more formal forms of adult education.

Overall, Long and Agyekum concluded that there is, indeed, validation support for the SDLRS. However, concerns about apparent inconsistency between instructor ratings and SDLRS score prompted the authors to conduct a second study (Long and Agyekum, 1984). The second study was essentially a replication of the earlier investigation, except that a different teacher-rating instrument was utilized. For the most part, the findings supported those of the earlier study. With regard to teacher ratings, though, a different picture emerged. Though the correlation between SDLRS score and teacher rating of self-directedness fell slightly short of statistical significance, it was considerably stronger than in the first study, leading the authors to suggest that the original teacher-rating instrument may have been flawed. Of course, there is a clear concern in attempting to draw conclusions from non-significant statistical analysis, so this point can only be taken with a minimal level of credence. Indeed, Long and Agyekum (1988) caution that more cross-validation studies of the SDLRS must be conducted before a complete interpretation of such findings is possible.

Intuitively, one may find it easy to believe that there is a relationship between learner self-directedness and the desire to learn for the pure enjoyment of and interest in learning. Reynolds (1986), in a study of ninety-five part-time community college students, found support for such a link. Administering the SDLRS and the Education Participation Scale (Boshier, 1971) to the sample, Reynolds found a significant positive correlation between SDLRS score and the motivational orientation factor "Cognitive Interest." At the same time, a significant negative correlation was found between readiness for self-direction and the motivational orientations of "Professional Advancement" and "External Expectations." Based on these findings, Reynolds suggested that self-directed readiness may be associated with the desire to learn for the sake of learning, while those who are motivated by external factors, such as the desire for professional advancement and the expectations of others, are likely to be lower in self-directedness.

McCarthy (1986) used the SDLRS to examine relationships between self-directedness and attitude toward mathematics among 183 younger undergraduate students (those individuals age 25 or younger) and older students (those individuals 26 or older). While no significant relationship was found between self-directedness and attitude toward mathematics, the older group was found to be significantly higher on SDLRS scores.

It was noted earlier that self-directed readiness appears to be linked to such factors as creativity, problem-solving ability, and degree of personal change (Torrance and Mourad, 1978). Guglielmino, *et al.* (1987) were interested in whether or not a link exists between these characteristics and actual job *performance*. In this study, which was first reported in Guglielmino and Guglielmino (1983), the researchers administered the SDLRS to 753 employees (managers and non-managers) of a large utility company who participated in training courses. It was found that those individuals rated as "outstanding performers" in jobs requiring high levels of creativity, problem-solving ability, and/or degree of change scored significantly higher than the remainder of the subjects in the sample. Further, while women scored "slightly higher" than men, there were no significant differences between blacks and whites, nor between managers and non-managers. Relative to age, it was found that those persons in the 46–55 age group scored significantly lower than those of the other age groups. Finally, a positive relationship was found between SDLRS scores and level of education. From their findings, the authors offered the following recommendation:

> In light of this study, personnel departments in business and industry might consider examining the use of a measure of self-directed learning readiness as part of the selection process for individuals who fill highly creative jobs, highly changing jobs, and jobs requiring a high level of problem-solving ability.
>
> (Guglielmino, *et al.*, 1987; 316)

A more recent study by Roberts (1986) found similar results with a sample of managers from the Hong Kong Telephone Company. Here, SDLRS scores were found to relate to the following: management level; management performance; self-perceptions of creativity; problem-solving ability; education level; and degree of change required in the job.

Most recently, the SDLRS has been used in several additional studies with various findings related to self-directed learning readiness and a wide range of variables. For instance, Young (1986) did not find a significant correlation between SDLRS score and locus of control. In another study, the "intuitive" approach and "judging" orientation of the Myers-Briggs Type Indicator were found to be related to self-directed readiness among adult degree students (Johnson, *et al.*, 1988). Self-directed readiness was negatively related to a preference for structure in a course setting, but was not related to achievement (Russell, 1989). Among a sample of pregnant women, Lacey found that SDLRS scores peaked during the second trimester and declined through the third and fourth, "suggesting that this finding has implications for the timing of prenatal/postnatal classes" (Lacey, 1989: 2496A). There was no significant correlation between the SDLRS scores of a sample of fifth grade students and their teachers (Eisenman, 1989). Finally, Bitterman found a relationship between self-directed readiness and achieving style, a concept that "is based on motivation theory and is rooted in the individual's reinforcement for goal accomplishment" within one's environment (Bitterman, 1989: 851A).

Diagnostic studies of self-directed readiness

The studies described above have emphasized the use of the SDLRS as a tool for basic research, designed primarily to explore the link between learner self-directedness and a wide range of psychosocial variables. In addition to this use, however, the SDLRS can be used as a diagnostic measure. The first three studies presented in this section offer a look at self-directed readiness in a particular context: graduate courses in adult education where a learning-contracts approach is utilized. Caffarella (1982, 1983b) examined the relationship between the value that learners ascribe to using a learning-plan (contracting) format in a graduate-course setting and their perceptions of self-directed readiness. Fifty-four graduate students who had enrolled in courses offered by the researcher over a 2-year period, at the completion of their course, were mailed copies of the SDLRS and the Learning Plan Format Follow-Up Survey, a questionnaire developed by Caffarella to determine learners' "opinions related to the worth and value of the learning plan format, their perceptions of their own self-directed learning skills, and what if any effect this had on their own continuing learning and teaching activities" (Caffarella, 1982: 48). Based on forty-two returned questionnaires, it was found that 69 percent of the respondents believed the contracting format to be an excellent tool, while the remaining individuals felt it to be very good or good. With regard to SDLRS scores, the mean for this sample was at the 90th percentile based on norms established by Guglielmino (1977). Caffarella concluded that the learning-plan approach is a useful strategy for promoting self-directed learning, and could be applied effectively in a wide range of adult learning situations.

In a more extensive follow-up study, Caffarella and Caffarella (1986) obtained data from 163 students from six universities. Using the SDLRS, the Learning Contract Follow-Up Survey, and the Self-Directed Learning Competencies Self-Appraisal Form, also developed by R. S. Caffarella, support for the use of contract learning in graduate education was again found. However, it was also found that the use of the learning contract did not have a significant effect on the student's self-directed learning readiness. The investigators speculated that the lack of a significant effect might be attributed to very high pre-test scores on the SDLRS. Thus, while the study provides support for the attractiveness of the learning contract approach, it does not establish a link between a preference for contracting and one's level of self-directed readiness.

Kasworm (1982, 1983), in another study involving graduate students in adult education courses, examined the development of self-directed knowledge and behavior resulting from participation in a graduate course using learning contracts and where students were expected to assume a high level of self-direction. The sample was comprised of thirty-three individuals enrolled in one of two sections of a "Methods and Techniques in Adult Education" course. Each individual was asked to complete the SDLRS at the outset of the course and again at the completion, along with a course evaluation form. In addition, the instructor and two students maintained "observational diaries" for the duration of the course.

A t-test analysis for the pre- and post-test SDLRS scores revealed a significant increase in scores over the duration of the course. In the course evaluation, most students expressed positive reactions to the self-directed learning approach and indicated a desire for further self-directed study opportunities; however, about one-quarter of the respondents stated that they found the approach to be difficult and would probably not opt for additional courses using a self-directed learning approach. Kasworm suggested that some areas for further investigation to better understand this dilemma include basic writing and oral communication skills, cognitive ability, and learning style preferences.

Another diagnostic study looked at a different group of students. In this investigation, Cunningham (1989) studied the self-directed readiness among three populations affiliated with the Southern Baptist Seminary: new students; students nearing graduation; and graduates with 2 years experience in the ministry. He reported a "significant increase" in readiness between the new and graduating students. However, it should be noted that this is not an increase, *per se*, but rather a *difference* since the comparison was based on two groups at one point in time rather than on one group at different times. Also, Cunningham noted that 2 years of experience in the ministry "did not significantly increase readiness for self-directed learning" (Cunningham, 1989: 3246A). But again, the word "increase" seems to have been misused; instead, there were no significant differences between the practicing ministers and the students.

Finally, a study by Rutland (1988) looked at the effects of a self-directed learning group activity on the self-directed readiness and self-concept of Adult Basic Education (ABE) and General Educational Development (GED) students. Using a pre-test post-test design, with an experimental group that participated in 10 1-hour group sessions, Rutland found no significant differences between experimental and control groups on either variable. Like other studies discussed in this and the following section, these findings contribute to mixed findings relative to the use of experimental treatments to increase self-directedness among adult learners. Thus, while some of these studies indicate the potential of the SDLRS as a diagnostic tool, it must be argued that the jury is still out.

Nurses and self-directed learning readiness

Self-directed learning readiness has been studied across a broad spectrum of adult groups. However, there is perhaps no other group that has been studied more extensively than nurses. SDLRS studies involving nurses span different methodologies (e.g., correlational, experimental, quasi-experimental) and different purposes (e.g., studies of psychosocial factors related to self-directed readiness, diagnostic investigations of the concept). Thus, we have chosen to present these studies within a separate subsection.

The earliest investigation using the SDLRS with nurses was a diagnostic study conducted by Savoie (1980), who was interested in determining if it would be possible to predict success in continuing education courses for nurses where learners were expected to assume a high degree of self-direction. Savoie administered the SDLRS and a biographical information instrument to 152 nurses enrolled in one of seven courses. A percentage grade for the course (e.g. 79 percent, 94 percent) served to measure degree of success in the experience.

It was found that a significant, positive relationship existed between SDLRS scores and course grades. Savoie also noted a relationship between self-directed readiness and individuals' self-concept as self-directed learners; a finding supported by several other studies (e.g., Sabbaghian, 1980; Brockett, 1983c, 1985a). Savoie concluded that the SDLRS can be useful in determining the extent to which learners enrolled in activities requiring a high degree of self-direction may need extra support or assistance to succeed in the learning experience.

Box (1983) investigated differences among first level students, second level students, and graduates of an associate degree nursing program. Based on data from 477 respondents, Box did not find significant differences in SDLRS score among the three groups; however, she did note a positive significant correlation between SDLRS score and grade-point average. To some extent, this corroborates Savoie's (1980) finding.

Most SDLRS research to date has employed a correlational design, where comparisons are made between two or more variables without the administration of a specific treatment or the use of control groups. However, a study of nursing students by Wiley (1982a, 1982b) was an exception. Using a nonequivalent, control-group design, Wiley examined the effects of a 12-hour, "process-oriented", self-directed learning project and the personal preference for structure on self-directed learning readiness. A total of 104 junior nursing students, about 85 percent of whom were 20–21 years old, comprised the study sample.

Both the control and experimental groups were pretested on the SDLRS and Ginther's Reaction to Statements (1974), a measure of preference for structure. The experimental group then participated in a 12-hour, self-directed learning process experience. Each group was posttested on the SDLRS upon completion of the treatment. After analyzing the data, Wiley drew the following conclusions:

1 Teaching the SDL process did not increase the overall SDL readiness of these baccalaureate nursing students;
2 Preference for structure did not affect students' SDL readiness; and
3 Students who preferred low structure and who experienced an SDL project gained in SDL readiness.

It also appeared, but was not conclusive, that students who preferred high structure and who experienced an SDL project lost in SDL readiness (Wiley, 1982a, 1982b). Based on these conclusions, Wiley suggests that a self-directed learning process experience is useful for learners who prefer low structure. However, students who prefer high structure may benefit from "assistance in self-structuring" in addition to the self-directed learning process project.

Crook (1985) was interested in exploring the predictive validity of the SDLRS. Like Savoie (1980), Crook wanted to determine the extent to which SDLRS score could predict success in the nursing classroom. Sixty-three first-year nursing students completed the SDLRS and a demographic questionnaire during their first week of classes. At the end of the academic year "students were asked to nominate the three 'most effective' self-directed learners" in their seven- to eight-member study group. Faculty members were also asked to do the same for their groups of students.

A significant correlation was found between SDLRS score and two variables: peer nomination scores and end of year grades. However, as was noted in another study (Brockett, 1985a, 1985b), these correlations explained only a small percentage (7 percent and 8 percent, respectively) of the variance. Based on these findings, Crook concluded that, although the instrument has face validity and is easy to use, "for the purposes of predicting success or failure in this school, the SDLRS has not been found useful" (Crook, 1985: 278).

Three additional diagnostic studies have recently been reported (Moore, 1988; Murray, 1988; Palumbo, 1989). Moore looked at predictors of success in home-study nursing courses. In this study of 121 nurses, SDLRS scores did not correlate significantly with final course grade. However, Moore notes that the nature of the sample, which involved both technical and professional nurses who were both highly self-directed and highly motivated, and who answered most test items correctly, could have limited "possible correlation between the criterion and predictor variables" (Moore, 1988: 1670A).

Murray used a quasi-experimental design to "investigate the effect of a clinical internship on the self-directed learning readiness of baccalaureate nursing students" (Murray, 1988: 1036-A). It was found that: (a) the experimental group (who participated in a clinical internship) differed significantly between pretest and posttest SDLRS scores; (b)SDLRS scores were related to grade-point average and plans for advanced education in nursing; and (c) SDLRS scores were significantly higher for those students who "felt they had a quality internship experience" (Murray, 1988: 1036A).

Like Murray, Palumbo (1990) employed a pretest posttest design to measure change in SDLRS score over time. Over a period of one and one-half years, this group of forty-five registered nurses studying for a baccalaureate degree showed a significant change in SDLRS score, but these scores were not found to be associated with several demographic variables. Palumbo concluded that the change in self-directed readiness may be linked with participation in formal education and with the readiness of these nurses to finish their degree programs.

Graeve studied "registered nurses' patterns of self-directed learning for professional growth and development" (Graeve, 1987: 820A). She found that nurses reported spending significantly more time: (a) in self-directed than in teacher-directed learning; and (b) in personal than in professional learning. A significant relationship was found between SDLRS score and the number of hours engaged in self-directed learning, a finding that lends further support to the Hassan (1982) and Hall-Johnsen (1986) studies.

In an investigation of self-directedness and job satisfaction among nurses, Middlemiss (1988) used the SDLRS along with a measure of job characteristics, motivating potential of a job, and job satisfaction. Based on data from a sample of 115 randomly selected professional nurses, Middlemiss found that respondents perceived themselves to be high in self-directed readiness and several job characteristics, and that the interaction of self-directed readiness, job characteristics, and motivating potential of the job "predicted 29 percent of the variance in job satisfaction for professional nurses" (Middlemiss, 1988: 1036A).

From these studies, it can be seen that self-directed readiness is viewed as an important concept in the study of adult learning among nurses. And while the picture presented by the results is somewhat mixed, this is essentially a reflection of the overall body of knowledge relative to self-directed learning readiness. Some possible explanations for this mixed picture are presented in the next section.

Analysis of the SDLRS: methodological and substantive issues

From the findings of studies such as those presented above, it should be clear that the Self-Directed Learning Readiness Scale has made a major contribution to the knowledge base of self-direction in learning. Yet, as with any self-reporting paper and pencil instrument, it is unwise to accept the appropriateness of the scale without first looking at such considerations as reliability and validity. In her original investigation of the SDLRS, Guglielmino (1977) found a reliability coefficient of 0.87, which suggests that scores derived from the instrument should be rather highly generalizable to populations similar to those in Guglielmino's study. Further validation support for the scale has been reported by Long and Agyekum (1983, 1984) in their multitrait-multifactor study, Finestone (1984) in a construct validation study of the instrument, and Reynolds (1986) and Long (1987) through item-to-total correlations for each of the fifty-eight SDLRS items.

However, at the same time, Long and Agyekum {1983: 87) have stated that a further area for SDLRS research includes "validation studies based on intensive experimenter observation". While no SDLRS studies based on "intensive" observation have been reported in the literature to date, the first author of this book, in the investigation of self-directed learning readiness and life satisfaction that was mentioned earlier, *did* have the opportunity to gain some insights from observation that led to additional analysis of the SDLRS (Brockett, 1983c, 1985b).

In the life satisfaction study, each of the sixty-four participants was given the option of either completing instruments on their own or having the researcher read each item and record the response. Throughout the process, it became clear that many of the people in the study were having difficulty and were becoming frustrated as they completed the SDLRS. Since more than 60 percent of the individuals chose the "oral" format, and since a t-test revealed that there was not a significant difference in the scores of those persons who completed the instrument in oral and written formats, "it was possible to observe various points at which problems relative to the format and layout of the SDLRS appeared to arise" (Brockett, 1985b: 19). These concerns led to the decision to take a closer look at the instrument.

Looking first at the reliability of the instrument, a coefficient of 0.87 (the same figure reported by Guglielmino, 1977) was noted. However, as Nunnally has pointed out, reliability does not necessarily imply validity (i.e., the extent to which a scale measures what it was intended to measure). Therefore, a high level of "reliability is a *necessary* but not *sufficient* condition for high validity" (Nunnally, 1970: 107).

In order to look beyond reliability toward internal consistency of the scale, an item analysis of the scale was conducted. Here, item-to-total correlations were obtained for each item of the instrument. It was found that 12 of the 58 SDLRS items (i.e., 21 percent of the instrument) did not correlate significantly with the total scale. Further, two related concerns seemed to emerge. First, of these 12 items, 9 were among 17 items of the scale written to be scored in reverse. Adding to this confusion is that many of the reverse-scoring items were written using double negatives. Second, many of the respondents were confused by the wording of the response choices of the SDLRS, which range from "Almost never true of me: I hardly ever feel this way" to "Almost always true of me: there are very few times when I don't feel this way".

The following comment addresses what we believed to be at least a partial explanation for these methodological concerns.

It is suggested that the educational level of the sample can be associated, to a large degree, with these difficulties. Previous research using the SDLRS, primarily with subjects having at least a high school education, did not report these kinds of problems. One exception to this trend was a study of rural adults of low formal educational attainment living in rural Vermont (Leean and Sisco, 1981). This study examined the learning efforts of 93 adults through the learning projects interview format, the SDLRS, and case studies of a portion of the larger sample. In a personal communication, Sisco ... stated that similar kinds of difficulties were encountered in using the SDLRS as have been noted above. He concurred that many of the subjects found the reverse-scoring items and response choices frustrating. Based on the somewhat tentative observations of these two investigations, it is speculated that potential concerns are accentuated when the instrument is administered to adults of low formal educational attainment

(Brockett, 1985b: 20).

While we believe that educational attainment might be a key link in terms of internal consistency of the SDLRS with this particular sample, it is important to note that Finestone (1984), in his content validation of the SDLRS based on labor education participants, did not find significant differences on SDLRS scores according to one's level of formal educational attainment. At the same time, Leeb (1985), in her study of health promoting behavior among a sample comprised largely of college graduates, found that eleven items of the SDLRS did not correlate significantly with scores on the total scale and, further, that eight of the 11 items were among those questioned in the life satisfaction study.

Landers (1990) undertook a comparison between the SDLRS and the Oddi Continuing Learning Inventory (OCLI). He administered both instruments and a demographic form to ninety-eight graduate students at Syracuse University. Findings relative to the comparison will be discussed later in this chapter. In terms of the SDLRS, though, Landers found that each of the eight factors correlated significantly with total SDLRS score. Further, he noted that only six of the SDLRS items were found to be weak statistically. It was concluded that in spite of identified concerns with the scale, internal reliability was very high; thus, the SDLRS is the most appropriate of the two instruments to use to measure self-direction in adult learning. The OCLI is discussed further in the next section.

Although methodological concerns with the SDLRS raise some important questions about the appropriateness of the scale for certain adult populations, there seems to be an even greater issue at hand. It is suggested that the SDLRS defines self-directed learning readiness in a way that is highly oriented toward formal education and the learning of knowledge as opposed to skills, largely through books. The issues might be summarized in the following way:

Self-directed readiness, as defined by the SDLRS, is very much oriented toward learning through books and schooling. Perhaps this is where the present findings depart from the majority of previous SDLRS research, since earlier studies have generally reported samples of college students and adults with at least a high school education. For these groups, the SDLRS has been demonstrated to be an appropriate instrument. But how relevant can the scale be to those adults who have spent little time in school?

One can argue that the SDLRS is appropriate for adults in general, citing the extensive body of literature of participation in continuing education and learning projects demonstrating that those adults with more formal education will be more inclined toward formal continuing education participation, overall learning projects activity, and positive attitudes toward learning. Indeed, there is something to be said for the notion of "education begets education." But such a strong emphasis on books and schooling tends to minimize the impact of skills and attitudes where books are, at best, supplemental tools and may, in fact, even be unnecessary. Auto mechanics, musicians, athletes, and artists are but a few of the kinds of individuals for whom the most meaningful learning comes not from a book, but from the actual experience of "doing". By using a definition of self-directed learning that is as school- or book-oriented as the SDLRS, and expecting it to be relevant to all adults, there is a risk of excluding individuals from many walks of life, such as those mentioned [in Chapters One and Two], who may excel at taking charge of their learning, but have generally done so in nonschool settings, with primary emphasis on resources other than books.

(Brockett, 1985b: 21–2)

Two additional studies have attempted to provide an even closer look at the appropriateness of the SDLRS, and offer very different conclusions. In a further look at the internal consistency issue, Long (1987) conducted an item-to-total analysis of the SDLRS based on a sample of 117 college students "similar to Guglielmino's original sample, except that the subjects may have been slightly older and had a higher education level" than those in the earlier investigation (Long, 1987: 333). Long's major findings were that: (a) 3 of the 58 items did not correlate with the total instrument and (b) 12 of the 58 items correlated significantly with age. Based on these findings, Long argues that the findings from the Brockett (1985a, 1985b) study "are more sample-related than scale-related", meaning that the problems encountered in the earlier study may be due more to the nature of the sample than to limitations of the instrument.

Long's study makes an important contribution, for – as we recommend in Chapter 13 – there is a need for replication studies that can lead to refinement of the methodologies used to study self-direction in learning. Although we are not in complete agreement with Long's conclusion, since the emphasis of his study was on *age* –rather than *educational attainment*, which was at the heart of the concerns raised in the Brockett (1985a, 1985b) study – we still believe, however, that Long has made a useful contribution, and we welcome further validation work of this type.

Finally, perhaps the most direct criticism levelled against the SDLRS – has been presented by Field (1989). In this study, Field examined structure, validity, and reliability of the SDLRS by administering the instrument to 244 individuals enrolled as students at the Institute of Technical and Adult Teacher Education in Sydney, Australia. A reliability coefficient of 0.89 was found, which is very close to figures reported previously (Guglielmino, 1977; Brockett, 1985b). However, item-to-total correlations revealed that twelve items did not achieve a 0.3 correlation coefficient with the total SDLRS. Interestingly, three of the items that did not correlate have been identified similarly in at least three other studies (Brockett, 1985b; Leeb, 1985; Long, 1987), and two additional items were found not to correlate with total SDLRS score in both the Brockett and Leeb investigations. Thus, at this time, the evidence is rather convincing that early concerns raised about certain items of the scale are warranted.

Field raises a number of other concerns relative to the SDLRS. Specifically, these concerns center on four areas: (a) the use of the Delphi technique to generate items, given conceptual confusion relative to the term "self-directed learning;" (b) lack of definitions for the terms "self-directed learner" and "readiness;" (c) the use of negatively phrased items; and (d) the instrument-development process used by Guglielmino, where 9 of 41 original items had been eliminated and 26 new items were added, without separate validation efforts, to give the scale its current 58 items. Based on these concerns, Field offered the following conclusion:

> These findings suggest that the use of the SDLRS as an indicator of readiness for self-directed learning is not justified. As has been revealed, most of the claims regarding the scale rest on Guglielmino's developmental work which is seriously flawed, both methodologically and conceptually .... This tentative interpretation does not imply any support whatsoever for continued use of the SDLRS. The problems inherent in the scale are so substantial that it should not continue to be used.
>
> (Field, 1989: 138)

Field's study prompted a series of responses. Guglielmino (1989) responded to the four criticisms mentioned by Field. First, she stated that the Delphi process was *not* used for the selection of items, but rather, in order to obtain a consensus about characteristics of the self-directed learner. Second, Guglielmino points out that "self-directed learner" was defined through the responses of the Delphi panel, and clarifies that "readiness" implies that self-direction can be viewed as a continuum and with learners existing at various points along the continuum. Third, Guglielmino justifies the use of "reverse items" as a way of minimizing the potential for "response set", where a person who responds similarly to several items of a measure "is likely to assume that the remaining responses will be similar and cease to read the items carefully" (Guglielmino, 1989: 237). Here she reports that, in another study – based on a sample of 3,151 individuals – only one of the reverse items had item-test correlations of 0.30 or higher. Fourth, Guglielmino points out that the "17 additional items were added after the initial field test, not 'after validation of the scale,' as stated by Field" (Guglielmino, 1989: 238). Finally, Guglielmino presents evidence intended to refute concerns raised by Field relative to the validity of the scale and concludes that Field's report "is so filled with errors of omission and commission that it does not merit serious consideration" (Guglielmino, 1989: 240).

Long (1989) and McCune (1989b) offer further reactions to the Field study. Long (1989) states that Field's review of literature omitted several important references and provided references to other studies that were "lifted out of context" or were "particularly misleading" (Long, 1989: 241). He also adds further support to the comments by Guglielmino (1989) relative to the validity of the SDLRS. McCune (1989b) takes issue with Field's statistical analysis. Among the concerns raised are Field's use of a "modified" version of the SDLRS rather than the standard version of the scale and his discussions of reliability, factor analysis, and reverse-scored items.

Clearly, the SDLRS has proven to be a source of controversy within the realm of research on self-direction in adult learning. Concerns with the instrument have led various writers to make recommendations ranging from proceeding with caution and ensuring that the scale is validated for different samples (Brockett, 1985b) to total dismissal of the instrument (Field, 1989). This controversy was perhaps further escalated in that, as recently as 1988, Guglielmino had not acknowledged or addressed concerns raised with the scale (e.g. Guglielmino and Guglielmino, 1988). Recently, however, Guglielmino pointed out that in response to earlier concerns (e.g., Brockett, 1985b; Brookfield, 1984c), she has developed a new version of the SDLRS for adults with lower reading and/or English proficiency levels. This is an encouraging development that may address some of the concerns raised with the original scale.

In summary, we believe that despite several apparent substantive and methodological concerns, the SDLRS has made a most important contribution to present understanding of the self-directed learning phenomenon by generating considerable research, controversy, and dialogue. We think that this contribution ultimately outweighs the limitations that seem to be inherent within the instrument. Indeed, the SDLRS has made it possible to advance the knowledge base of self-direction in ways that otherwise probably would not have been possible. Guglielmino is to be commended for her willingness to help us become better able to explain what lies beneath the surface of the adult learning iceberg. At the same time, we believe that the criticisms raised about the scale cannot be overlooked. There remain too many questions, particularly relative to the validity of the scale, that are not easily dismissed. We are unwilling to dismiss the scale, as Field has suggested, for to do so would mean to ignore such findings as those presented by Long (1987). However, we do recommend that the SDLRS be used with the same discretion as any other standardized instrument. And, as we point out in Chapter 13, we would hope that future adult education researchers would join in the search for new and improved ways of measuring the iceberg.

THE ODDI CONTINUING LEARNING INVENTORY

The Self-Directed Learning Readiness Scale has played a major role in making it possible to quantitatively measure self-reports of learners' tendencies toward self-direction. While there are certain limitations in attempting to quantify a construct that is linked to personality dimensions, the approach can nevertheless help us to gain understanding that is not likely to be otherwise obtained. Yet these instruments are limited by the way in which they define the meaning of a construct, such as is the case with the SDLRS relative to those learners who are not oriented toward books or formal learning.

As a way of providing an alternative measure of self-direction in learning, Oddi (1984, 1985) developed the Oddi Continuing Learning Inventory (OCLI). Using a theoretical framework based on "personality characteristics of individuals whose learning behavior is characterized by initiative and persistence in learning over time through a variety of modes" (1985: 98), Oddi identified three clusters that she hypothesized to be essential personality dimensions of self-directed continuing learners. These dimensions include:

1 *Proactive Drive versus Reactive Drive* – ability to initiate and persist in learning without immediate or obvious external reinforcement" (1985: 98);
2 *Cognitive Openness versus Defensiveness* "openness to new ideas and activities, ability to adapt to change, and tolerance of ambiguity" as opposed to "rigidity, fear of failure, and avoidance of new ideas and activities" (1985: 99); and
3 *Commitment to Learning versus Apathy or Aversion to Learning* – while many individuals enjoy learning for its own sake, there are also individ-

uals who have little interest in learning involvement. Those who fit the personality dimension of self-directed continuing learners generally fall into the former category.

Based on these theoretical dimensions, Oddi constructed 100 items that were subjected to a content validation by panels of graduate students and experts in psychological constructs or self-directed learning. The 65 remaining items were organized into a seven-point Likert scale and, in this pre-pilot form, were administered to 30 volunteers. Emerging from this preliminary scale was a 31-item instrument, which was administered to 287 graduate students in law, nursing, and education. Five items from this instrument proved unreliable; however, the 26 remaining items yielded a raw score coefficient alpha of 0.75.

In order to obtain validation support for the OCLI, Oddi then identified a new sample of 271 graduate students in adult education, law, and nursing. Each person in this sample was asked to complete the OCLI and one of four instruments selected in order to estimate external validity for the scale. Included in this validation were the following instruments: the Leisure Activity Scale (Litchfield, 1965), a measure of adult participation in educational activities; the Internal-External Scale (Rotter, 1966), which measures perceived locus of control; four scales of the Adjective Check List (Gough and Heilburn, 1983), designed as a self-report of selected personality characteristics; and the Shipley Institute of Living Scale (Shipley, 1982), a measure of adult intelligence.

It was found that the mean score on the OCLI for the sample was 123.6, with a standard deviation slightly above 19 and a median of 126. A significant degree of skewness suggests that a fairly high number of the respondents in the sample could be described as "self-directed continuing learners." Gender and age correlated significantly with the scale, while educational level, family income level, and parent's educational level did not correlate significantly. Furthermore, while two of the items did not correlate significantly with the total scale, the remaining 24 items demonstrated an internal consistency of 0.875 and a test–retest reliability of 0.893.

A factor analysis of the instrument revealed the presence of three factors. The first of these is essentially the notion of a proactive approach toward learning, which was identified in the theoretical formulation used in the study, along with "the ability to work independently and to learn through involvement with others" (Oddi, 1986: 103). A second factor was labelled "Ability to be Self-Regulating," and a third factor was called "Avidity for Reading." Since these factors only accounted for 30.9 percent, 8 percent, and 6.8 percent of the variance, respectively, Oddi suggests that the factors are not likely to be as useful as the total score on the instrument. However, we would note that accounting for nearly 50 percent of the variance with any instrument is somewhat remarkable, given the many intervening variables that are typically at work in human behavior.

With regard to validity, Oddi reported positive correlations between OCLI scores and scores on the Leisure Activity Survey, as well as three of the four subscales on the Adjective Check List. On the other hand, the scale did not correlate with scores on the locus-of-control measure and a subscale of the Adjective Check List dealing with open-mindedness and flexibility. From the validity-related findings, Oddi suggests that the scale demonstrates convergent validity, and supports the elements of proactive drive and commitment to learning as elements of self-directedness in learning.

A particularly encouraging finding is that the OCLI did not correlate significantly with scores on the Shipley adult intelligence measure. When combined with the lack of significance between OCLI scores and educational level, it would appear that the scale does not demonstrate bias toward those persons who possess a high level of intelligence or a strong orientation toward formal learning. Given the concerns that have been raised relative to the SDLRS, this finding could potentially prove important in using the OCLI with adults of low formal education, as well as with populations involving individuals with average or lower levels of intelligence.

Based on her findings, Oddi concluded that when used in its entirety, the scale demonstrates a satisfactory level of reliability and validity. However, she warns that the scale should be "used with caution until further studies are undertaken" (Oddi,1984: 174). We agree with this assessment, for to do otherwise would run the risk of promoting the same kind of controversy that has surrounded the use of the SDLRS.

While the OCLI has been used in relatively few studies to date, compared with the SDLRS, it is noteworthy that two of these investigations have offered findings that differ from those of earlier investigations. Shaw (1987), for example, examined the relationship between self-directedness and intellectual development. She administered the OCLI and the Measure of Epistemological Reflection (MER) (Taylor and Porterfield, 1983) – a measure of intellectual development, based on the Perry (1970) scheme, which utilizes a short-answer essay format – to a randomly selected sample of 100 students at Montana State University. Shaw reported a statistically significant correlation between OCLI and MER scores, which suggests that as self-directed readiness increases, intellectual development also increases. In addition, Shaw noted significant positive correlations between age and scores on both the OCLI and the MER; however, she found that there were no significant differences in scores for either instrument between those individuals under age 25 and those 25 or older. Finally, she noted a positive relationship between class rank (freshman through post-baccalaureate) and both the OCLI and MER.

Shaw's findings are interesting in that they contrast with those of Leeb (1985), who did not find a significant relationship between self-direction and intellectual development. One possible reason for these differences in findings, according to Shaw, is that Leeb's study was based on a different methodology, as well as a smaller sample (N = 34), the vast majority of whom had completed at least four years of college at the time of the study. Shaw concluded that her findings offer tentative support to earlier theoretical speculation by Kasworm (1983) and Cameron (1984).

Blackwood (1989) looked at the relationship between self-directedness and hemisphericity. In this study, hemisphericity was measured by the Refined Wagner Preference Inventory (WAPI II) (Wagner and Wells, 1985), a twelve-item, forced-choice inventory that views hemisphericity on a continuum rather than as an absolute dichotomy. The WAPI II, the OCLI, and a demographic questionnaire were administered to 390 individuals who were "currently involved in a learning situation, and whose ages ranged across the life span" (Blackwood, 1989: 69).

A significant positive relationship was found between self-directedness and left brain hemisphericity. In addition, increasing age was again found to be related to greater self-directedness, as well as left-hemisphere orientation. With regard to the differences between the findings of this study and the earlier investigation of Torrance and Mourad (1978), where self-directed readiness was found to be related to *right* hemisphere dominance, Blackwood suggests that there may be two explanations: (a) the earlier study used a measure that divided hemisphericity into three categories (right hemisphere dominant, left hemisphere dominant, and integrated) while the more recent study used a measure that views hemisphericity as a point along a continuum rather than as a dichotomy; and (b) since the small sample of the Torrance and Mourad study (N = 41) were all enrolled in a university course on creative thinking, they may have been influenced in the direction of this right hemisphere-oriented characteristic (i.e., creativity). Also, it should be noted that Blackwood used a different instrument from the Torrance and Mourad study, and this could have contributed to some of the differences in findings.

Our own view is that hemisphericity is one of those nebulous concepts that does not offer a clear and simple picture. It would seem that there are certain characteristics associated with both hemisphere orientations that have been variously linked to self-directedness. And it is here that the value of doing replication studies becomes clear. Were it not for the later study, earlier findings would probably remain unquestioned. Thus, while we are enthusiastic about studies that find ways to make technical refinements on earlier work, we suggest that hemisphericity may be one of those areas where there could be a risk of "mixing apples and oranges."

Another study employing the OCLI offered a look at self-directedness among clinical laboratory science professionals (McCoy, 1988). In this investigation, McCoy sought to determine "if a professional's environment had an influence on self-directedness in learning and participation in continuing education activities" (McCoy, 1988: 187A). It was found that the OCLI scores of respondents were generally high and, further, that organizational environments with varying degrees of perceived mandatory continuing education did not appear to influence scores on the OCLI.

Since the OCLI is a relatively new instrument, it has not yet been subjected to the same degree of scrutiny as the SDLRS. However, three studies have investigated methodological and substantive issues relative to the instrument. Six (1989a) administered the OCLI to 328 students at a private, 2-year business college with a mean age of 19.6 years. Several weeks after completing the OCLI, 36 of the participants were selected at random to be assessed by their instructor on their level of self-directedness. Instructors were asked to complete a form designed by the researcher, the Classroom Learning Scale (CLS). A test of the relationship between scores on the OCLI and the CLS indicated a criterion-referenced validity coefficient of 0.14 ($p = 0.41$). Six concluded that the OCLI was not an effective predictor of self-directed learning behavior in the classroom setting and that the OCLI was not sensitive to demographic characteristics of the respondents.

In a follow-up investigation, Six (1989b) took a closer look at the three factors of the OCLI, as identified by Oddi (1984). Using data from his earlier study (Six, 1989a), along with data from the Oddi (1984) and Landers (1990) investigations, he sought to determine the extent to which the three factors "replicate across study samples" (Six,1989b: 44). Six found that the factors derived from his earlier data matched the factors identified earlier by Oddi, thus suggesting that "the factors derived by Oddi do not break up to form new factors under different study conditions" (Six, 1989b: 50). These findings therefore support the earlier factor analysis of Oddi (1984).

In conclusion, Six (1989b) offers the following comment relative to the OCLI:

> the underlying dimensions of the OCLI demonstrate robustness and applicability to a wider range of populations. One weakness, however, is that the total explained variance is bothersomely modest, justifying to some extent a lack of confidence to what is being measured. It is recommended that efforts be initiated on a number of fronts to improve the measuring properties of the OCLI and of self-directedness in learning.
>
> (Six, 1989b: 51)

The third OCLI validation study was the comparison of the SDLRS and the OCLI by Landers (1990), which was mentioned earlier. Relative to the OCLI, Landers found a significant positive correlation between two of the three factors and total OCLI score. He also found evidence that the internal reliability of the scale was weak: three items correlated negatively with total OCLI score and two other items were statistically weak. As was mentioned earlier, Landers concluded that, in measuring the concept of self-directedness, the SDLRS is preferred over the OCLI.

The findings of the Six (1989a) and Landers (1990) studies raise formidable questions about the appropriateness of the OCLI as a measure of self-direction. Yet, as with the SDLRS, we are unwilling to dismiss the instrument. Oddi has made an important contribution to the knowledge base by attempting to further clarify the meaning of self-direction and to develop an instrument reflecting that perspective. The concerns with the scale seem real and legitimate; however, only through further research will it be possible to confirm, refute, or modify the legitimacy of these concerns.

A META-ANALYSIS OF QUANTITATIVE STUDIES ON SELF-DIRECTION

From the studies presented in this chapter and in Chapter 3, it should be clear that the knowledge base relative to self-direction has mushroomed since the publication of Tough's original study. With this growth of knowledge, however, has come the problem of interpreting and synthesizing this vast body of research. This problem of interpretation is further compounded in that the approaches to studying self-direction discussed in these two chapters (i.e., Chapters 3 and 4), while clearly the major approaches, are not the only instruments by which self-direction has been studied. Using meta-analysis, a statistical procedure designed to allow for the integration of findings from a large number of individual studies, McCune (1989a) sought to synthesize the findings of quantitative studies on self-direction reported between 1977 and 1987.

Through an extensive computer search of literature covering the study period, McCune identified 103 studies addressing self-direction in adult learning. Of these, 67 met criteria necessary for inclusion in the data analysis (e.g., based on empirical data and reported in a way that provided enough information for the meta-analysis). Nearly half of the investigators for these studies (47.8 percent) came from the field of adult education, while another 25.4 percent were from nursing. The 67 studies used 18 different approaches to measure self-direction, the most frequent of these being the SDLRS, the Tough interview schedule (or a modified version of the schedule), the reported number of hours devoted to self-directed learning activity, and course participation/persistence/completion.

McCune found that "adult self-direction in learning has been investigated with a diversity of demographic and psychosocial/behavioral variables" that can be grouped into eighteen different categories (McCune, 1989a: 121). In assessing the relationship across studies between self-directedness and these variables, McCune offered these observations:

> The findings of this study indicate that the following variables are asso-ciated with self-direction in learning: (a) degree of self-directed learning activity ($r = 0.242$); (b) positive self-concept ($r = 0.230$); (c) educational attainment level ($r = 0.200$); (d) self-development ($r = 0.194$); (e) auton-omy ($r = 0.165$); (f) ability to master the environment in work, school, play, or social relations ($r = 0.147$); and (g) factors related to longevity on the job ($r = 0.138$).
>
> (McCune, 1988: p.126)

The relationships between self-direction and other variables (such as age, gender, positive attitude about life or learning, dependence, and environmen-tal factors that discourage learning efforts) were "uncertain", because these relationships seem to have been influenced by "selected independent vari-ables within the studies" (McCune, 1988: 125).

All in all, this study is an important contribution to the literature for it provides further confirmation *across studies* of relationships that have been hinted at previously. While, as McCune cautions, causation should not be implied from this correlational study, it seems clear that her findings give us a much clearer picture about the relative importance of certain variables *vis-à-vis* self-direction than was previously possible. While meta-analysis, as is true with any research methodology, has its limitations, its effective use rests on the assumption that a phenomenon has been studied sufficiently to warrant a large-scale synthesis. McCune's investigation can be used as evidence to further confirm what we have been stressing throughout the book – that while many questions remain unanswered, self-direction has been demonstrated to be one of the brightest lights in research efforts throughout the adult education field.

CONCLUSION

Studies designed to measure an individual's level of self-directedness have clearly moved the body of knowledge in this area well beyond descriptions of the frequency and nature of self-directed learning activities. At the same time, concerns have been raised about both of the key instruments designed to measure self-directedness. To a large extent, these concerns can be linked to questions about how self-direction is defined and the theoretical underpinnings of the concept. The third stream of research, qualitative investigations, takes the knowledge base one step further by attempting to develop theory relative to self-direction in adult learning. These studies are considered in the next chapter.

5   Beyond the iceberg: expanding the knowledge base through qualitative approaches

The previous two chapters have highlighted research on self-direction employing designs involving the quantitative analysis of data. Clearly, these kinds of studies have had a major impact on current understanding of the phenomenon of self-direction. Some of the most important research findings in this area, however, have emerged as a result of still another methodology. The third major branch of research on self-direction in adult learning has consisted of studies employing naturalistic research designs and qualitative data analysis procedures. Qualitative research, which includes such strategies as participant observation, case study, and in-depth interviewing, is characterized by the following: studying phenomena in their natural setting; collecting descriptive data that are usually not analyzed through statistical methods; a focus on process as well as outcomes; inductive data analysis; and an emphasis on the importance of "meaning" that participants attach to their experiences (Bogdan and Biklen, 1982). Whereas quantitative approaches such as survey, correlational, and experimental/quasi-experimental designs stress the testing of existing theory, qualitative researchers focus on building theory from the "bottom up" – an approach that is referred to as "grounded theory".

In the current effort to gain greater understanding of self-direction in adult learning, qualitative approaches have been the most recent stream of inquiry to evolve and, we believe, offer much toward creating a greater understanding of the context in which self-directed learning takes place, and the many meanings that learners and educators attach to the concept of learner self-direction. Several major studies on self-direction in learning employing the qualitative approach are reviewed in the following sections.

QUALITATIVE STUDIES OF SELF-DIRECTION

Experts without formal training

"One of the most promising sources of knowledge about self-education is the lives of people who became expert in a field which did not include formal training" (Gibbons, *et al.*, 1980: 44). Based on this rationale, Gibbons and his colleagues analyzed the content of twenty individuals "who became expert without formal training past high school or the equivalent" (except for one person who completed one year of college). These individuals were classified according to four categories:

1 entertainers;
2 inventors, explorers, and creators;
3 people of letters, science, and philosophy; and
4 administrators, organizers, and builders.

Included among those whose biographies were analyzed were the following individuals:

Muhammed Ali	John L. Lewis
Charlie Chaplin	H. L. Mencken
Aaron Copeland	Pablo Picasso
Walt Disney	Will Rogers
Gerald Durrell	George Bernard Shaw
Amelia Earhart	Harry S. Truman
Ralph Edwards	Virginia Woolf
Henry Ford	Frank Lloyd Wright
Eric Hoffer	Wilbur Wright
Harry Houdini	Malcolm X

As each biography was read, items considered to pertain to the "nature, life, or times" of subjects were recorded. In all, 154 themes emerged from the data. Of these, the 20 most prominent characteristics, as determined by the ratings ascribed by the readers, were as follows:

1 Primary experience in the area
2 Industriousness
3 Perseverance
4 Self-disciplined study
5 Curiosity
6 Single-minded pursuit
7 Creativity
8 Ingenuity
9 Self-confidence

10 Natural ability
11 Assertiveness
12 Intelligence
13 Independent exploration
14 Observation
15 Confirmational support from others
16 Integrity;
17 Nonconformity
18 Ambition
19 Effect of the economic environment
20 Effect of personal major achievements

Based on these characteristics, Gibbons and his colleagues drew several conclusions about differences in the assumptions underlying self-directed learning and formal schooling. First, there is much greater diversity in the kinds of expertise and skills needed by the self-educated experts than is generally stressed in formal schooling. Second, the expertise developed by these individuals appears to have grown out of extracurricular activities; school generally played an insignificant or negative role in developing this expertise. Third, the twenty experts tended to focus their efforts on their area of expertise rather than develop less in-depth knowledge about a broader range of topics. Fourth, there was a strong, active, experiential orientation to the learning efforts. Fifth, these individuals tended to possess characteristics that enabled them to pursue their areas of expertise despite great odds, failures, and public disapproval.

Based on these findings, Gibbons, *et al.* laid a tentative foundation consisting of fourteen principles that they suggest could contribute to a theory of self-education. Among the suggestions were the following: "that self-education can help individuals assume control for their own learning, undertake learning for specific use in the present, promote personal integrity, and develop expertise in an area while remaining open to exploring many fields of activity" (Brockett, *et al.*, 1982: 174).

In a critical assessment of the Gibbons, *et al.* study and how it has been utilized by adult education researchers to date, Long and Agyekum (1990) concluded that the work has not had a great influence on practice relative to self-direction in learning. While the study has been cited by a number of authors in the field, emphasis of this writing has typically been on the research methodology rather than on the findings themselves. In providing an analysis of the first three principles, Long and Agyekum conclude that the principles have limited use in their current form; however, the principles may, in fact, be useful in analyzing other literature and in promoting the development of research efforts based on the findings.

A fellowship of learning

A second qualitative study of self-direction in adult learning employed a different approach. Using a "semi-structured interview," Brookfield (1981b) studied 25 adults who, like the subjects in the Gibbons, *et al.* study, had become acknowledged experts in their fields without formal preparation. As with the study by Gibbons, *et al.*, Brookfield's research differed from the learning projects studies in that it concentrated not on the subjects' entire range of learning activities, but rather emphasized only learning related to the individuals' area of expertise. Unlike Gibbons and his colleagues, however, Brookfield gathered his data first-hand, from the subjects themselves.

Brookfield identified two criteria that had to be met by prospective subjects in order for them to be included in the study sample. For each individual:

> [learning] has to have resulted in the development of such a high level of expertise that the learner had been awarded the acclaim of fellow enthusiasts at local or national level, and such expertise had to have been developed without participation in externally planned programmes of instruction (such as adult education classes, correspondence courses or in-service training schemes).
>
> (Brookfield, 1981b: 17)

Some of the areas of expertise identified by Brookfield's sample were organic gardening, chess, philosophy, record collecting, animal breeding, narrow gauge railways, and pigeon racing. Length of involvement in these activities ranged from four years for a person engaged in drama production to 50 years for a beekeeper.

A number of themes were identified from the data. One such theme revolved around three attitudes toward learning that seemed to be shared by many of the independent learners. First, these learners tended to view their involvement as ongoing, with no identified end point to their study. Second, they did not feel constrained to limit their study to "conventional study boundaries" (Brookfield, 1981b: 20). Rather, many of the individuals preferred to expand their explorations into other related areas. For example, a person interested in botany also felt it important to spend time studying birds and insects. Similarly, an expert in steam engines was also interested in other modes of transportation, such as canals. Third, these adults believed themselves to belong to a larger "fellowship of learning" (Brookfield, 1981b: 20). While individuals assumed primary responsibility for planning and carrying out their learning activities, the learners did not work in isolation from others who shared their interest. Indeed, one of the criteria for being considered an "expert" was acknowledgement of such status by one's peers.

This finding supports the contention of many (e.g., Knowles, 1975) that self-direction does not necessarily mean learning that takes place in isolation.

Related to this third attitude is probably one of the most important findings of the study. Brookfield has noted that the learners he interviewed expressed both a spirit of cooperation and competitiveness. On the one hand, learners emphasized their identification as part of a group of individuals with a common interest. As such, they were willing to share their knowledge and experience with their peers. On the other hand, however, it was seen as important by the experts to have their abilities recognized by their peers through awards and competitive success. In fact, several of the learners identified the opportunity for competitive success as a primary reason for undertaking the learning endeavor.

A portion of Brookfield's discussion centered on the evaluation of independent adult learning. A distinction was made between subjective indices of evaluation (exemplified primarily through the learners' increased confidence in their abilities, to the point where they felt capable of judging the ideas and writings of experts in the field) and objective indices (such as recognition and comparison by their peers). To some extent, these indices can be related to the cooperative and competitive elements mentioned above. Some objective indices, for example, include requests for advice, written contributions, and talks to interested groups. Each of these reflect a sense of cooperation – a willingness to share one's expertise. At the same time, possessing a level of expertise sufficient to question other experts – essentially stating that one's own ideas or observations are more appropriate – demonstrates a competitive nature. Perhaps it is here that Brookfield has made a major contribution to theory relative to self-direction in learning. Certainly he has raised some important areas for further examination and reflection.

The Vermont study

While the methodologies employed by Gibbons and his colleagues (1980) and Brookfield (1981b) differ considerably, they share an emphasis on studying individuals with limited formal preparation in their field of endeavor. In a third major qualitative study, Leean and Sisco (1981) investigated self-directed learning among rural adults in Vermont who had completed less than 12 years of formal education. This 18-month project consisted of three major phases: (a) a replication of the learning projects methodology based on a sample of 93 adults; (b) a case study process involving 14 of the original 93 individuals; and (c) dissemination of findings, including conference presentations and retreats involving consultants with expertise in self-directed learning and naturalistic inquiry. It is perhaps the case study component of this investigation that has provided some of the most insightful findings.

In the case study phase, fourteen individuals were selected on the basis of representativeness by age, gender, and educational background. Over a 6-month period, three researchers spent about 14 hours with each of the participants. Data collection included several protocols, such as interactive exercises and conversational interviews, that allowed the investigators to obtain a wide range of qualitative data.

Using Lewin's Field Theory (1951) as a conceptual base, Leean and Sisco were able to look at the influence of learning on the lives of the interviewees across a chronological progression of time – past, present, and future. This framework allowed the researchers to consider learning from a holistic perspective. While the importance of integrating these three time phases cannot be separated, Leean and Sisco pointed out that the major findings relative to self-directed learning were noted within the "present" time perspective. Major findings related to self-direction can be summarized as follows:

1 Learning is seen as a part of everyday living as people are continually challenged by their environments to solve problems as well as explore interests. *Suggests that "undereducated" should be perceived as learners who already have skills.*

2 Thinking is connected to times when people are alone, usually doing a mundane or repetitive chore or task. *Suggests that self-directed learning involves work done in the mind before it is done with the hands.*

3 The ways people talked about how they go about their self-directed learning varied, but most referred to visualizing the end state of the learning goal before they entered into the effort. *Suggests further exploration of the process of visualization as a guide or motivating phenomenon in self-directed learning.*

4 Learning since leaving school has been varied, challenging and meaningful. People commented on how much more they have learned outside of the public school context. They enjoy self-directed learning because they can do it at their own pace and without anybody judging them. This is consistent with findings from other research on self-directed learning. *Suggests self-directed learning should be taken seriously as an alternative form of learning.*

5 The cognitive profiles of the group looked like a normal distribution of other populations tested. *Suggests that the number of years of formal education is not necessarily correlated to one's cognitive abilities.*

6 Both men and women expressed a belief in the value of commonsense thinking and rational problem solving, providing many examples of how

they do this. *Suggests that self-directed learning is guided by innate abilities of the rational mind.*

7 Most recognized times when they got answers to problems through non-rational means. Again, many experiences were related. Descriptive names given to this way of thinking were: "back-burner thinking," "dream thinking," "psychic," "spontaneous," "passage thinking." *Suggests alternative states of consciousness may be helpful in one's self-directed learning efforts.*

8 Developmentally, the group was dispersed in a bell-shaped curve using Loevinger dimensions of preconventional, conventional and postconventional. Factors which seemed to impede and enhance developmental movement were evident in many of their statements about themselves. These obstacles tended to be a limited sense of self and the inability to resolve contradictions in one's life. *Suggests more attention be paid to how developmental theory can enrich the understanding of adult learning, especially through the study of growth enhancing and impeding factors.*

9 Having access to resources and information does not appear to be a major problem of these rural learners. They seem to know where to go for what they need. However, when this was probed more, they did speak about some frustrations in getting full and accurate information. *Suggests that information services for rural "long-distance learners" may be helpful if they are responsive and relevant to specific needs and contexts of rural learners.*

(Leean and Sisco, 1981, Section II: 28–9)

These findings address several areas that previous studies had not explored; in particular, the idea that much self-directed learning occurs through "non-rational" means. Self-directed learning, in its ideal form, involves a transcendence not unlike Maslow's (1970) "peak experience." Leean and Sisco found evidence to support this idea. Perhaps there is a link between this finding and the notion of nondeliberate learning as addressed by Ingham (1984), which was discussed in Chapter 2.

The organizing circumstance

To what extent do self-directed learners consciously preplan their learning activities? With the development of models designed to provide a process for undertaking self-directed learning projects, some of which are considered in later chapters, it would seem worthwhile to consider the extent to which such processes are, indeed, used by self-directed learners. In a secondary analysis of qualitative data based on interviews with 78 self-directed learners who had less than high school completion, Spear and Mocker (1984) found that such preplanning usually does not exist.

Spear and Mocker have suggested that the concept of the "organizing circumstance" can be used to understand this finding. According to the investigators, the organizing circumstance "postulates that self-directed learners, rather than preplanning their learning projects, tend to select a course from limited alternatives which occur fortuitously within their environment, and which structures their learning projects" (Spear and Mocker, 1984: 4). From their findings, Spear and Mocker have presented a typology that can be used to distinguish four patterns through which the organizing circumstance can be found to exist. The categories of the typology are as follows.

Type I – Single event/anticipated learning

This category refers to situations where an adult enters into a learning activity perceived to be required, where he or she has little understanding of what needs to be learned or how to learn it. The learner thus enters with the expectation that the "means for learning will be contained within the situation and available to them" (Spear and Mocker, 1984: 5). Many on-the-job training experiences fall into this category.

Type II – Single event/unanticipated learning

This category is similar to the Type I category in that tasks are performed by individuals on a frequent and repeated basis. However, within this category, individuals do not view themselves as engaged in a learning process.

Type III – Series of events/related learning

Some self-directed learning projects can be seen as a series of episodes that, on the surface, give the appearance of being a linear progression toward a future goal. In actuality, the series of events builds upon previous events. However, this progression was not deliberate on the part of the learner. In fact, such learners are usually unable to have foreseen the "logical" progression from episode to episode.

Type IV – Series of events/unrelated learning

Type IV situations develop over a longer period of time than Type III situations but are the accumulation of various unrelated learning experiences. According to Spear and Mocker (1984: 7), this category "is both a cumulative and culminating circumstance uniting previously unrelated sets or series of circumstances".

Spear and Mocker's conclusions, which seem to challenge the oft-accepted view that self-directed learning is a clearly deliberate, well-planned, and linear series of episodes are reflected in the following statement:

> Because self-directed learning occurs in a natural environment dominated by chance elements and is in contrast to the artificial and controlled elements which characterize formal instructional environments, it seems useful to investigate the possibly differing effects of the natural environments on the learning process. This is opposed to seeking to understand self-directed learning by imposing what is known about formal learning upon it.

> (Spear and Mocker, 1984: 9)

The issues Spear and Mocker raise are relevant ones that could provide some valuable directions for future inquiry.

Self-directed learning in higher education settings

While most qualitative investigations of self-direction have emphasized learning outside of the classroom, there remains a need to look more fully at self-direction within the institutional setting. As was noted in Chapters 1 and 2, self-direction can be viewed as existing on a continuum and can, indeed, take place in institutional settings. Kasworm (1988a, 1988b) undertook two exploratory investigations in order to support a conceptual framework for self-directed learning in institutions. In the first study, Kasworm (1988a) conducted semi-structured interviews with seven adults enrolled in graduate courses at a university in a large metropolitan area. Drawing in part from the models presented by Knowles (1975) and Tough (1979), Kasworm essentially found support for the presence and potential of self-direction in the graduate classroom. However, she pointed out that because this study was based on a very limited sample, and was based on a graduate student population, the findings must be viewed in a most tentative way.

For this reason, Kasworm (1988b) undertook a follow-up investigation that sought to examine the same phenomenon with a group of undergraduate adult learners who pursued college credit on a part-time basis and held full- or part-time jobs. Ten individuals were randomly selected and interviewed. Of these individuals, 70 percent reported that "their reentry into college was related to an expected delayed gratification that they projected would be fulfilled upon completion of the degree" (Kasworm, 1988b: 9). Noting that each of the interviewees was able to share examples of themselves as self-directed learners, and pointing out that most of the respondents felt that self-directed learning is desirable for most adults, Kasworm asked respondents to discuss how they perceived their role as active/passive learners in credit courses.

Four patterns of responses were identified. One pattern was a clear preference for a self-directed approach stressing informal learning and minimizing competitive, test-oriented learning. A second pattern involved a "selective" combination of self-directed and more structured approaches. A third pattern was a preference for "quality structured learning" with a clear set of expectations. Finally, a fourth pattern was a preference for structured classes and an attitude of compliance with the system in order to "just get through."

While the limited size of the samples from these studies make it necessary to view the findings in an exploratory way, this research reemphasizes that self-direction can indeed be a vital part of learning in institutions. At the same time, it is a mistake to assume that all learners have the same level of readiness for self-directed learning. These findings have implications for the teaching/learning transaction as well as for the development of institutional policies relative to self-direction. Such implications are discussed in Chapters 6 and 8, respectively.

Librarians and self-directed learners

In order to better understand the role of the facilitator in self-directed learning, Smith (1990) focused on one type of facilitator – the public librarian. Twenty-two librarians from a public library system in a northeastern U.S. metropolitan area were interviewed using a semistructured interview process. Using a modified, constant comparative method of qualitative data analysis, Smith's findings centered on four major themes relative to the following questions.

1 What is a public library?
2 Do self-directed learners use the library?
3 What materials, services, and programs do librarians make available to learners?
4 How do public librarians interact with learners?

With regard to the first question, three aspects of the library were noted consistently: "the public library as physical space (building, arrangement, and furniture); people (staff, library users, and the community-at-large that supports it); non-physical environment (the atmosphere, e.g., warmth, friendliness, quiet, that the library projects to the community)" (Smith, 1990: 243). Of particular interest is the non-physical environment aspect. Here, Smith pointed out that nearly "all of the librarians interviewed were concerned that their libraries be warm, friendly places, a welcoming, rather than a threatening institution in the community" (Smith, 1990: 244).

Regarding the second question, Smith noted that every one of the librarians "had at least one or two stories or examples" of self-directed learners with whom they had worked, and many had "at least a working definition of what this type of learning meant to them" (Smith, 1990: 245). Based on these findings, Smith proposed a tentative model that distinguishes between "timid" and "confident" learners. She contends that interactions with a librarian might be a way for timid learners to develop into confident learners.

As for the resources made available to learners, it is clear that the book remains the primary resource utilized by library learners. Yet *programming* (either of an educational or entertainment nature) and *services* (such as reference/reader guidance or educational brokering) were sometimes identified as relevant learning resources.

Finally, with regard to the ways in which librarians interact with users, Smith found that typically, a set of maxims (i.e., unwritten rules) somewhat analogous to Schön's (1987) idea of "knowing-in-action" were combined with a process of "negotiating the question," which is a way of responding to the unique situation of each individual user.

This study makes an important contribution to the knowledge base because it addresses implications both for the facilitation of self-directed learning and the ways in which institutions can respond to self-directed learners. These issues are also discussed further in Chapters 6 and 8, respectively.

Other qualitative studies

Several other studies have investigated self-direction through the use of naturalistic designs and qualitative data analysis. The following five investigations are dissertation studies, three of which were conducted at Teachers College, Columbia University. For example, Zabari (1985) examined the role of self-directed learning as an approach to continuing education for practitioners in the field of gerontology. Semistructured interviews with eighteen senior center directors revealed the following four types of self-directed learning activities: "job-framing, resource seeking, feedback and evaluation seeking, and making sense of experience" (Zabari, 1985: 1061A). Zabari found that the interviewees developed "along a continuum of autonomous functioning determined by the way in which they negotiated learning activities" (Zabari, 1985: 1061A).

In another study, Bauer (1986) used a case-study approach to examine the first 3 years of operation of the Adult Education Guided Independent Study (AEGIS) program, an alternative doctoral program in adult education offered by Teachers College, Columbia University. Through document analysis, observation, and interviews with students, faculty, and administrators, Bauer described how various functions of the program interfaced administratively with the college in general. She concluded that the development of innovative programs requires an intensive personal commitment on the part of professionals; therefore, "institutions must provide stronger support to faculty in substantive areas of tenure criteria, monetary reward for involvement of this kind, and adjustment of teaching and administrative load" (Bauer, 1986: 2518A). The AEGIS program is discussed further in Chapter 8.

Two recent qualitative investigations have attempted to provide greater conceptual clarity for the concept of self-direction. Gerstner (1988) conducted a critical review of self-directed learning as reflected in the North American and British literature between the years 1920 and 1986. Drawing from progressive, humanist, behaviorist, and critical philosophical orientations, Gerstner identified four variations on the self-directed learning theme: "(1) instrumental learning; (2) self-knowledge; (3) self-management; and (4) as a personal attribute" (Gerstner, 1988: 27A). This model is both similar to and different from the PRO model that serves as a foundation throughout this book.

Candy (1988) also investigated the concept of "self-direction". As was noted in Chapter 2, Candy distinguished between self-direction as a personal attribute, an approach to learning that takes place outside of institutions (autodidaxy), and as a way of providing learner control over the learning process. From a critical analysis of literature as well as a conceptual analysis process, Candy's eight major findings were as follows:

> (1) lack of internal consistency in the literature precludes the development of a coherent 'theory of self-direction' from within the literature; (2) autodidaxy can be usefully distinguished from learner-control; (3) autonomy in learning does not necessarily lead to personal autonomy, nor does personal autonomy always manifest itself in the learning situation; (4) autonomy has both personal and situational dimensions; (5) understanding the perspective of learners is vital to understanding strategies used and outcomes attained; (6) personal autonomy in learning comprises both cross-situational and situation-specific dimensions; (7) research into learning outcomes should stress qualitative rather than quantitative dimensions of knowledge acquisition; and (8) constructivism sanctions action-research and other naturalistic inquiry modes.
>
> (Candy, 1988: 1033A)

Based on these findings, he suggests a research agenda developed from a constructionist perspective.

Finally, in a study that seems to take the Gibbons, *et al.* (1980) study a step further, Cavaliere (1989) used content analysis of biographical and historical data from a 28-year period in order to examine "the independent learning processes utilized by the Wright brothers which led to their invention of the airplane" (Cavaliere, 1989: 2894a). She noted that the behaviors employed by the Wright brothers during this process were "repetitive, cyclical, and progressive. The data analyses demonstrated that learning does not occur in isolation and defined goals can be accomplished through practice and perseverance" (Cavaliere, 1989: 2894A). To a large degree, these characteristics support those identified by Gibbons and his colleagues.

Contributions and limitations of qualitative investigations

Clearly, the studies in this chapter indicate that qualitative research methods have greatly extended the boundaries of knowledge relative to self-direction in learning. In our view, qualitative approaches to studying self-direction have made at least two major contributions to the knowledge base in this area. First, this stream of inquiry has contributed to theory-building efforts relative to self-direction. Concepts such as Brookfield's fellowship of learning, or Spear and Mocker's organizing circumstance, along with Leean and Sisco's findings relative to the potential impact of altered states of consciousness on self-directed learning processes, and Kasworm's findings about self-direction among adult college students, probably would not have been as likely to be uncovered through the use of standardized measures of self-direction.

A second contribution of the qualitative paradigm can be seen in the thread that runs through many of the studies discussed in this chapter. The samples selected for the studies by Gibbons, *et al.*, Brookfield, Leean and Sisco, and Spear and Mocker were comprised of adults with low levels of formal education or no formal training in their area of expertise. It can be argued that many adults who fit into the category of "undereducated" are less likely to respond to standardized scales than those individuals whose more extensive participation in formal learning experiences may have helped them to feel more experienced with such instruments. In other words, it is likely that qualitative methods can play a valuable role in studying segments of the adult population that are frequently overlooked in research efforts.

While the qualitative paradigm has made what we believe to be a significant contribution to research efforts in this area, the approach is not without its parameters. First, although this method is certainly appropriate for studying problems from a sociological or anthropological perspective, qualitative approaches are probably not as useful in studies focusing on personality dimensions, such as those that fall within the bounds of learner self-direction, since they generally focus on social processes and interactions rather than internal psychological processes.

In addition, some would argue that qualitative findings are not generalizable to other populations, since such considerations as random selection of subjects, manipulation of independent variables, and tests of statistical significance are not part of the methodology. However, Bogdan and Biklen (1982) suggest that generalizability can also be considered in terms of application to related *situations* rather than populations. In this way, the findings of qualitative investigations can, indeed, have implications beyond the specific study addressed.

THE UNDERLYING KNOWLEDGE BASE: AN ASSESSMENT

In this and the previous two chapters, we have attempted to present a look at the research efforts that support the underlying knowledge base of self-direction in adult learning. The questions that remain center on assessing how valuable this research has been in helping us to better understand the phenomenon of self-direction and how it might impact upon the practice of adult education. As a way of bringing this review of research to a close, we will present our assessment of the knowledge base by first looking at some of the critiques that have been written about this research area and then by summarizing some of our own conclusions.

In 1984, Brookfield offered what he called a "critical paradigm" of self-directed adult learning (Brookfield, 1984c). The rationale for this paradigm was that while research such as the learning projects approach had made a clear contribution to the knowledge base, there was a clear need to move further – "to infuse a spirit of self-critical scrutiny into this developing field of research" (Brookfield, 1984c: 60). Essentially, Brookfield identified the following four criticisms of the research up to that time:

1 Research on self-directed learning was based almost entirely on middle-class samples; studies of "working class" adults were largely ignored;
2 There was an almost exclusive emphasis on studying self-directed learning through quantitative approaches – the qualitative orientation was generally overlooked;
3 The research had been characterized by an overemphasis on the individual dimension of self-directed learning without consideration of the social context in which such learning takes place; and
4 Little consideration had been given to implications of existing research findings for "questions of social and political change".

(Brookfield, 1984c: 60).

Brookfield argued that until these four issues could be addressed and resolved, research on self-direction would be limited to merely reinterpreting what had already been well documented.

In a response to this critique, the first author of this book (Brockett, 1985c) presented an alternative view of the four criticisms. Regarding the overemphasis on middle-class samples, it was agreed that while there was some truth to this view, groups traditionally viewed as "hard-to-reach" had been studied more widely than suggested by Brookfield. Several examples were used to support this view (e.g., Hiemstra, 1975; Umoren, 1978; Baghi, 1979; Leean and Sisco, 1981). As for the concern about excessive use of quantitative research approaches, the "three streams" model that has served as a guide in this book was used to refute Brookfield's claim. Here, it was noted that "self-directed learning at this time is an excellent example of a research area where qualitative and quantitative approaches have been used to explore distinct pieces of the puzzle" (Brockett, 1985c: 57). On the final two concerns raised by Brookfield, there was basic agreement; the sociopolitical dimensions of self-direction were, and continue to be, essentially overlooked. These issues "are amplified in situations where individuals view themselves as powerless in determining the direction of their lives" and, as such, present both positive and negative potential consequences for "promoting self-direction in societies where individual human rights may be in question" (Brockett, 1985c: 58).

A final commentary by Brookfield (1985b) helps to illuminate the spirit in which the above exchange was undertaken. While points of disagreement remained, the exchange "was presented in the spirit of furthering genuine dialogue" (Brookfield, 1985b: 60). "Essentially, we have the same concern. We are disturbed at the creeping orthodoxy which threatens to exercise a conceptual stranglehold on research and theoretical speculation in this field" (Brookfield, 1985b: 64). Today, with the advantage of several years perspective since the original publication of the exchange, this "spirit" remains the real contribution of this exchange. In our view, concerns about the research being dominated by middle-class samples and quantitative designs are less of a concern than they were in 1984. On the other hand, concerns about the sociopolitical dimension of self-direction remain valid today, though some theoretical headway *has* been made on this front (see Chapters 2, 6, and 10 for examples). But it was the tone of the Brookfield–Brockett dialogue that made the series of articles more constructive than confrontational, and, in retrospect, this is the real contribution of the exchange.

So, then, where do things stand relative to the knowledge base of self-direction? We believe that several conclusions can be drawn. First, it is clear from the vast body of learning projects research, that self-directed learning activity is, indeed, "a way of life" that cuts across socioeconomic strata. It is, to be sure, highly visible in middle-class U.S. society. But it is also thriving in groups traditionally deemed "hard-to-reach" for adult education programming: older adults; minorities; rural residents; low-income adults; persons with low levels of formal education; and adults who demonstrate expertise in a particular area despite lack of formal preparation in that area. It is also found, in varying degrees, within societies outside of North America and Western Europe.

Second, and related to the above point, it would appear that most findings related to measures of self-directedness and various demographic variables are inconclusive. The possible exception is educational attainment and, even here, the findings are not overwhelming. This perhaps lends further support to the point made above, that self-direction does indeed cut across the entire adult population and holds promise for individuals regardless of their demographic background.

Third, it can be said with a high degree of confidence that there is a link between self-direction and self-concept. A bit more tentatively, the same thing can be said for the link between self-direction and life satisfaction (although these latter findings have been drawn only from older adult samples). These findings indicate that self-direction is clearly reflected in how adults perceive themselves and the quality of their lives.

Fourth, the findings relative to self-direction and certain psychosocial variables – such as locus of control, intellectual development, and hemisphericity – paint a mixed picture. The study of hemisphericity might be particularly instructive to future researchers. As was pointed out in Chapter 4, it is possible that the inconclusive findings are linked to the idea that self-direction might be tied to certain elements of *both* left and right brain hemispheric orientation. Hence, it may be entirely appropriate to arrive at different findings, especially given that various researchers may operationalize the variables in different ways. Our conclusion is that some variables simply do not easily fit into the conceptualization of self-direction.

Fifth, despite the concerns raised by Brookfield (1985b) that research in this area has over-relied on quantitative measurement of the concept, we are encouraged by the methodological diversity that continues to evolve in the study of self-direction. As can be seen from studies reported earlier in this chapter, the last half of the 1980s has witnessed an increase in studies utilizing the qualitative paradigm. There is every reason to be optimistic that this trend will continue.

Sixth, legitimate concerns have been voiced about both of the instruments that have been used to measure self-direction (i.e., the SDLRS and the OCLI). However, in spite of these concerns, both the SDLRS and the OCLI have been vital to the development of the knowledge base. The developers of each instrument continue to work at refinements of their scales and we are encouraged by this (Guglielmino, 1989; Oddi, personal communication with R. Brockett, January, 1990). Until alternative measures of self-direction can be developed, based perhaps on some of the new ways in which the phenomenon is being conceptualized, further research with these scales is encouraged, so long as validation work continues on a study-by-study basis.

Finally, our review leads us to conclude that self-direction can and should serve as a model for the field of adult education in terms of how to systematically develop a research base over time. While some may wish to view the research over the past two decades as a fad that has just about run its course, we believe that this kind of thinking in the past has cost adult education a great deal in terms of its development as a field of study. In Chapter 13, we offer a number of recommendations pertaining to how this research base may continue to develop in coming years.

CONCLUSION

In this chapter, we have examined the third stream of research on self-direction in learning: studies employing the qualitative or naturalistic paradigm. Although this stream does not compare in mere volume with the other two approaches, it has perhaps been the most valuable in terms of theory development. In our overall assessment of the knowledge base in self-direction, we believe that the picture is generally bright, especially when compared with most other research areas in adult education. Yet, there is much more that remains to be done.

Part III
Process and personal orientation

The PRO model is built around the premise that personal responsibility for learning is both desirable and effective. Such personal responsibility can be fostered by a skilled facilitator or aided by the right kind of learning resource. It also is a learning attribute that can be enhanced in most adults. This part builds on such notions.

The first chapter, 6, describes how self-directed learning can be facilitated through a learning process orientation. After a description of how andragogical notions, principles, and literature have been foundational to our thinking, we detail an individualized teaching and learning process. The process is one we have developed based on our experiences, understanding of literature, and faith in the ability of learners to accept personal responsibility.

Various steps within the process are detailed. These range from ideas about initial planning that must take place even before contact with learners is made to such basic features as helping learners become acquainted with each other and the process, facilitating needs assessment activities, and even engaging learners in individual planning or evaluation functions. The chapter concludes with information pertaining to the type of learning variables that individuals can control and some ideas about the nature of possible learning resources.

Chapter 7 examines the internal, personal orientation component of the PRO model. It focuses on how learner self-direction and the acceptance of personal responsibility can be enhanced. A variety of influences on self-direction as reported in the literature is reported, including such varied areas as the research on participation, humanist influences, and behavioral influences.

Finally, three important strategies for the enhancement are described. The first centers on notions of how critical reflection can be facilitated. Several specific activities are discussed. The second strategy deals with ways for promoting rational thinking. The third strategy is related to ways that various helping skills can be used to enhance learner self-direction.

6 Facilitating self-directed learning

To some readers it may seem quite a paradox to talk about the facilitation of self-directed learning when self-direction implies learning alone. However, one of our reasons for writing this book is to explore appropriate roles for educators of adults, given this widespread interest in self-direction. This chapter is designed to provide some initial ideas about the process of facilitating self-direction from the instructor's perspective. Chapter Seven will deal with self-direction from the learner's perspective.

As we pointed out in earlier chapters, some critics of the "self-directed learning movement" argue that the research related to such concepts as andragogy and learning projects is flawed in some ways. As we note throughout the book, certainly more research is needed to better understand implications for instruction, program development, and so forth. However, it has been our experience, both in and out of the classroom, that most adults do prefer to assume considerable responsibility for their own learning if given the opportunity and appropriate support.

In this chapter we describe how we have translated our knowledge and experience into a teaching and learning process that works for us in facilitating self-directed learning. The collective "we" is used in that we talk about various procedures and techniques that at least one of us uses or has tried. We also will use "you" to communicate directly in terms of our recommendations for your use of the information in the chapter. Obviously, we can only present you with an accounting of how we translate beliefs and experiences into instructional activities, and you will need to make adaptations that fit your preferred teaching style, philosophical framework, and institutional requirements.

ANDRAGOGY: A FOUNDATION FOR SELF-DIRECTED LEARNING?

Much attention has been given to the North American version of andragogical teaching and learning as developed by Knowles (1980). His initial description of andragogy (Knowles, 1968), subsequent modifications from the first edition of *Modern Practice* (1970) to the second (1980), and descriptions of various ways in which the process has been used (Knowles and Associates, 1984) have certainly popularized the term. Appendix A provides an annotated bibliography of writings that deal directly with andragogy and some of its implied concepts. For the reader interested in pursuing further variations, Savicevic (1981, 1988, 1989) describes how certain Eastern European countries have used some form of andragogy.

Popularization of andragogy has been accompanied by numerous debates for and against the concept put forth by many writers (Brookfield, 1986; Candy, 1981; Carlson, 1979; Cross, 1981; Darkenwald and Merriam, 1982; Davenport, 1987; Davenport and Davenport, 1985a, 1985b, 1985c; Day and Baskett, 1982; Elias, 1979; Griffin, 1983; Houle, 1972; Jarvis, 1984; Knudson, 1979; London, 1973; McKenzie, 1977, 1979; Podeschi, 1987; Podeschi and Pearson, 1986; Pratt, 1988; Rachal, 1983; Tennant, 1986; and Yonge, 1985). Many North American critics of the concept argue that differences between adults and children are not significant enough to warrant different teaching and learning approaches. Some people also believe that Knowles is too dependent on the ability of all people to accept individual freedom in learning. For example, Pratt (1988) believes that self-direction is a situational attribute or "an impermanent state of being dependent on the learner's competence, commitment and confidence at a given moment in time" (Pratt, 1988: 162).

Knowles has responded to some of this criticism by saying he made a mistake in subtitling the 1970 version of *Modern Practice* "Andragogy versus Pedagogy." He now believes the subtitle should have been "From Pedagogy to Andragogy," (a subtitle he actually used in the 1980 second edition) and that he should have presented these ideas as two points on a continuum (Knowles, 1979), rather than as a dichotomy.

Criticism of andragogy outside of North America has taken a somewhat different turn. Griffin (1983), for example, suggests that Knowles fails to account for crucial distinctions between individual purposes and social consequences of learning. This results in extreme individualism and, in effect, "the social functions of adult education are reduced to the sum of the purposes of individual learners" (Griffin, 1983: 60). Day and Baskett (1982) suggest that andragogy is not a theory of adult learning at all; rather, it is an educational ideology rooted in an inquiry-based learning and teaching paradigm. Tennant (1986) worries that andragogy places the individual at the center of a value system that relegates the group to second place.

We are largely in agreement with Knowles' current view of andragogy as a continuum. We also believe that individuals can be assisted to become increasingly more self-directed when given appropriate learning tools, resources, experiences, and encouragement. This is because an underlying theme in our interpretation of teaching and learning as a process is that of facilitating learning, or as Knowles would put it, "self-directed" as opposed to "teacher-directed" learning. In fact, self-directed learning is seen as a goal, an underlying assumption of andragogy, and a prevailing philosophy for adult education by many in North America (Mezirow, 1985).

Mezirow (1981) has also described 12 activities fundamental to the enhancement of learners becoming more self-directed in what he calls a "charter for andragogy." For facilitators this involves helping learners participate in various activities, including the assessment of personal needs, planning subsequent learning activities, securing or creating necessary learning resources, and assessing personal progress in achieving learning goals. Schuttenberg and Tracy (1987) believe there are many different roles a facilitator should assume, including that of a leader, collaborator, or colleague, in promoting varying types of self-directed behavior. In other words, a facilitator is not just a classroom teacher, but also can be a counselor, consultant, tutor, and resource locator.

However, for such activities and roles to be successful, a partnership must be developed between learner and facilitator. We believe this is important so that issues like quality of the experience, a personal desire to continue learning activities, and obtaining necessary support are considered. It has been our experience that such a partnership works best within an individualized teaching and learning process. It involves mentoring, building collegiality, helping learners free themselves from expected dependent relationships with teachers, and developing greater learner independence. Individualized, as used here, refers more to the degree of – or potential for – learner control of the process than to independence of the study method (Candy, 1981).

The purpose of this chapter is to describe such a process and how facilitation of self-direction or increased learner control is carried out. This, then, is a discussion of the "self-directed learning" side of the PRO model described in Chapter 2. The focus will be primarily on what Mocker and Spear (1982) refer to as an expected formal relationship between a learner or group of learners and an instructor. We do recognize that not all self-directed learning activity involves developing such formal roles but, for purposes of this chapter, we stress the involvement of a facilitator in describing the process.

PLANNING SELF-DIRECTED LEARNING

Some basic assumptions underlie the notion that self-direction in learning is possible. For example, we accept that the mature adult is quite capable of assuming personal responsibility for planning and carrying out learning activities. Thus we believe that an adult is a person who fulfils adult social roles and who possesses self-directed abilities and beliefs (Mezirow, 1985). However, it has been our experience that most adults, when entering a formal educational setting, initially expect the teacher to be an authority who passes knowledge on to them as receptive learners. On the other hand, research noted earlier, as well as our personal experiences as facilitators, has shown us how quickly learners will adapt to assuming self-direction in learning. The landmark *Learning To Be* report (Faure *et al.*, 1972) made this point more than 15 years ago:

> From the standpoint of lifelong education and in the present state of human knowledge, calling teachers "masters" (whichever of its meanings we give the word), is more and more an abuse of terms. The teacher's duty is less and less to inculcate knowledge and more and more to encourage thinking ... [this includes becoming increasingly] an advisor, a partner to talk to, someone who seeks out conflicting arguments rather than handing out ready-made truths.... [The teacher] will have to devote more time and energy to productive and creative activities: interaction, discussion, stimulation, understanding, encouragement.
>
> (Faure *et al.*, 1972: 77–8)

This interactive role does require lots of time and energy on the part of the teacher throughout the process. In fact, we believe our process requires considerably more effort than do more traditional, teacher-directed approaches. A facilitator must be able to provide numerous kinds of support because of the many barriers to self-direction that a learner will face.

As with any teaching and learning process, an instructor's activities do not begin during initial contact with learners. Some anticipatory planning takes place, resources are secured, and some thinking is done regarding what is to be expected of learners. Each learner or group of learners will be unique, the state of knowledge regarding the subject will constantly change, and needs uncovered during the learning process will provide new information for identifying learning resources and activities.

Self-directed learning by individuals frequently is inhibited by the absence of a guiding model or plan. Stubblefield (1981a) has suggested a model with four phases. Table 6.1 describes each phase and provides some questions that should be asked during the planning process. The first phase, *initiating*, involves focusing on needs, objectives, and benefits from the learning activity. The second phase, *planning*, involves identifying learning resources, specifying learning activities, and establishing criteria for successful

Table 6.1 Guiding model, or plan, for self-directed learning

Initiating phase	Planning phase	Managing phase	Evaluating phase
What is the purpose or goal of the learning endeavor?	What learning resources are available or attainable?	Has each learning activity been carried out?	Were the learning goals achieved?
What questions are to be answered or what needs met?	What activities can best stimulate learning?	How can the acquired information and knowledge be analyzed, interpreted, and incorporated?	Are there other goals that can be established?
What are the intended outcomes or personal benefits?	What are the criteria for successful accomplishment of any learning goals?	What conclusions or personal change is obtainable from the experience?	How can personal proficiencies as a learner be improved?

Source: Stubblefield (1981a: 24–5)

accomplishments. The next phase, *management*, involves carrying out the learning activities, analyzing the information obtained, and recording progress toward some personal changes. The final phase, *evaluation*, should answer questions as to whether or not objectives were achieved and where do we go from here.

Spear and Mocker (1984) looked at planning in terms of patterns of involvement. They derived four patterns from qualitative research on adult learning that can serve as a basis for organizing the circumstances that affect learning activities. Type I, which they defined as a single event with anticipated learning, is where the environment containing learning resources governs the learning process to a large degree. An example would be a new car owner being shown a video tape about and being given a brief lesson related to operating the vehicle. Type II, a single event with unanticipated learning, is where learning grows out of observations of and contact with a set of actual circumstances. For instance, a new secretary sees an experienced colleague utilizing a different word processing package than the one taught in business school. It seems to have some superior qualities. The colleague is asked to demonstrate its capabilities and to teach the fundamentals. The new secretary also takes the manual home and reads it until, finally, there is a great enough feeling of comfort to switch over to the new software.

Type III, a series of events with related learning, is where one learning experience naturally leads to another. Neal, one of our examples in Chapter 1, became somewhat of an expert on alternative energy sources utilizing primarily Type III learning experiences. Type IV, a series of events with unrelated learning, includes a number of different learning experiences which provide considerable background knowledge on a particular topic. Mary from Chapter 1 demonstrated Type IV learning. She gained most of her genealogical skills over long periods of time, through various learning experiences – many of which were mainly unrelated to each other.

Spear and Mocker (1984: 8) point out that more research is needed to understand better "how the structure for learning is constructed and how and why self-directed learners make their decisions as their learning activities proceed". However, their current framework on involvement patterns still provides some help in understanding the different types of teaching and learning that are possible.

The teaching and learning process we advocate in this book encompasses most aspects of Stubblefield's four stage model. It also allows for the varied organizing and decision-making circumstances suggested by Spear and Mocker, although Type IV learning usually occurs after more formal experiences take place. As Little (1985) notes, the strategies employed to learn in a self-directed manner will necessarily vary as a function of what is being learned.

Following, therefore, are some specific roles that we believe the facilitator needs to undertake in promoting self-direction in learning:

1 Provide information on certain topics through lecturing and the use of media or other learning techniques;
2 Serve as a resource for an individual or for a small group on certain portions of the learning content;
3 Assist learners to assess their needs and competencies so each person can map out an individual learning path;
4 Provide feedback on successive drafts of each person's learning plan or contract;
5 Locate available resources or secure new information on topics identified through needs assessment;
6 Build a resource collection of information, media, and models related to a variety of topics or areas of study;
7 Arrange for contacts with resource people on special topics and set up learning experiences for individuals and small groups beyond normal large group sessions;

8 Work with learners outside of formal or group settings as a stimulator or sounding board;

9 Help learners develop an attitude about and approach to learning that fosters independence;

10 Promote discussion, raising of questions, and small group activity to stimulate interest in the learning experience;

11 Help develop a positive attitude toward learning and self-directed inquiry;

12 Manage a learning process that includes such activities as continuous diagnosis of needs, acquisition of continuous feedback, and fostering of learner involvement; and

13 Serve as a validator or evaluator of learner accomplishment both throughout and at the end of a learning experience.

Thus, the interactive process that we advocate calls for an instructor to serve as facilitator and for learners to assume personal responsibility related to their own achievements. It has been our experience that the mature learner flourishes in a setting where identification of needs, personal ownership of learning involvement, and use of a wide variety of available resources are thoroughly and thoughtfully integrated into the instructional process.

AN INTERACTIVE TEACHING AND LEARNING PROCESS

The process described in this chapter has evolved through several years of experimentation and feedback from learners, primarily in the graduate classroom with students majoring in adult education. Together we have over 30 years of experience instructing adults in a wide variety of settings. This has included weekly classes, intensive summer classes, weekend classes, independent study via learning contracts, instruction via television, tele-lecture, and computer conferencing software, workshops, conferences, and informal training sessions. We stress, however, that the ideas presented here are but a few possible strategies for facilitating self-directed learning. Nonetheless, they are strategies that work for one or both of us.

We believe that the process can work, with various modifications, in virtually any setting. The librarian, for example, can use approaches for determining needs and helping learners select learning resources similar to those we describe. The County Extension agent can incorporate learners' experiences and needs in teaching about appropriate pesticide use. The literacy volunteer can adapt variations of learning contracts for helping learners make progress on reading and writing.

As noted earlier in this chapter, the andragogical teaching and learning procedures advocated by Knowles (1980) have clearly influenced our approach. In addition, Knowles and Associates (1984) describe adaptations of the andragogical process in various formal and informal settings. In Chapters 8 and 10 we also summarize some individualized approaches used in various settings and with various groupings of people. Understanding the influence of Knowles' work on us and studying all these variations will be useful as you think about adaptations you can make to the process we describe. We therefore present our process with the expectation that it will be necessary to make appropriate adjustments that fit your personality, preferred teaching techniques, and organizational requirements.

Finally, we must note that your teaching and learning philosophy, and the teaching style growing out of this philosophy, will impact on the adaptations you will make. Understanding and being able to delineate a personal philosophy promotes both the flexibility and consistency we believe is needed in working with adult learners. Hiemstra (1988b) provides some guidelines for thinking about personal philosophy and how that philosophy can be used to guide action within the classroom. White and Brockett (1987) also share some ideas about applying philosophy in an informal adult education setting. Hayes (1989) provides a wide range of insights relative to teaching style.

Initial planning

One of the first things we usually do in preparing for a facilitator role is develop what we call a "learning rationale" sheet. In this rationale statement we go further than simply developing a description of the learning experience. We develop for learners a statement that describes some reasons why we believe they will be interested in the learning experiences. We also describe how we will work as instructors in the individualized experience. Philosophically, it is not our intent to manipulate learners into following some preset direction, but we believe facilitators must constantly be diligent in finding an appropriate balance between learner freedom and whatever organizational requirements that might exist. Thus, in the rationale statement, we also include comments about self-direction in learning and what learners can expect from us.

Another preparation activity involves specifying necessary competencies, learning requirements, and goals. In reality, most learners will expect you to put on an "expert" hat from time to time. In other words, as we noted above, you need to make sure that the course covers those topics included in the catalog description and curricular guide, or implied in the title.

Before a learning experience actually begins, it is important to design some appropriate needs-assessment materials. When we are teaching a formal course, for example, we normally use two needs-assessment techniques. The first technique involves written responses by learners to a needs-assessment tool. The second technique involves learners in some small group discussions in which each person's needs can be contrasted with others in the group. This usually leads to more clearly defined personal needs and, frequently, discovery of previously unrecognized needs. More information on needs assessment is presented later in the chapter.

Another initial course-planning activity involves finding, building, designing, and developing relevant support materials. This function actually is ongoing, with new materials constantly being developed and old ones phased out as needed. It involves continuous reading and collecting materials related to various subjects or content areas. The job is almost overwhelming, especially as one adds courses to a teaching repertoire. However, the process is predicated on a philosophy that places instructors in the role of learning facilitators, resource providers, and encouragers of as much self-direction as is possible in a learner. Thus, we believe that an important part of the teaching process is providing a wide variety of learning materials to the learners.

One more activity we have often found quite helpful both to us and to learners is the preparation of a workbook or study guide of supplemental materials related to the course. This includes course syllabus materials, descriptions of learning activities, bibliographic citations, learning contract forms, any necessary descriptions or instructions, and special materials we think will be useful to learners. In most instances, we also provide material specific or supplemental to certain learning activities. There are two distinct advantages to creating your own workbook for a learning experience. First, such an endeavor promotes advance planning and preparation related to a course or content area. Obviously, not everything can be prepared in advance if you plan to use needs-assessment activities to determine specific learning requirements. However, after a course is taught once or twice you will have a fairly good understanding of the core material that typically needs to be covered.

A second advantage is that much of the material pertaining to a course that normally is handed out in a piecemeal fashion, is distributed all at once. We often make arrangements with a local printing company to copy and bind all the material within an attractive cover. Then the workbook is sold to learners as a normal text requirement for the course. Most learners do not seem to object to the arrangement because the materials are bound together and most photocopying processes result in material of a uniform quality. Such a procedure potentially has a spin-off advantage of saving the institution some money and some secretarial time. Even if such a workbook or study guide is done entirely in-house, it has proven to us to be easier than developing the materials from session to session.

Climate setting

Once the course is underway, there are several activities important in establishing a positive learning climate. This section's purpose is to describe these activities and to provide a picture of the approach used in those crucial first few hours together. As Pratt (1984: 7) notes, "the first session can be critical to the eventual success of ... [the course]".

In many learning experiences, the actual content acquisition begins within the first few minutes of the first session. In essence, many instructors assume that each student is there with textbooks in hand, an appropriate mental attitude in place, and pencil poised to receive the "gospel". Consequently, what often happens is that the "gospel" is given via a lecture that continues throughout the initial period. Any mention of assignments, expectations, and course direction is made almost incidentally. Very often learners are even discouraged from talking with each other, seeking an understanding of course goals, or asking questions.

We realize that a somewhat negative picture of teaching is being painted in the above paragraph. However, many of our graduate students report that they frequently experience something similar in many of their courses. Both authors also have participated in training experiences in which we were subjected to a "fill in the empty reservoir" approach.

We realize that most teachers or trainers are given the freedom to make presentations in whatever style or manner desired. However, based on our teaching experiences, we contend that the independent, self-directed learner deserves and desires a different approach. This is especially true during the first few hours together, when personal attitudes about subject, instructor, teaching style, and learning activities are formed.

Some additional strategies we have used with success include the following:

1 Physical arrangements and personal comfort are important ingredients in successful teaching and learning. Plan ahead to make sure the classroom or meeting place arrangements will meet the needs of the participants and your learning expectations. Hiemstra and Sisco (1990), Vosko (1984, 1985) and Vosko and Hiemstra (1988) provide some ideas related to the physical setting and environment;

2 Arrive at the classroom setting early enough to ensure that the space is appropriately set up. This may include moving chairs, checking the room temperature, checking for adequate lighting, arranging for any needed break-out areas for group discussion, and making sure all audio-visual equipment is in place and working;

3 Make provisions for coffee/tea, smoking, and toilet breaks, taking into account both those who may be very much opposed to smoking and those

who cannot go for long periods of not smoking without it having an effect on their ability to learn.

Helping learners become acquainted

There are a number of techniques that we use to help learners become acquainted and to begin to feel comfortable in the learning setting. One of the first things we usually do is spend a very brief time introducing ourselves. We then ask all participants to fill out one side of a card with their name, address, and other useful information. We note that the information will be used for a group roster so they can contact fellow students outside of group meeting times. We encourage such networking for purposes of raising questions, studying together, or working jointly on course projects.

We then ask them to turn the card over, fold it in half so that the above information is on the inside, and make a tent card that will stand up by itself. They are then asked to print their first name, a nickname, or whatever name they would like to be called, in large block letters on both sides of the card. The instructor should make a tent card, too (we both prefer to use our first names rather than titles or last names to help create an informal climate). Such name cards are used for at least the first several group sessions to help in the learning of each others' names.

Next, we have students introduce themselves. One technique is to have the students turn to their closest partner and work in dyads. We ask them to spend about 15 minutes becoming acquainted. Then each partner in a dyad introduces the other to all group members and tells something about each other's background. This provides a chance for participants to get to know another person and for remaining group members to learn something about everyone through the subsequent introductions.

If the group is not too large (probably no larger than sixteen people), or if several people already know each other quite well, we ask partners to find out and report something unusual or special about each other. If there are uneven numbers, a group of three can introduce one of the other two, or an instructor can participate in the activities to form the last dyad. There also will be occasions, such as in small seminars or training workshops, where stick-on, or pin-on, name-tags can be used so group members can read the names as they enter into personal conversations.

Such techniques may sound simplistic at first glance. However, we have found that they do a nice job of breaking the ice, setting a tone of informality and mutual respect, and helping people learn names. In addition, you as the instructor can learn some valuable things about members of the group.

We also have found it very important during the first session to spend some time talking about the teaching and learning process we use. The workbook of supplemental materials described earlier contains a write-up that both describes the process and the instructor's personal teaching philosophy. Typically we include various examples of how the process is employed, how self-directed learning is encouraged, and how the instructor's role as facilitator evolves during the course. Discussion and answering questions about the process or course requirements can go on until students appear to have an understanding of the proposed process.

Needs assessment

It is our premise that learners should become actively involved in determining specific needs around which subsequent learning activities are planned. This involvement usually takes place or at least is begun during the first session. There are two aspects to the needs assessment process that we use.

Individual needs assessment

As noted earlier, we spend considerable time before each session thinking through the probable topics of student interest. The resulting needs-diagnosis form provides a starting point for learners to assess individual ability and experience. Within the first 3 hours together (or as a take-home assignment in between the first and second sessions) learners are asked to rate themselves on several competency areas listed on the form. We also encourage them to add other items that are not covered on the form but that they think should be included.

The point of this activity is to begin building personal responsibility for learning through a process involving self-recognition of strengths and weaknesses. Thus, we ask them to look at their own needs rather than guessing what their needs might be. In this way, our learners begin to see how a certain set of experiences can be used to fill in gaps or to enhance personal strengths.

If it is impossible to pre-design an instrument, group members can be asked to list their learning expectations and personal needs, and/or to begin a process of designing learning objectives. In one graduate course, for example, a gaming and simulation device on community-needs analysis is employed during the first session as a means of stimulating the students' awareness of what they do and do not know. In another course, a pre-test of knowledge most likely to be covered during the semester is administered as a means of stimulating thinking about the range of topic possibilities.

Group activities

We also believe that it is very important to involve participants in group-needs assessment. In our experience, hearing how others are both similar and dissimilar helps most individuals obtain a perspective on why certain topics should be covered in formal group sessions, even if they do not meet every person's individual needs.

The technique that we use most often involves the formation of groups of five to eight people. This is usually done at the conclusion of the first session together or at the beginning of the second. If possible, we like to put together in groups people who already have been through courses taught with the individualized process and people who have not. Frequently, people will be asked ahead of time (perhaps before the first session actually starts or during the first break) to serve as a leader for a small group.

Thus, after people have had time to complete an individual needs-diagnosis form, and after everyone has some notions about the range of possible topics, we ask people to move into a group setting. We often use a numbering technique to divide people into groups, where we go around the room and each person counts off in sequence up to the number of groups desired. Each person who numbered themselves as a one in the counting sequence goes into group number one, those numbered two would go into group number two, and so on. Sometimes we put up on a chalkboard the names of individuals within each group, or let learners form their own groups. If possible, we have extra rooms available or we use areas like hallways, private offices, or faculty lounges, so that each group's discussion will not be disruptive to other groups. We either appoint a group leader and a recorder or, more often, ask that they be picked by the group.

The leader and group members are instructed to use the needs-diagnosis form as a starting point, by ranking listed topics according to how each person rated a topic on the form and how much class time should be devoted to them. The process facilitates discussion of the various topics. It helps participants recognize the individual differences within the group, and occasionally prompts a request for clarification from the instructor. We make ourselves available as a resource but attempt to keep a low profile during the process. We want the students to struggle with the terms and language, to seek out clarification, and to realize that they will need to spend time during the course on certain topics.

We also encourage each group to determine whether there are additional topics that require some attention during future meetings. Each group is asked to supply a report that provides a ranking of the topics, describes other topics needing attention, and seeks clarification of any concepts. We also encourage them to provide suggestions relative to teaching techniques, learning resources, and sequencing ideas. Typically each leader or recorder makes a brief report to the larger group so that everyone can see similarities or differences among the various rankings.

Implementing self-directed learning

Designing future learning activities begins to take place after the session devoted to needs diagnosis. Using the needs-assessment information, the instructor builds a tentative group plan for the remainder of the course. We do this by examining the various small group reports, compiling a majority report of needs, and estimating the amount of time required to cover each topic. We also suggest the various resources that can be used or developed.

Next we take a careful look at any requirements for the course to see how closely they match the compiled needs information. This is where the instructor's expertise comes into play to be sure that students will finish the course with any basics necessary for subject mastery or to move on to a next level. Then we begin detailing activities for remaining sessions and pulling together resources that will complement and supplement each group period.

The result is a plan of action for the course that is shown to learners for a final review and approval the next time they gather. This tentative plan typically lays out a weekly schedule of learning experiences, suggests appropriate support materials and objectives, and highlights any required course deadlines. We also attempt to ensure that the weekly schedule is flexible, contains slack time so particular topics can be explored in depth as interest dictates, and that time is allotted for what Danis and Tremblay (1985: 142) call "reflective activity" and what Little (1985) would call primary and support learning strategies.

Next, the instructor tries to bring about a logical flow of events. This includes securing the necessary resources, arranging for any guest presenters, communicating the class plan to learners, and rediagnosing learner needs whenever it is deemed necessary. Rydell (1983) provides several ideas on how to develop and use various educational materials with self-directed learners.

The learners then develop a learning plan or contract through which they design an individualized approach to meeting identified needs. These plans typically describe personal goals, resources to be employed, learning strategies, evidence planned to show accomplishment, anticipated validation means, and time-frames for completing activities. Knowles (1986) presents a variety of contracting forms that can be used. The instructor provides feedback and help in insuring that a meaningful and realistic plan for the course is completed. Throughout the course, learners are urged to partake of group activities as appropriate to their learning plan. Some learners will participate in every remaining session. Others will participate in only selected group activities and use time away from class to pursue individualized learning activities.

During the remainder of such a course the instructor takes on two roles.

One is the management of each remaining session in such a manner as to promote both learning and involvement. We also support Brookfield's (1987) urging that a conscious effort to promote critical reflection by learners must be made so that all the intricacies of managing a process do not get in the way of promoting thinking, theory building, and intellectual transformation.

A second role involves one-to-one communication with learners through written feedback and individual appointments, renegotiation of learning plans as needs evolve, assistance in securing learning resources, and evaluation of any products developed. Courses that meet daily (such as an intensive summer session workshop), every other weekend, or electronically will require some variations on those that meet weekly during a 15-week semester or a 10-week quarter.

Evaluation activities

We use three means of evaluation during a graduate course to help us keep our teaching fresh and to provide indications of how well the self-directed learning process is working for participants. One involves formative evaluation throughout the course. This includes being sensitive to non-verbal cues of problems, soliciting written feedback occasionally, employing a mid-course evaluation tool, and encouraging appointments outside of class as concerns or problems arise. Another technique is an instrument we employ during the last class session. It is designed to evaluate us as instructors and facilitators of self-directed learning. The third technique is another instrument also administered at the end of the course. This instrument seeks evaluation of the process used, content covered, and resources employed during the course.

We ask learners to exclude their names on evaluation instruments unless they want us to have such information. Our belief is that an anonymous response is preferred by most people. Also, in our experience most learners take these evaluation assignments quite seriously. Consequently, over the past decade we have refined our process so that self-directed learning skills are maximized for most learners.

DEVELOPING SKILLS BY INDIVIDUAL CONTROL OF LEARNING VARIABLES

Within the confines of any formal or individual learning experience, there are several ways in which learners can maximize their self-directed learning skills. Borrowing from work by Cooper (1980) and adapting material from Hiemstra (1988a), we suggest there are at least nine learning variables that can be controlled by learners. The extent to which control is shared between learner and facilitator may shift from time to time, but it has been our experience "that these variables are important to the overall encouragement of self-directed learning" (Hiemstra, 1988a: 119).

1 *Identification of learning needs* As noted in the previous section, we do some initial thinking on the range of possible topics for a course or learning experience. However, once the experience begins, we use one or more techniques that enable learners to identify individual needs associated with the course topic and to begin taking that personal responsibility that is so crucial to the process.

2 *Learning goals* Once needs have been identified, specific topics, purposes, and goals should be chosen by the learner and incorporated into a learning contract or plan. The facilitator and learner can then share in the refinement of this contract.

3 *Expected outcomes* "The nature of the outcomes desired or expected should be determined by the learner and tied back to needs, topics, and purposes. The facilitator provides advice or offers concrete suggestions as needed" (Hiemstra, 1988a: 119).

4 *Evaluation/validation methods* We encourage learners to select evaluation or validation methods and techniques that best suit their own learning styles or preferences. These can range from traditional tests to the use of experts or advisors completely divorced from the learning situation to serve as validators or evaluators. The latter type can be encouraged when learning topics fall outside the facilitator's area of expertise.

5 *Documentation methods* We also encourage learners to choose methods for documenting and demonstrating accomplishments in order to keep records of what they have learned and to refer to them after the learning experiences have ended. Consequently, diaries, logs, journals, and scholarly papers are often chosen. Christensen (1981) and Progoff (1975) provide some guidelines for developing and using diaries and journals.

6 *Appropriate learning experiences* Learners are encouraged to select learning experiences that suit their specific situations. A mini-internship in a particular adult education organization might work well for one person, whereas learning through reading or listening to audio tapes might suit another person. We also elicit feedback from learners in various ways to monitor the appropriateness of various learning experiences.

7 *Variety of learning resources* To foster acceptance of personal responsibility for learning, we provide various resources from which a person can choose as personal needs and interests dictate. For example, in a typical graduate course we will provide: text recommendations; an instructor-designed study guide, or workbook, of supplemental materials;

bibliographic and library reading suggestions; media materials placed on reserve in the library; personal materials to be loaned; lists of outside resource specialists; and examples of student-generated materials from previous courses.

8 *Optimal learning environment* The promotion of individualized learning includes providing an environment that stimulates learning in various ways. Thus, throughout a course, we provide a mixture of instructor input, supplemental learning materials, discussion opportunities, evaluation options, and mechanisms for critical reflection from which a learner selects those aspects of personal value.

9 *Learning pace* The self-directed learning process described in this chapter allows for much of the learning pace to be determined by the learner. Given the existence of organizational constraints like designated course time slots, we encourage learners to select a pace best suited to their individual needs. In an institutionally sponsored course, this will require negotiations between the instructor and the learner relative to completion dates, evaluation techniques, and grading choices.

The learner can also control many aspects of individualized learning activities outside the course parameters. We can thus:

encourage learners to seek ways of tying learning activities to practical realities of job, home, and community. In addition, learners have the freedom to select a wide variety of written or media resources to enhance their intellectual growth related to the subject matter, especially once the course has been completed and subsequent application needs arise.

(Hiemstra, 1988a: 120)

RESOURCES FOR SELF-DIRECTED LEARNING

As noted throughout this chapter, the fostering of self-directed learning requires that many resources be made available to learners. These resources frequently need to be made accessible during an entire learning experience because of varied learner needs, pacing requirements, and plans. This also means there has to be continuous evaluation of resource selections and feedback by the facilitator. The final section of this chapter provides some thoughts regarding the types of resources that can be used for self-directed learning activities.

When looking in book stores, media catalogs, and general magazines, there are many resources which self-directed learners can use, including a multitude of do-it-yourself books, video tapes, and audio tapes. In addition, public agencies like libraries and adult learning centers have compiled many resources on a variety of subjects that may be of value to learners.

Table 6.2   Range of potential resources identified during a workshop on self-directed learning

Mediated	Individualized	Agency/Group	Mentored
Journals/ magazines	Travel	Classes	Peer reviews
Programmed learning	Competency ratings	Free universities	Modeling
Cassette tapes	Gaming devices	Libraries	Mentors
Computers	Observations	Proprietary schools	Personality analyses
Workbooks	Personal inventories	Agency visits	Learning partners
Interactive video	Self-talk	Conferences	Counseling/ testing
Television	Learning projects	Museums/ galleries	Information counselors
Radio	Personal journals/diaries	Discussion groups	Networks/ networking
Learning modules/kits	Internships		
Films/video tapes	Stimulated recall		
Conferencing software			
Electronic networks			

Source: Hiemstra (1985c)

Unfortunately, from our viewpoint, there has not been much work to date in evaluating the effectiveness of these resources. Gross's (1977) book on lifelong learning, Knowles's (1975) self-directed learning guide, and a sourcebook for independent learners by Smith and Cunningham (1987) are examples of some efforts to provide resource suggestions. In most learning experiences, however, the facilitator still needs to play some sort of role in evaluating, locating, providing, and even creating learning resources.

A group of people thought about possible resources for self-directed learners during a workshop on the topic (Hiemstra, 1985c). Although the purpose was not to evaluate resources, a classification scheme was developed to aid in the selection of resources. Table 6.2 represents the range of potential resources identified. Such resources only scratch the surface in identifying possible aids or learning activities in support of self-directed activity. As you begin to use aspects of the process described in this chapter, you will no doubt be able to add to the list those resources specific to your locations or teaching situations.

CONCLUSION

This chapter has presented various examples and ideas related to the facilitation of self-directed learning. Much of the individualized process elements described have evolved from our own instructional experiences. However, many of them have been influenced by the andragogical teaching and learning process, as well as several other ideas.

Obviously, we would like to be influential in helping you think about and alter your own approaches to instructing adults or we would not be writing this book. In reality, though, you will need to filter our thinking and instructional-process ideas through your own experience base, philosophical beliefs, and day-to-day instructional realities. We hope that our ideas and experiences and those described in Hiemstra and Sisco (1990) will enhance your instructional skills and abilities.

7   Enhancing learner self-direction

In the "Personal Responsibility Orientation" (PRO) model, self-directed learning as an instructional method is one of two key components in the broader concept of self-direction in learning. This component, which was addressed in the previous chapter, stresses the processes occurring *outside* the individual that can facilitate greater self-direction. The other key component of the PRO model is what we have referred to as "learner self-direction." Here, the focus is on what is going on *within* the person and is perhaps best understood in terms of personality. Another way of distinguishing between these two components is that the emphasis of self-directed learning is *external* to the individual while the focus of learner self-direction is *internal* to the individual. In this chapter, we will shift our focus from the external, process orientation to an examination of the internal, personal orientation.

It is our intention to explore some of what we believe are key influences on the phenomenon of learner self-direction. Further, we will address the interplay between influences on the individual learner and the social context in which self-direction develops. Finally, emphasis will shift to an examination of three strategies that can be used by facilitators to promote greater self-directedness among adult learners. A key assumption underlying the discussion in this chapter, as well as the PRO model in general, is our belief that there is an inseparable link between learner self-direction and the development of human potential. In other words, self-direction in learning can be seen as a means, or vehicle, by which individuals can more fully realize their greatest potential as human beings.

Why do we believe that personality is so vital to a clearer understanding of self-direction in learning? There are at least two reasons for this. First, as was pointed out in the chapters on research, one of the most convincing findings growing out of quantitative investigations on self-direction is the strong link between self-direction and self-concept. For purposes of this discussion, self-concept refers to how one is "seen, perceived, and experienced" by oneself (Fitts and Richard, 1971: 3). Essentially, what much of the research shows is that a relationship exists between a positive self-concept and the extent to which one subscribes to principles of self-direction.

A second reason for stressing the importance of personality can be found in clues emanating from research on participation in more formal adult and continuing education activities. For instance, Houle (1961) in his classic study *The Inquiring Mind*, developed a typology consisting of three groups of learners: goal-oriented, activity-oriented, and learning-oriented. The latter group, learning-oriented individuals, were those who chose to pursue learning for its own sake, believing that such activity would help them to grow as individuals. More recently, Houle has stated that at the time he conducted his (1961) study, there was tacit acceptance of "the idea that men and women should assume responsibility for their own learning" (Houle, 1988: 89). However, he also states that the major thrust of the literature during the 1960s was not on individuals, but rather on "social actions and responses" (Houle, 1988: 89). In another study, Morstain and Smart (1974) derived six major reasons for adult education participation from a factor analysis of Boshier's (1971) Educational Participation Scale. Among the six factors identified was "cognitive interest," which closely parallels Houle's learning-oriented individual. Indeed, as was noted in Chapter 4, Reynolds (1986) found a strong link between cognitive interest and self-directed learning readiness.

Looking at the issue of participation from another angle, it is possible to gain insights based on studies of why adults *do not* participate in adult and continuing education activities. Cross (1981) has identified three major categories of barriers to participation: situational, institutional, and dispositional. The last of these categories is particularly relevant to our discussion. According to Cross, dispositional barriers are "related to attitudes and self-perceptions about oneself as a learner" (Cross, 1981: 98). These can include such concerns as a belief that one is "too old" to learn, lack of confidence, previous negative experiences in school, and uncertainty/fear about what might result from participating in learning. What the various types of dispositional barriers share, though, is that they are based on beliefs that come from within the individual, based on personal perceptions and/or past experiences.

More recently, Darkenwald and Valentine (1985), using a modified version of the Deterrents to Participation Scale (DPS) (Scanlan and Darkenwald, 1984), identified six factors related to non-participation in organized adult education courses among a "general" adult population. These factors include: lack of confidence, lack of course relevance, time constraints, low personal priority, cost, and personal problems. Similarly, Hayes (1988) administered a modified version of the DPS (DPS-LL) to a group of adult basic education students and found five factors identified as deterrents: low self-confidence, social disapproval, situational barriers, negative attitude to classes, and low personal priority. While these more recent studies utilized methodology and instrumentation different from the earlier work, there seems be a degree of overlap between the major sets of factors that appear to impact upon participation in formal adult education.

We believe that the research on participation and barriers to participation provide important insights relative to learner self-direction. Even though this work has largely been drawn from institutionally-based adult education programs, the emphasis on attitudinal factors reinforces the importance of personality as a determinant of, or deterrent to, participation. By addressing these considerations, it might be possible to increase participation in adult learning. So, too, we believe will be the case when one chooses to engage in learning through a self-directed method. Let us now look at some of the ideas that have influenced the concept of learner self-direction.

CONCEPTUAL INFLUENCES ON LEARNER SELF-DIRECTION

In Chapter 2, we pointed out that the idea of personal responsibility, which we view as central to the idea of self-direction in learning, is derived largely from principles of humanistic philosophy. Similarly, we believe that an understanding of learner self-direction can best be gained from the humanist perspective. At the same time, other theories – namely behaviorist/neobehaviorist thought and perspective transformation/transformation theory – can help to provide greater understanding of this personal orientation. Each of these directions is considered below.

Humanist influences

Humanistic philosophy has deep roots that can be found in the ideas of Confucius, Greco-Roman philosophers such as Aristotle, and many of those involved in the Italian Renaissance of the fifteenth century (Elias and Merriam, 1980). In the twentieth century, the humanistic viewpoint has been further developed by existentialist philosophers such as Sartre.

Elias and Merriam (1980) have discussed what they see as seven basic assumptions underlying humanistic philosophy. These can be summarized as follows:

1 Human nature is inherently good;
2 Individuals are free and autonomous and, thus, "capable of making significant personal choices within the constraints imposed by heredity, personal history, and environment" (Elias and Merriam, 1980: 118).
3 Each person is a unique individual with unlimited potential for growth and development;

4 Self-concept – one's subjective perception of self – is an important influence on growth and development;
5 Individuals possess an urge toward self-actualization, the highest level of personal growth;
6 Personally defined realities play an especially important role in humanistic thought; and
7 Individuals possess a sense of responsibility to themselves and others.

It should be clear that each of these principles is very much consistent with the values underlying the PRO model.

Within the field of psychology, humanistic ideas have been stressed through what is sometimes referred to as the "third force" in psychology (Goble, 1970). This third force, or humanistic psychology, grew out of discontentment with the psychoanalytic and behavioristic emphases that have been predominant in twentieth-century psychological thought. Perhaps the two individuals whose ideas have been most seminal to the development of humanistic psychology are Abraham Maslow and Carl Rogers.

Maslow (1970) is perhaps best known for his theory that human motivation occurs according to a "hierarchy of needs." In this hierarchy, needs are arranged in the following order: physiological, safety, belongingness and love, esteem, and self-actualization. The point that Maslow stresses is that since these needs are arranged hierarchically, one must be able to fulfill the needs at a given level in order to work effectively toward the fulfillment of needs at the next highest level. For example, it will be necessary for a person seeking to fulfill belongingness and love needs to first have met needs at the two previous levels.

What is crucial about Maslow's work to our discussion of learner self-direction is the concept of "self-actualization." This, according to Maslow, "may be loosely described as the full use and exploitation of talents, capacities, potentialities, etc." (Maslow, 1970: 150). In other words, self-actualization refers to the highest level of human growth, where one has reached one's fullest potential. As with self-direction, though, it is important to think of self-actualization as an extreme on a continuum, an ideal state toward which one is continuously striving.

Maslow has also identified a number of characteristics shared by self-actualizing people. According to Maslow, self-actualizers tend to, among other things: possess a more efficient view of reality and a corresponding tolerance of ambiguity; be accepting of themselves and others; demonstrate spontaneous behavior that is in tune with their own values and not necessarily tied to the common beliefs and practices of the culture; focus on problems that lie outside of themselves, thus demonstrating a highly ethical concern; maintain a few extremely close interpersonal relationships rather than seek out a large number of less intense friendships; and possess high levels of creativity. Another characteristic, one that is especially important in terms of learning, is what Maslow (1970) has referred to as the "mystic or peak experience." Peak experiences are extremely intense episodes where the individual is transformed through new insights. In describing persons who had reported peak experiences, Maslow noted the following observation:

> There were the same feelings of limitless horizons opening up to the vision, the feeling of being simultaneously more powerful and also more helpless than one ever was before, the feeling of great ecstasy and wonder and awe, the loss of placing in time and space with, finally, the conviction that something extremely important and valuable had happened, so that the subject is to some extent transformed and strengthened even in his daily life by such experiences.
>
> (Maslow, 1970: 164)

While most learning activities are not of such an intense and insightful nature, peak experience is an important notion for educators to grasp and, in our view, is potentially a key to understanding learner self-direction.

Self-actualizers, then, are people who have a great deal of self-understanding and insight. They are creative individuals who are not afraid to deal with unstructured situations or to march to the beat of the proverbial different drummer. Self-actualized individuals are consistently working toward higher levels of personal growth and, in doing so, are able to utilize existing resources to their greatest potential. In essence, self-actualization, and the people who demonstrate high levels of this characteristic, epitomize personal responsibility – as we have used the term within the context of the PRO model.

Rogers, through the approach that has been referred to as "client-centered therapy" (e.g., 1951), has stressed the importance of the client-therapist relationship and the need to shift responsibility for growth in a therapeutic relationship away from the therapist toward the client. Through such an approach, Rogers expresses his belief in the potential of clients and his trust in their ability to assume responsibility for their own lives.

According to Rogers, a major goal of therapy is to help clients foster greater self-direction. He notes that to be self-directing "means that one chooses – and then learns from the consequences" (Rogers, 1961: 171). This is the essence of what we mean by the term *personal responsibility* throughout this book: that learners retain control over their learning processes, and are subsequently responsible for the consequences of their learning. To expand further on this point, Rogers offers the following observation:

The individual who sees himself and his situation clearly and who freely takes responsibility for that self and for that situation is a very different person from the one who is simply in the grip of outside circumstances. This difference shows up clearly in important aspects of his behavior.

(Rogers, 1983: 278)

Rogers (1969, 1983) has applied the principles of his therapeutic approach to educational practice and, as such, has helped build a foundation for the development of theory relative to self-direction in adult learning.

How might concepts from humanistic psychology translate into concepts of learner self-direction? The study by Gibbons, *et al.* (1980), which was discussed in earlier chapters, includes a list of fourteen principles, derived from research, that contribute to a tentative theory of self-education. These principles, are as follows:

1 Locus of control lies within the self-educator rather than in institutions;
2 The focus of self-education is on a very specific area rather than a broad one;
3 Self-education is undertaken for immediate application;
4 The self-educator is motivated by the desire to achieve in a given field;
5 Recognition and rewards – a general sense of accomplishment – are important to the self-educator;
6 Previous experience, interests, and abilities contribute to the selection of one's chosen field of endeavor;
7 Self-educators draw from a wide variety of methods and techniques most compatible with their own style of learning;
8 "Self-education involves the development of attributes traditionally associated with people of character: integrity, self-discipline, perseverance, industriousness, altruism, sensitivity to others, and strong guiding principles" (Gibbons, *et al.*, 1980: 54);
9 Such individuals tend to develop independent, nonconformist, and creative attributes;
10 Reading and "other process skills" are important to self-educators;
11 Experiences that occur in youth contribute to an eventual conscious choice of what one focuses upon as a self-educator;
12 The optimal environment for self-education is one that is warm and supportive, where there is a close relationship with at least one other individual;
13 Self-educators tend to possess good interpersonal relating skills and are often well liked by others;
14 The above characteristics correspond closely with those that comprise a "mature personality" and are associated with self-actualization.

To summarize, our view of self-direction is largely framed within the context of humanistic thought. Notions relative to belief in a positive view of human nature and the belief that human potential is virtually unlimited serve as cornerstones to the concept of personal responsibility, as we have used it throughout this book. Nonetheless, current thinking about self-direction has, indeed, been influenced and informed by other perspectives. Two such perspectives are behaviorism and neobehaviorism, and transformation theory.

Behaviorist and neobehaviorist influences

Classic behaviorism suggests that human nature is neither inherently positive or negative but, rather, is shaped by influences from the person's environment. Learning, in this view, emphasizes the attainment of measurable objectives, which are ideally achieved through a systematic instructional design process. While the assumptions underlying behaviorism depart from the basic humanistic thought from which the PRO model is derived, we nevertheless believe that behaviorism provides some insights relative to self-direction in adult learning. Two practices rooted in behaviorism that we find particularly valuable to self-direction are (a) learning contracts and (b) a systematic instructional planning process. These are discussed elsewhere in the book, particularly in Chapter 6.

One example of this behaviorist perspective on self-direction is presented by Watson and Tharp (1985). In this view, self-direction is discussed as a set of skills related to the process of self-modification. According to Watson and Tharp, self-modification is a change closely linked to "adjustment." Here, adjustment refers to harmony, both within the thoughts, actions, and feelings of the individual and between the self and the environment. Watson and Tharp go on to describe a process that individuals can utilize in modifying their behaviors toward the end of greater adjustment.

A variation on the theme of behaviorism has been presented by Penland (1981), who suggests that self-direction can be understood from a neobehaviorist perspective. Neobehaviorism departs from classic behaviorism in that while the latter is concerned exclusively with observable behaviors, the former acknowledges the importance of also understanding elements that are internal to the individual. Thus, whereas classical behaviorism is only concerned with the environment as a determinant of behavior, neobehaviorism stresses the interaction of the individual and environment. This is not unlike the aspect of adjustment discussed by Watson and Tharp as harmony between the self and the environment.

In our view, it is this link between the self and the environment that provides the strongest support for a behaviorist influence on self-direction. A purely humanistic view of self-direction looks only at factors internal to the individual. Yet it is clear that environment *does* play a role in self-direction. Certain teaching-learning transactions can be seen to support or frustrate self-direction. Similarly, there are certain sociocultural contexts where self-direction is probably more desirable than others. The social context, which is a vital aspect of the PRO model, can be further understood in terms of the next category of theoretical influence.

Transformation theory influences

In the late 1970s, Mezirow (1978) presented his notion of "perspective transformation" to the literature of adult education. This concept, which had come out of several years of conceptual work (e.g., Mezirow, 1975) is based on the idea that, in adult development an essential kind of learning involves "how we are caught up in our own history and are reliving it" (Mezirow, 1978: 101). Mezirow goes on to suggest that adults "learn to become critically aware of the cultural and psychological assumptions that have influenced the way we see ourselves and our relationships and the way we pattern our lives" (Mezirow, 1978: 101). Influenced by such writers as Habermas (1970, 1971), Freire (1970), and Gould (1978), perspective transformation holds that learning is not merely the accumulation of new knowledge, which is added on to existing knowledge; rather, it is a process whereby many of the basic values and assumptions under which a person operates are changed through the process of learning. Perspective transformation is an emancipatory process (Mezirow, 1981) and is very much similar to "consciousness-raising." And while it is a very personal process, it can clearly be linked to social action. Mezirow uses such examples as the women's movement and the civil rights movement, where the goal of learning is the empowerment of individuals, to illustrate how the transformation of individuals can subsequently be translated into social action.

How is perspective transformation related to self-direction in adult learning? First, Mezirow suggests that self-directed learning underlies the process of perspective transformation:

> Enhancing the learner's ability for self-direction in learning as a foundation for a distinctive philosophy of adult education has breadth and power. It represents the mode of learning characteristic of adulthood.

> (Mezirow, 1981: 21)

In order to enhance the ability of adults to function as self-directed learners, Mezirow offers the following guidelines:

1 progressively decrease the learner's dependency on the educator;
2 help the learner understand how to use learning resources – especially

the experience of others, including the educator, and how to engage others in reciprocal learning relationships;

3 assist the learner to define his/her learning needs – both in terms of immediate awareness and of understanding the cultural and psychological assumptions influencing his/her perceptions of needs;

4 assist learners to assume increasing responsibility for defining their learning objectives, planning their own learning program and evaluating their progress;

5 organize what is to be learned in relationship to his/her current personal problems, concerns and levels of understanding;

6 foster learner decision making – select learner-relevant experiences which require choosing, expand the learner's range of options, facilitate taking the perspectives of others who have alternative ways of understanding;

7 encourage the use of criteria for judging which are increasingly inclusive and differentiating in awareness, self-reflexive and integrative of experience;

8 foster a self-corrective reflexive approach to learning – to typifying and labeling, to perspective taking and choosing, and to habits of learning and learning relationships;

9 facilitate problem posing and problem solving, including problems associated with the implementation of individual and collective action; recognition of relationship between personal problems and public issues;

10 reinforce the self-concept of the learner as a learner and doer by providing for progressive mastery; a supportive climate with feedback to encourage provisional efforts to change and to take risks; avoidance of competitive judgment of performance; appropriate use of mutual support groups;

11 emphasize experiential, participative and projective instructional methods; appropriate use of modeling and learning contracts;

12 make the moral distinction between helping the learner understand his/her full range of choices and how to improve the quality of choosing vs. encouraging the learner to make a specific choice.

(Mezirow, 1981: 22–3)

A second way in which perspective transformation and self-direction might be linked is that transformation theory attempts to bridge the personal and social dimensions of learning. Thus, it can offer some insights into the "social context" dimension of the PRO model presented in Chapter 2. The following section offers a further look at the linkage between individual and social emphases in self-direction.

THE DILEMMA OF SOCIAL CONTEXT

Historically, one of the controversial issues that has pervaded the field of adult education is the question of whether the primary emphasis of adult education activity should be on individual learners or on the larger society (e.g., Cotton, 1964; Elias and Merriam, 1980; McGinnis, 1981; Stubblefield, 1981b). One school of thought holds that the emphasis should be on the growth and development of individuals while another school argues that social change should be the primary function of adult education. As was noted in Chapter Two, this issue has been relevant to discussions of self-direction in adult learning. Indeed, some of the strongest criticisms of work in this area to date have centered on the belief that such efforts have failed to consider the social context of self-direction.

We believe that the notion of individual vs. social emphasis is a false dichotomy. Instead, we share the view that *both* the individual and the social dimension are important and that one cannot exist without the other. At the same time, given that we are working largely from the assumptions of humanistic thought, it is our view that the individual is the *starting point* for adult education practice. Indeed, this point serves as a foundation underlying the PRO model, and the extent to which one agrees with this view will probably influence the extent to which he or she is likely to support the model.

On what do we base this belief? A general basis for this view can be found in Maslow's (1970) characteristics of self-actualizing people. One such characteristic is found in the notion of *Gemeinschaftsgefuhl*, which was coined by Alfred Adler (1939), and describes self-actualizing people in the following way:

> They have for human beings in general a deep feeling of identification, sympathy, and affection in spite of the occasional anger, impatience, or disgust described below. Because of this, they have a genuine desire to help the human race. It is as if they were all members of a single family. One's feelings toward his brothers would be on the whole affectionate, even if these brothers were foolish, weak, or even if they were sometimes nasty. They would still be more easily forgiven than strangers.
>
> (Maslow, 1970: 165)

While there is a certain condescending tone in this quote that, taken out of context, does not seem entirely consistent with basic tenets of humanism, the concern for humanity is nevertheless expressed.

Another characteristic of self-actualizing persons described by Maslow that may have relevance for our discussion is that such persons reflect a "democratic character structure." That is, they can relate well with people of diverse backgrounds and beliefs and, in fact, may seem oblivious to differences such as race or class. Further, such persons often express a sense of humility that allows them to "learn from anybody who has something to teach them" regardless of differences between the individuals (Maslow, 1970: 168).

While Maslow has addressed issues of social responsibility and oppression in a very general, indirect way, Rogers (1977) has written directly on the theme. Rogers has stated that his "person-centered approach," of which self-direction is a key characteristic, is very much parallel to the thinking of Freire (1970). While the contexts in which Rogers and Freire operate are very different, Rogers found himself "open-mouthed with astonishment" at the similarities around which their works were built (Rogers, 1977: 106).

In the years since Rogers first published his comparison with Freire's ideas, these similarities have been debated extensively – often with Rogerians and those with a North American perspective supporting the similarities, and Freirians and those with a Third World orientation disagreeing with the similarities. O'Hara (1989) has offered a synthesis of these arguments. For example, many Freirians are skeptical about psychology and psychotherapy that stress the individual to the exclusion of the social context. However, O'Hara suggests that the basic differences that do exist between Freire and Rogers can be resolved by understanding a single thread that runs throughout the work of both men:

> Both unabashedly celebrate human existence and our evolutionary potential. They write of their fascination with human capacity for self-regulation, self-understanding, and transcendence. Neither begs the intervention of a God, magic, manipulative technology, or supernatural forces. They are both *radical humanists*.
>
> (O'Hara, 1989: 13, authors' italics)

She goes on to state that neither Rogers nor Freire "gives up on people," and offers the following conclusion:

> What both Freire and Rogers offer us, separately and together, is the faith that truth both heals and emancipates, the uncompromisable position that we are all capable of becoming conscious, the conviction that we achieve only through dialogue with each other, and the hope that through such dialogue, whenever, wherever, and however we have the opportunity, we can create a world where every one of us may live in dignity and may exercise our natural vocation to become ever more fully human.
>
> (O'Hara, 1989: 33)

Finally, returning to the notion of transformation theory for just a moment, it seems clear that this approach offers insights relative to the interplay between individual and social dimensions. As we interpret perspective transformation, we see it as a very personal process, which ultimately can lead to action in the social arena. Yet the approach is not without its critics. Collard and Law suggest that Mezirow's work has been valuable in that by drawing from a German intellectual tradition, it attempts to address the atheoretical nature of North American adult education research. At the same time, they argue that the approach lacks the socio-political critique central to critical theory and does not address radical ideology. They conclude that "the essentially liberal democratic character of Mezirow's ideas suppress the concept of a radical praxis" (Collard and Law, 1989: 106). Mezirow responds by stating that social action is only one goal of adult education and that it, like other adult education goals such as intellectual development, self-actualization, and human rights, is instrumental to the end of fostering "the conditions and abilities necessary for an adult to understand his or her experience through free, full participation in critical discourse" (Mezirow, 1989: 174).

The comparison between the ideas of Rogers and Freire and the critique of transformation theory illustrate the inevitable dilemma that arises in attempting to reconcile individual growth and social change as goals for adult education. Clearly, this is not an either/or dichotomy. Nor can it adequately be resolved by simply concluding that "both are important." Based on evidence such as that presented throughout this section, it is our belief that the individual should be viewed as the *starting point* for adult education efforts, and that an individual who is able to strive toward greater realization of potential (i.e., relative to self-direction in learning) will also be increasingly able to contribute to the creation of a more just society, where each person has the opportunity to maximize their potential.

THREE STRATEGIES FOR ENHANCING LEARNER SELF-DIRECTION

The personal orientation of self-direction in learning, which we are referring to as "learner self-direction," involves a process of growth that takes place *within* the individual. Can the adult educator contribute to furthering this growth process? Our response is a resounding "yes!" Just as the educator of adults can serve as a facilitator of the process described in the previous chapter, it is possible to help learners expand their potential by helping them discover that which is as yet untapped. This section will introduce three sets of strategies that educators can use in their efforts to help learners more fully realize their potential for self-direction. The strategies to be considered include: facilitating critical reflection, promoting rational thinking, and using helping skills in the facilitation process. Each of these strategies fit within the framework of the PRO model because they are aimed at helping learners strive toward assuming greater *personal responsibility*.

Before considering these strategies, though, it is necessary to set forth two important points that facilitators need to bear in mind. First, the extent to which educators can help enhance learner self-direction is clearly linked with the degree of trust placed in the learners. Whether it is due to fear of losing control, or the belief that the experiences that learners bring with them are of little relevance, the person who is unable or unwilling to place trust in the learners or in the facilitation process is likely to have trouble fostering greater self-direction among the learners. On the other hand, the facilitator who views learners more as *partners* in the process, with valuable insights and ideas to share, will go much further toward demonstrating a basic sense of trust. This, in turn, should prove valuable in the facilitation process.

A second point is that by modeling such behaviors, a facilitator can help learners maximize their personal levels of self-direction. Just as we can be inspired by leaders from various walks of life who are models for values and behaviors we see as desirable, the facilitator who can provide a positive model of what it means to be self-directed serves as a first-hand example of unlocked potential. Such a person can thus serve as a most important resource for learners. The old adage "actions speak louder than words" clearly holds true in this instance.

Facilitating critical reflection

One strategy for enhancing self-directedness involves helping learners develop an ability to critically reflect on their experiences to help them use the knowledge that has been gained in future actions. Critical reflection, as used here, is similar to Mezirow's (1978) notion of not being trapped by one's past. More recently, Mezirow has used the term self-reflective learning to describe a process of "gaining a clearer understanding of oneself by identifying dependency-producing psychological assumptions acquired earlier in life that have become dysfunctional in adulthood" (Mezirow, 1985: 20).

Closely linked to critical reflection is the idea of "critical thinking," which Brookfield (1987: 4) describes as occurring "whenever we question why we, or our partners, behave in certain ways within relationships." Thus, when people question existing ideas or behaviors, or information that has been presented to them, they are engaging in critical thinking. Four components of critical thinking identified by Brookfield include: identifying and challenging assumptions; recognizing the influence of context on thoughts and actions; considering "alternatives to existing ways of thinking and living" (Brookfield, 1987: 8), and developing "reflective skepticism," an unwillingness to accept a behavior or an idea merely on the basis of having "always been done that way" or "because an expert says it is so."

Taken together, critical reflection and critical thinking are important elements of learner self-direction because they involve analysis and judgment of a problem or situation. In other words, by being critical, one is demonstrating an unwillingness to accept "what is" as inevitable. By being critical, one is thus able to assume personal responsibility for one's beliefs or actions rather than pass off such responsibility to a source outside oneself.

Educators of adults can play a role in helping learners to develop critical reflection and thinking skills. Brookfield has suggested the following strategies for facilitating critical thinking:

1 Affirm critical thinkers' self-worth;
2 Listen attentively to critical thinkers;
3 Show that you support critical thinkers' efforts;
4 Reflect and mirror critical thinkers' ideas and actions;
5 Motivate people to think critically;
6 Regularly evaluate progress;
7 Help critical thinkers create networks;
8 Be critical teachers;
9 Make people aware of how they learn critical thinking;
10 Model critical thinking.

(Brookfield, 1987: 71–88)

While readers may find many of these strategies to be self-explanatory and self-evident, the strategies are worth noting here because they are the kinds of ideas that can be easily taken for granted or overlooked in efforts to work with learners. Yet so much of what goes on in traditional education runs contrary to the development of critical thought.

What are some ways through which critical reflection and thinking skills can be nurtured? In discussing ways through which continuing education practitioners can systematically analyze their practice, Apps (1985) suggests the following activities: reading, participating in the arts, thinking, writing, discussing, and acting. This same list could easily be applied in response to the above question. For purposes of this discussion, we would like to focus on two of these activities (which also happen frequently to incorporate the other types of activities).

Reading

As Apps (1985) suggests, reading is an obvious way in which one can gain new perspectives and, thus, be in a stronger position to reflect critically; yet, reading is often overlooked because time pressures frequently keep many people from reading beyond what seems essential just to stay on top of the activities of daily living. Some types of reading materials that can be particularly relevant to the development of learner self-direction include general fiction and non-fiction, self-help materials, and biography.

General fiction and non-fiction (and we are including poetry and plays within this category) can help a person to gain a broader perspective on the world. The person who is "well-read" has gained a vast array of insights and ideas through reading, which should be helpful in allowing the person to identify alternative perspectives to a given situation. For example, a person who has read widely on political and social issues is likely to be in a position to understand why different sides have emerged with respect to a given controversy, such as abortion or capital punishment. One who has had an opportunity to look at an issue from various perspectives should be able to advocate a particular position with even greater strength. Here, the value of general reading is similar to the goal of traditional liberal education: development of persons who are educated in the "broadest" sense of the word (Elias and Merriam, 1980).

In recent years, perhaps no aspect of the non-fiction market has grown more rapidly than self-help writing. One need only look in virtually any bookstore to see a major section devoted to such writings. The assumption in most self-help writing is that readers will be able to come away with new tools for improving their lives, whether by changing careers, losing weight, dealing with a difficult relationship, overcoming substance abuse, performing better in a sport or hobby, or understanding oneself in a new way. It is important to bear in mind that self-help materials are not limited to the printed word: media such as audio and video tape are growing sources of self-help material. While the quality of self-help materials certainly covers a vast range, and while motives behind the development of such works will also vary considerably, the self-help market would never have reached its current heights were it not for the belief that many people *do* believe themselves capable of making changes in their own lives.

Finally, biography can be a tool for critical reflection and thinking because it provides insights into the lives of other individuals. The study by Gibbons, *et al.* (1980), which was mentioned earlier, shows how it was possible to identify and understand factors that helped a select group of experts to develop self-direction within their area of expertise. Through biography and autobiography, we can learn lessons and gain insights from those who have gone before us. Biography can both inform and inspire.

To illustrate this point about how biography can be inspirational, let us share an example from our own experience. During the development of the first draft of this chapter, the first author found himself faced with a fairly strong case of "writers' block." This block occurred about the same time as several other factors – such as new job responsibilities and professional commitments, the process of buying a house, minor but distracting health problems, and periodic self-doubt – were going on. During this period, a journal that had been kept by John Steinbeck during the writing of *The Grapes of Wrath* (Steinbeck, 1939) was published (DeMott, 1989). In this journal, Steinbeck reveals the process and many struggles he went through in producing this most important work. The various entries revealed a writer facing numerous issues of daily living (including the process of buying a new house) and expressions of personal anguish about his ability to complete a worthwhile piece of writing. Indeed, as he neared the end of the book, the tone of Steinbeck's entries were characterized by sheer determination and perseverance on the one hand, and physical and emotional exhaustion on the other. While there is no presumption to compare Steinbeck with Brockett, reading the journal was nevertheless inspiring and comforting; knowing that, despite the hurdles, both externally and internally imposed, Steinbeck was able to persevere and make it through a difficult process. Through the words he shared in this journal, Steinbeck thus served as facilitator and role model, providing an excellent stimulus for personal reflection.

Writing

The written word is an invaluable tool for critical reflection and thinking. The potential of reading has been addressed above; however, writing can be at least as valuable a tool as reading. For some people, this writing takes the form of publishing. However, some of the most valuable writing for personal insight comes through such activities as keeping a personal journal. Steinbeck's journal revealed a man who was able to use the personal journal as a means of critical reflection. Certainly, many of the insights gained by Steinbeck through his journal contributed, either directly or indirectly, to the final product as well as to his further development as a writer.

An approach that may have potential for enhancing learner self-direction is the "Intensive Journal" process created by Progoff (1975). According to Progoff, this process "plays an active role in reconstructing a life, but it does so without imposing external categories or interpretations or theories on the individual's experience" (Progoff, 1975: 9). Thus, the process is therapeutic "not by striving toward therapy but by providing active techniques that enable an individual to draw upon his inherent resources for becoming a whole person" (Progoff, 1975: 9).

In the "Interactive Journal" process, one engages in a dialectical movement that involves continuous shifting between externally- and internally-oriented reflections. For instance, on one occasion, a person may begin the journal entry by describing an external event, then move into an analysis of what that experience has meant personally. At other times, internal reflection may be the point of departure, with subsequent discussion emphasizing how insights gained from this reflection might be applied in specific external situations.

Like the first author using reading, the second author has used the interactive journal as a personal means for moving his own thinking and critical reflection on various topics. For example, a long-term attempt to understand more clearly the learning activities of older adults was aided by a personal journal kept during an initial research project and subsequent data-analysis effort (Hiemstra, 1975, 1976b). The reflection that took place via this journal activity resulted in a case study of thirty older adults that has been ongoing since 1976 (Hiemstra, 1982a). Both of us also encourage students to use the work of Christensen (1981) and Progoff (1975) as models for recording personal reflection and understanding within our courses in adult education.

To summarize, critical reflection and thinking are relevant strategies for enhancing learner self-direction because (1) they can lead to greater self-awareness and (2) they can help a person recognize alternative ways of thinking and acting that may not have been apparent prior to engaging in the process. In either case, the end result is a person who is better able to take personal responsibility in life, and indeed, in learning.

Promoting rational thinking

The notion of personal responsibility means that one assumes the primary decision-making role for one's life. It also means accepting responsibility for those decisions. Perhaps one of the greatest barriers to learner self-direction, then, is the tendency among many of us to seek out external explanations for why the world is not going the way we would like it to be going. The wife who attributes unhappiness in her marriage to her husband's unwillingness to act more as she would like him to act, the man who claims that his inability to read is due to an extremely negative second-grade teacher, and the manager who is unwilling to change a seemingly outmoded policy because "we've always done it that way" exemplify three situations where individuals have not taken personal responsibility.

Personal responsibility is a *choice*: in any given situation, including the process of learning, individuals can choose how they wish to respond. At the other extreme, they can "cast their fate to the wind." That is, they can allow themselves to be controlled by the situation. A model that we believe holds much potential for enhancing learner self-direction can be found in the ideas underlying a therapeutic process known as "rational-emotive therapy."

Rational-emotive therapy (RET) is an approach, first developed by Ellis

(1962, 1973), that "places great emphasis on *rational thinking* and has as its primary goal *emotional change*" (Wexler and Wexler, 1980: 1). In RET, humans are viewed as being in the center of their "own emotional fate" and, thus, are almost fully responsible for choosing or choosing not to make themselves "disturbed" (Ellis, 1973: 4). Further, this "choice" is due in large part to the extent to which the person holds rational or irrational beliefs about events that have taken place. Ellis (1973) discusses his model as "the ABC's of RET," where: A = An *activating event* about which a person becomes disturbed; B = The *belief* that the person holds about the event; C = The emotional *consequence* of the beliefs (see also Wexler and Wexler, 1980).

Essentially, what Ellis argues is that emotional consequences (C), either positive or negative, result not from an event that has taken place (A), but rather, from the beliefs (B) that the person holds about the event. In other words, it is not the action itself that is responsible for "causing" the disturbed feelings. Instead, it is a series of irrational beliefs that the person has constructed *about* the event. These irrational beliefs are expressed in the messages that people tell themselves. These messages are liberally sprinkled with words such as "should" and "must," and a host of self-condemning statements.

To illustrate, take the case of a man who sought a promotion and was denied by his supervisor. According to RET, the real distress that the person feels is not so much from the event itself as it is from the beliefs the person holds about the event. If the man responds, for instance, with such statements as: "It's not *fair*;" "I *should* have been given the promotion;" "Because I did not get the promotion, I'm a *failure* in life," he is responding with what Ellis would describe as irrational beliefs. By contrast, responses such as "I am disappointed by the decision" and "It would have been nice had I received the promotion" are considered appropriate or rational. The point is that while we cannot always control the events around us, we *can* control our *responses* to those events. And by doing so, we can choose to retain control of our lives. RET is an approach designed to help people replace irrational belief systems with more rational approaches to dealing with their lives.

Rational thinking, as addressed within the principles of RET, can be an important tool in enhancing learner self-direction, because it supports the link between self-direction and personal responsibility. In discussing self-direction as a goal of the RET process, Ellis offers the following comment:

> The healthy individual assumes responsibility for his own life, is able independently to work out most of his problems, and while at times wanting or preferring the cooperation and help of others, he does not *need* their support for his effectiveness or well-being.
>
> (Ellis, 1973: 159)

Ellis (1982) offers further insights on his view of self-direction:

> most people – and especially those who aim for outstanding achievements – highly prefer to be self-directed rather than strongly controlled either by others or by external situations.

(Ellis, 1982: 27)

And with regard to personal responsibility, Wexler and Wexler (1980) point out that choices and decisions are a given of daily living and that what really matters "is taking personal responsibility for the decisions we make."

To our knowledge, the principles of RET have not to date been discussed within the context of self-direction in adult learning. We have introduced the possible linkage here with the hope that this can be an area worthy of further exploration. For those readers seeking a concise resource providing further information about rational thinking, a good source is *A New Guide to Rational Living* (Ellis and Harper, 1975).

Using helping skills to enhance learner self-direction

A final strategy to be considered in this section is of particular relevance to those who seek to facilitate the development of increased learner self-direction. This strategy involves the application of basic helping skills to the learner-facilitator relationship. In a previous article, Brockett suggested that, in order to maximize the learning process, "it is important that the facilitator establish an effective helping relationship with the learner" (Brockett, 1983a: 7). The assumption here is that the facilitator of self-directed learning is in fact engaged in a helping process, in some ways not unlike that of a counselor, social worker, or clergy member. The point is that there are certain core skills that such helpers can use to enhance their effectiveness.

Using the helping model proposed by Egan (1975) as the basis for this discussion, several helping skills were divided according to three categories: attending, responding, and understanding. More recently, however, Egan (1986) has revised his model. In this section, we will look briefly at the skills essential to the application of Egan's revised process model for systematic helping.

Core values: Respect and genuineness

Egan's model is based on the premise that respect and genuineness must be present for there to be an effective helping relationship. *Respect*, according to Egan (1986: 59) "means prizing others simply because they are human beings." In other words, respect is a nonjudgmental attitude where a facilitator accepts the learner as a unique individual. Respect does not necessarily mean that the facilitator must *agree* with the learner; it does mean that the facilitator *accepts* the learner despite these kinds of differences. This is what Rogers (1961) has termed "unconditional positive regard." According to Egan (1986), respect can be communicated through a number of actions. The following list has been adapted from Egan (1986: 60–3) and has been translated into the facilitator–learner process:

1 Being "for" the learner;
2 Regard for the learner as a unique individual;
3 Regard for the self-determination of the learner;
4 Assuming the goodwill of the learners to want to learn;
5 Maintenance of confidentiality;
6 Attentive physical presence;
7 Suspending critical judgment of the learner;
8 Communication of understanding;
9 Helping learners more effectively draw from their own resources;
10 Expressing a reasonable degree of warmth; and
11 Being genuine in the learning relationship.

Genuineness, the second core value, is simply "the quality of being oneself. The genuine helper does not need to hide behind a facade" in order to feel acceptable to others (Brockett, 1983a: 8). By being genuine, a facilitator can communicate a sense of self-confidence and comfort to the learner, and thus, is modeling behaviors beneficial to learner self-direction. According to Egan (1986), genuineness has both positive and negative implications, as can be deduced from the following list of actions: refusing to overemphasize one's professional role; being spontaneous, but not haphazard, in relationships; being assertive without being aggressive; remaining open and avoiding defensiveness, even when feeling threatened; being consistent between values and actions; and being willing to engage in self-disclosure when doing so is likely to be beneficial.

Respect and genuineness, according to Egan, form the core of a facilitative, helping relationship. In helping to promote greater self-direction among the learners with whom we work, these values can help to set a positive tone for greater growth.

Basic communication skills

Egan (1986) discusses four basic communication skills essential to the helping process. These are: attending, listening, empathizing, and probing. *Attending* "involves the development of both physical and psychological presence or, in other words, a sense of 'being with' another person" (Brockett,

1983a: 8). At the most basic level, attending means paying attention to the person and demonstrating this to the person. Physical attending involves such behaviors as facing the individual squarely, adopting an open posture (arms and legs not crossed, for example), maintaining good eye contact, and being relaxed with these behaviors. Psychological attending involves being aware of both the learner's verbal and nonverbal behavior.

Closely related to attending is active *listening*, the second skill identified by Egan. In the context of the helping relationship, individuals are likely to share their experiences (i.e., what has happened to them), their behaviors (i.e., what they do or do not do), and their effect (i.e., the feelings and emotions that grow out of these experiences and behaviors). In understanding the self-directed learning process as outlined in the previous chapter, each of these perspectives are clearly relevant to the success of such efforts. Listening, in this context, involves understanding the person's verbal communication.

As with listening, the purpose of *empathy* in communication is to gain greater understanding. Empathy "involves getting a feel for the world of the other while maintaining a sense of objectivity" (Brockett, 1983a: 8). In other words, being empathic means that one is able to view the world from another person's point of view without feeling so "sympathetic" that this understanding becomes distorted.

A fourth communication skill discussed by Egan is *probing*. By probing, a facilitator can help one to explore oneself and one's situation even further. Such probes can include: statements intended to encourage a person to talk further and to clarify what he/she is saying; questions that can help one to either elaborate or become more specific about something; "accents" that highlight a key word or two of a person's statement about which the helper is attempting to gain a greater focus; and "minimal" prompts (such as "uh-huh;" or nonverbal cues such as a nod of the head) that serve to reinforce the speaker or encourage further exploration.

The value of the basic communication skills mentioned above may be self-evident; yet, these skills are so often absent from our day-to-day interactions. For the person who is hoping to promote greater learner self-direction, these skills can help to foster a positive, growth-oriented relationship. Further, if used appropriately, the skills should be able to help learners more clearly and confidently explore their roles as learners and, hence, to take increasingly greater personal responsibility for their learning.

CONCLUSION

Essential to an understanding of self-direction in adult learning is a recognition of those forces internal to the individual that can help to foster a greater sense of personal responsibility for one's life. In this chapter, we have suggested that while self-direction is probably most consistent with the basic tenets of humanistic thought, other systems of thinking about human behavior enter into a more comprehensive understanding of self-direction. We also stressed the importance of recognizing how social context impacts upon the way in which one operates. (To look at the individual independent of this context would severely limit our understanding of self-direction.) At the same time, we believe that the notion of learner self-direction is vital, for it views the individual as the starting point for understanding actions and beliefs. Finally, while learner self-direction is an internal process that ultimately must be chosen and acted upon by the individual, we believe that there *are* strategies that facilitators can use to enhance an individual's ability to maximize self-directedness.

Part IV

Fostering opportunities for self-direction in adult learning

This part turns to notions regarding how various opportunities for self-direction need to be fostered or addressed. Most facilitators of adult learning and, indeed, many adults will bump up against various barriers, dilemmas, or issues that inhibit self-direction or the taking of personal responsibility. Four chapters are included that focus on some of the most important of these.

Chapter 8, Institutional Perspectives on Self-direction in Learning, describes how self-direction in learning takes place in various institutional locations and how it is inhibited or limited in others. For example, a variety of community agencies or entities, such as libraries and museums, are described in terms of their potential for educational pursuits. Various educational institutions with existing programs that promote self-direction are detailed. The chapter also provides an analysis of the types of barriers that do exist which limit such learning.

The next chapter, 9, describes some of the policy issues that are associated with efforts to foster self-directed learning. An attempt to address some of these issues through a workshop involving adult learners is detailed. Fourteen policy recommendations centered around adults as learners, adult educators, and adult education agencies are included.

The tenth chapter focuses on an examination of self-direction in learning from a global perspective. Based on reviews of available literature or interviews with adult educators from countries other than the United States, the self-directed learning situation in various countries around the world is presented. The chapter concludes with some recommendations on the further work that is needed to obtain a more thorough understanding of global perspectives.

Chapter 11, Ethical Dilemmas in Self-Direction, focuses on an exploration of the potential ethical dilemmas or conflicts inherent in fostering self-direction. The chapter starts with an overview of the current literature and thinking regarding ethics in adult education. It also includes the thinking that emanated from a workshop that involved several adult learners. Several principles were derived during the workshop. The chapter also describes numerous ethical dilemmas and presents some ways of dealing with them.

8 Institutional perspectives on self-direction in learning

Self-direction in learning exists in a variety of settings. For example, adult learning projects which involve considerable self-planning can occur among a wide variety of population sub-groups and in various situations. We have also demonstrated in previous chapters how self-direction in learning can be facilitated even in fairly formal circumstances. However, the willingness to accept this broader view varies considerably, depending on such factors as institutional mission or the philosophies of individual administrators. Thus, the purpose of this chapter is to demonstrate how self-direction in learning takes place in various institutional locations. To do this we will explore examples of selected institutions and will consider some of the barriers that can limit an institution's ability to support self-directed learning.

Some argue that the learning that takes place in informal settings, without adequate guidance and support, is generally of little value to society (Lawson, 1979; Little, 1979). Verner even went so far as to suggest that: "self-education is beyond the range of responsibility of adult education, since it is an individual activity and affords no opportunity for an adult educator to exert influence on the learning process" (Verner, 1975: 31).

It also is argued by some that true self-direction in learning can only exist outside of formal organizations or in isolation from some adult education specialist. Here, there is a belief that an institution and its employees cannot operate without certain guiding policies and regulations that affect learning or training. In addition, allowing learners to operate totally on their own invites anarchy into the organization sponsoring any learning or providing facilities. Some would also suggest that self-directed learning involvement would be inconsistent with the structure of an institutional setting. For example, Little (1979) and Penland (1981) place learning in institutional settings only within a category dubbed "other directed learning". In other words, "true" adult self-directed learning occurs outside of educational institutions. Finally, Spear and Mocker believe that self-directed individuals "tend to select a course [of learning activity] from limited alternatives which occur fortuitously within their environment, and which structures their learning projects" (Spear and Mocker, 1984: 4).

However, the above assumptions are rooted in philosophical models that place teachers or authorities in positions of control or leadership. The basic philosophy we share does not place teacher above learner or suggest that the adult educator must have a critical influential role. We believe that self-direction in learning is possible at any stage of a person's development and within almost any type of setting. Thus, although we demonstrated early in the book how many current notions about self-directedness stem from learning projects research and individuals as planners of their learning (Tough, 1979), Chapter 6 described procedures for facilitating learning in formal, group settings.

Mocker and Spear (1982) identify self-directed learning as one of four categories on a matrix of lifelong learning. However, we described in previous chapters our belief that self-direction is best viewed as a continuum, where involvement is possible at any point on the continuum, from very formal, even regimented, settings to highly informal, non-institutional settings. Kasworm (1988a) and Brookfield (1986) are among those who also support this notion of a continuum.

Moore (1986) provides an example of personal, intentional changes made through individual learning activities that take place among inmates of a correctional institution. Garrison (1987) and Moore (1983) make the case for facilitating self-direction in distance-learning activities. Knowles (1975) and Knowles and Associates (1984) suggest that self-directed activity is possible in any setting.

ACTIVATING THE EDUCATIVE COMMUNITY

Activating community resources for educational purposes assumes that most people and agencies have the capacity – or at least potential – for involvement in the educational processes necessary or desired in furthering human development. We suggest that these persons and agencies should assume considerable responsibility for the necessary educational functions. In this view, the community can be seen as a continuous learning setting in which the attitudes, talents, and behaviors of people are developed.

According to this view of education and learning, community resources are potential learning forces and factors. There are a number of organizations or agencies beyond the normal educational and social service ones that have such potential: business and industry can serve as job-training resources; churches can provide educational leadership on such issues as family life, human sexuality, and substance abuse; parks can serve as a learning resource related to physical fitness or outdoor education (Hiemstra, 1985a). Stewart

(1985) suggests that daily newspapers and other print media can be used very effectively for adult education purposes. In fact, in the following sections we will point out a variety of community resources used by self-directed learners.

The connection of educative community ideas to this book should be evident. We believe that self-directed learners can and do take advantage of a wide variety of community institutions to further their educational needs. Brookfield (1985a) provided several examples of how self-directed learning is carried out in the community. Smith and Cunningham (1987) and Gross (1982) provide a variety of ideas, references, and resources related to using community resources for learning. The purpose of this section is to provide three examples regarding what is being attempted and what is possible.

Libraries

Libraries are in a unique position in most communities to assist adults in various ways with their self-directed learning pursuits. Burge (1983) and several colleagues point out a variety of related activities. In reality, most libraries possess a multitude of learning resources, have access to many more resources through various sharing networks, and are managed by professionals who have information-searching and retrieval skills. The continual increase in electronic access mechanisms and the growing number of specific adult education activities are creating even more opportunities to meet the needs of users. Thus, there typically exists in most communities a public library service that provides support for people to educate themselves continually (Conroy, 1981; Martin, 1972).

Public libraries have, in fact, supported adult learning pursuits for many years. As J. C. Smith notes:

> From its beginnings in the Nineteenth Century, the public library has been a source of information and assistance for adults learning on their own ... The adult education movement of the 1920's and 30's further spurred the interest of librarians in adults who sought self-education or who were reading with a purpose.
>
> (Smith, 1986: 249)

A popular service that evolved during this period was the "Office of the Reader's Advisor" at the New York Public Library (Flexner and Hopkins, 1941; Monroe, 1963). The Office was established under the direction of Jennie M. Flexner in 1928 and existed for some 20 years. Adults pursuing particular learning activities were referred to the Reader's Advisor, who would interview them, determine specific needs, and develop a tailored reading plan.

During the 1940s and 1950s such specific services were absorbed into more generic services for adults, and interest in self-directed learning did not resurface on any large scale until the 1970s brought a special project into existence:

> Then, from 1972 to 1976, the College Board sponsored the Adult Independent Learning Project, which operated in several public libraries throughout the United States. As part of this project, librarians were given special training, and, rechristened Learner's Advisors, served as learning facilitators for library users.
>
> (Smith, 1986: 249)

The advisors worked with interested adults for weeks or even months, helping them map out individualized learning programs (Mavor, *et al.*, 1976); and, as Dale (1979: 85) notes, the service was intended "for self-directed adults who wished to study independently, outside the traditional education system".

The rediscovery of the value of providing consultation for self-directed learners raises some useful questions about the library as an important resource (Carr, 1980, 1983). J. C. Smith found that most librarians share a belief that accurate, effective guidance of learning must be directed by the learner. She suggests that librarians are in a unique position to be facilitators of self-directed learning:

> It is apparent that they recognize this, take it seriously, and through understanding born of experience, are usually good at it ... to successfully facilitate self-directed learning is to allow it to be as individual a process as possible.
>
> (Smith, 1986: 253)

What, then, are some likely future roles for the library? Obviously, technological change, financial conditions, and the professional preparation of future librarians are some important factors in determining just how successful libraries will be in meeting the needs of self-directed learners. One current project in New York State, begun through a Kellogg Foundation grant and sponsored in part by the State Education Department, provides some glimpses into that possible future. The development of Education Information Center (EIC) programs in several public libraries has resulted in several new features: (a) an information telephone service with experienced advisors providing resource ideas; (b) free half-hour advising appointments at selected community centers and libraries; (c) community workshops on specific educational or career topics; (d) the use of SIGI (System of Interactive Guidance and Information – a computerized information and guidance program); (e) educational help columns in newspapers; (f) a cable-access television series; (g) an outreach program to various target population groups; and (h) considerable cooperation between various community providers (Kordalewski, 1982).

Bundy (1977) describes another project where certain library storefront organizations provide information to learners outside the formal structure of a library building. Beyond the United States, S. M. Dale (1980) details some cooperative efforts taking place between libraries and Open University programs in the United Kingdom. Such innovations may well change the way libraries think of their programs and services in the future. Brookfield (1984a) even suggests that the public library is the most obvious community agency for assisting independent learners.

Museums

A museum is another institution where self-directed learning can thrive. Gross (1982), for example, has documented various contributions made by cultural institutions to the work of self-directed learners. Obviously, a wide variety of such settings provide unique opportunities for learning. Carr suggests several: museums, zoos, parks, historical sites, aquariums, restored villages, botanical gardens, forest preserves, wildlife refuges, famous homes, and planetariums (Carr, 1985: 51). Art galleries, science centers, archæological digs, special geological conditions, and theaters are some of the other possibilities. However, in this section we focus on only one such institution in pointing out some of the activities and potential.

Museums have been and are being used in various ways as a community resource available for the support of adult learning. However, many museums still provide fairly static "walk through but don't touch" exhibits or displays. In fact, adults do not appear to place museum displays and exhibits very high on their lists of frequently used learning materials (Hiemstra, 1975, 1981b). In another source, one of us has raised a number of questions that museum professionals must address in finding ways of better serving adult participants:

> Do you just set up displays and let people come in and view? Do you become engaged with the learners in some way beyond the exhibits? Do you provide study guides for them? Do you train your docents to answer certain kinds of questions or to engage in dialogue? Do you give visitors handouts, as they come in, that provide organizing tools for their visit? Do you offer them hands-on opportunities?
>
> (Hiemstra, 1981a: 65)

Questions such as these can help create greater awareness of the museum as a resource for self-directed learning.

Knox offers several guidelines for enabling museum visitors to engage in effective learning activities. He suggests (a) that visitors assume the main responsibility for deciding what to learn and how (this assumes they will choose according to their personal values, purposes, learning styles, and pacing), (b) that visitors be encouraged to sequence their learning activities so they progress from an overview of major features of an exhibit to more detailed explorations, and (c) that visitors be assisted in judging the value of their learning through such means as self-assessment inventories (pp. 106–7). He believes such assessment tools will "help people become more self-directed" (Knox, 1981: 107).

In reality, many museum educators understand quite well that if they are going to provide an effective product to their communities, it will be necessary to think of visitors as learners (Bertram, 1981; Bertram and Sidford, 1977; Daniels, 1981; Horn, 1979). Many efforts have been made to provide new or special programs for adult learners:

> Museum materials and staff members have been used as supplemental resources for adult education classes at other locations; museum-related courses or lectures have been given in locations other than museums; weekend museum courses have included field visits and work at archaeological sites; antique identification courses have been taught in museums by museum staff; special exhibits or annual shows have been done on topics aimed at attracting new adult audiences, such as minority groups, blue-collar workers, or the handicapped; traveling exhibits, loan exhibits, educational loan packets and tape or slide kits about museums have been provided for use in adult activities; displays have been set up in store fronts, shopping centers, zoos, libraries, etc., to promote special museum activities for family groups or other combined audiences; trained docents, volunteers and research assistants have worked extensively with educational programming related to adults; noon-hour programs or lectures (with or without lunch) have been held in and out of museums; exhibits have been presented that have special cultural or ethnic features; and a wide variety of media and materials (radio shows, TV shows, newspaper columns, supportive bibliographies) have been used as educational and promotional tools.
>
> (Hiemstra, 1981a: 123)

For more extensive details of such programs and activities, see the works of Bestall (1970), Carr (1985), the Center for Museum Education (1978), Chase (1978), Grabowski (1972), Heine (1977), and Wriston (1969).

Some special efforts have taken place in several locations. For example, in 1976 and 1977 selected museums in the United States were awarded "Learning Museum Program" grants from the National Endowment for the

Humanities. A variety of activities were made available to interested adults at such museums, including lecture series, film series, special exhibits, and discussion groups. As Parks notes, a "learner's packet," consisting of lecture notes, bibliographic information, film notes, guides to selected portions of the museums, and suggestions for further research and independent study was produced "to encourage use of the museum as a continuing resource" (Parks, 1981: 208).

Another popular theme or concept used by some museum educators is the notion of "hands-on," interactive, or participatory learning experiences. For example, at the Children's Museum in Boston, exhibits seek to promote self-experimentation and self-learning. Museum officials try to create an environment that accommodates many individual learning styles and speeds. Most adult visitors, therefore, gain new knowledge primarily through individual or small group activities.

The museum also makes a special effort to use such self-experimentation efforts in helping adults (parents, teachers, and others) become better prepared for aiding young people in learning related to museum resources. Gurian describes analogous museum objectives for such adults as follows:

1 Do their own learning about subjects they know little or nothing about.
2 Share with their children (a) those things they know more about than is apparent on the exhibit surface, and (b) what they have just learned themselves.
3 Add their own life experiences to the information the museum provides and tell their children about those connections.
4 See their children in a new light – step back a moment and watch their children learning in an entertaining and informal but still educational situation.
5 Observe their children with others in a nonthreatening, nongraded environment.
6 Gain ideas and materials they can use at home for family projects.
7 Feel free to let their children go, so that each member of the family can learn at his or her own pace.

(Gurian, 1981: 279)

Museums appear to be on the verge of starting many learning opportunities for the self-directed learner. Certain policy and procedural changes may be necessary for such opportunities to be universally accepted by both administrators and the public. For example, museum administrators and educators must recognize the value of serving the adult participant. Some of the special projects noted in this section and others taking place are evidence that such changes are evolving. Museums also need to do a better job of promoting themselves as a community learning resource center rather than just a collection or storage site. This will facilitate (a) learners taking advantage of the learning possibilities, and (b) resource sharing among museums and other cultural institutions in the community.

It is our hope that professionals responsible for education in museums will become better trained in adult education. Graduate programs of adult education throughout the world can provide specialized knowledge and training related to adults as self-directed learners. Similarly, conferences and workshops provide a less intensive but nevertheless valuable resource for adult education-related professional development. We believe that museum personnel could benefit from such training and that the resultant programs and opportunities would enhance the organization's place in the community.

Self-help efforts

The notion of grass-roots organizations forming around specific needs has been a reality in the United States and most other parts of the world for centuries. Biddle and Biddle (1965), McClusky (1960), and Warren (1979) provide some excellent discussions of self-help efforts at the local level during the past several decades. In fact, McClusky presented an excellent synopsis of several programs, including St. Francis Xavier University at Antigonish, Nova Scotia, the University of Wisconsin's successful Bureau of Community Development program, and similar efforts at the University of Michigan, Southern Illinois University, Earlham College, and West Georgia College (McClusky, 1960: 422–4). Brookfield also describes the Antigonish movement, the Highlander Research and Education Center (formerly Highlander Folk School), and the Liverpool Education Priority Area project (Brookfield, 1984a: 106–24) as learner-centered, self-help organizations.

There are several more current self-help programs, many of which promote self-directed learning involvement in meeting needs at individual and/or community levels. Dean and Dowling suggest that an important outcome of such community development efforts is the personal growth of participants:

> The potential exists for people to become more self-directed as learners, develop their communication skills, develop their ability to solve problems, increase their awareness and sensitivity to others, acquire new information about themselves, their community and others, and develop their self-confidence.
>
> (Dean and Dowling, 1987: 82)

For example, the Citizen Involvement Training Project (CITP) as a project of the University of Massachusetts Cooperative Extension Service, is designed to help people develop personal proficiencies related to community involvement. As Dale points out, the project has taken special efforts to promote self-directed learning:

> One is to promote the concept of a within-group education coordinator – an individual who would identify needs, locate resources, coordinate individual and group activities, and perhaps actually facilitate educational sessions .... The other means by which CITP has promoted self-directed or independent learning is by developing and publishing a set of manuals that present learning activities, work sheets, planning guides, background discussions, and annotated resource lists on the training issues that citizen groups most commonly raise.
>
> (Dale, 1981: 49–50)

As a second example, Boggs describes a project in Michigan, the Huron Agricultural Resources Tomorrow (HART), which used nonformal, self-directed study techniques in helping community members deal with waste-disposal problems and other issues. As Boggs notes:

> Groups such as HART have arisen in opposition to plans for hazardous waste disposal sites, nuclear power plants, commercial development of recreation land, and so on. It is critical to recognize that while political agitation and the like may be endemic to their efforts, so too are collaborative self-education and community education.
>
> (Boggs, 1986: 2)

In response to various needs of self-help groups in the United States, the National Self-Help Resource Center (NSHRC) created the Community Resource Center (CRC) in 1974 (Briggs, 1981; Brookfield, 1984a). The CRC provided a mechanism for individuals and organizations to network together in obtaining information and cooperation on various self-help efforts (Davis, 1974, 1976). The result has been a resource for individuals and groups desiring to promote change primarily through their own initiatives and without formal help from public organizations.

Libraries, museums, and self-help activities serve as but a few examples of institutional resources in a community that can play a role in serving the needs of self-directed learners. This, indeed, is what we mean by activating the learning community. It means, quite simply, that opportunities for self-direction can be enhanced if the resources of a community can be mobilized in a way that allows facilitators to take a proactive approach in serving such learners.

INSTITUTIONAL PROGRAMS BUILT ON SELF-DIRECTED LEARNING IDEAS

The programs described above reflect educational components of what Darkenwald and Merriam (1982) refer to as "quasi-educational organizations," where the educational function is closely related, but not always central, to the mission of the organization. But what about institutions whose primary function *is* to provide educational opportunities within the structure of a formal organization? Can self-direction thrive in such situations?

As we have stated throughout the previous chapters, we believe that institutions have the capability and, indeed, the obligation to help learners take increasing obligation for what they learn and how they learn it. If "lifelong learning" is to be more than a popular slogan or rallying cry, and if self-direction is truly to be viewed as part of lifelong learning, then it will be necessary to stress the potential for such activity within our formal educational institutions. The following sections offer a glimpse of how elementary and secondary schools, colleges and universities, external degree programs, and various other providers can successfully incorporate some of the principles of self-direction in learning within the context of their institutional mission.

Elementary and secondary education

As stated above, it is our belief that the promotion of self-directed, lifelong learning must begin early in the home, and be reinforced throughout a person's elementary and secondary schooling:

> The very early years of life are particularly crucial in the total span of human growth. This is when the child begins to acquire the ability to mentally process and use information ... the parents will also be a very important factor in developing a child's attitudes toward school, education, and lifelong learning. Education can be a very powerful instrument for influencing the quality of a person's total life, but there must be continuity between what transpires in the home and what takes place in the school.
>
> (Hiemstra, 1985a: 67)

What is begun in the home needs to be reinforced in the school setting:

> Thus, learning opportunities provided by schools to youth ... could be developed around stages of the human life cycle, around contemporary social issues, and around the promotion of future-relevant behavioral skills. The ability to adapt to change is a much needed skill in our society;

schools must help people acquire this skill through a variety of educational endeavors.

(Hiemstra, 1985a: 73)

Totten suggests further that teachers work with parents to encourage reading and study related to school activities as a regular "part of the family's routine" (Totten, 1970: 77). Knowles believes that the "primary mission of elementary and secondary schools would then be to develop the skills of self-directed learning" (Knowles, 1984: 363). For example, the Bishop Carroll High School (1984) in Calgary (Canada) developed an individualized program for students. Gibbons and Phillips (1984) created a "challenge education program" that demonstrated the ability of students in the younger grades to respond to self-directed learning activities. The Jefferson School-Based Management and Self-Directed Learner Project (Sanda, 1984) showed that self-direction can be nurtured in the younger years and maintained in later years. The success of such programs hopefully will prompt similar efforts in the future.

At the forefront of efforts to apply self-direction concepts to the elementary and secondary school settings has been the work of Gibbons and Phillips (1979, 1982, 1984). Essentially, they have argued that while self-education occurs *outside* of educational institutions, schools can provide opportunities for relevant skills to be taught, practiced, and simulated. They suggest that some of the major factors that can stifle or facilitate opportunities for self-education include the following:

1 Control over the learning process;
2 Responsibility for initiating learning activities;
3 Type of management skills utilized by facilitators;
4 Knowledge of learning styles;
5 Nature of the purposes (content mastery vs. identified learner needs and interests);
6 Type of relationships promoted (dependence vs. independence);
7 Emphasis placed on subject matter or problem solving areas;
8 Distinctions made between minimal competence and proficiency or excellence; and
9 Strategies used for evaluating outcomes.

Gibbons and Phillips (1982) have discussed a four-stage process for helping children and adolescents move from an authority-directed approach to greater self-direction as learners. During the pre-school years, the first stage – *influential parenthood* – involves parents modeling self-directed learning and providing an environment that fosters initiative and increasing responsibility by children. *Initiative training*, the second stage, occurs during the elementary years and stresses the development of individual and group projects by students in areas of personal interest. This approach is designed to change "the child's habit of learning casually through play to a self-conscious, intentional effort to learn through planned activities" (Gibbons and Phillips, 1982: 81). At the secondary level, students are challenged to excel within interest areas. In this stage, which Gibbons and Phillips call *challenge education*, learners meet with a planning committee (usually including a teacher and parent), design a learning contract, and determine outcomes that measure achievement of a negotiated goal. Finally, as the transition to adulthood is made, "the most valuable community contribution to self-education will be the organization of learning services – opportunities, consultants, resources, and facilities" (Gibbons and Phillips, 1982: 84). These *self-education services* are not unlike the learning community concept that we advocated earlier in this chapter.

Hamm, in response to Gibbons and Phillips, has argued that the above techniques have limitations because of (a) confusion over the meaning of the concepts, (b) "false empirical assumptions and an inadequate conception of education," and (c) a possible "radical" impact on schools and society (Hamm, 1982: 87). In essence, Hamm is arguing that, in order to gain control over oneself, it is necessary to go through a long, painful process of gaining knowledge through discipline. While we agree that learning is sometimes a long and painful process, and that this can in fact be an important part of maturation, we remain convinced that the development of a desire and ability to accept personal responsibility for learning clearly outweighs the above limitations. Self-direction as a way of life necessitates the fostering of such attitudes and the development of relevant skills throughout the *entire* lifespan.

Colleges and universities

While the promotion of self-direction in learning is not overtly emphasized much in elementary or secondary schools, for many years there have existed special university programs designed for those people who thrive on individualized instruction or independent study. In the United States, Antioch College's work-study program, Goddard College's adult degree program, and the independent-study degree programs of such institutions as the University of Nebraska were among efforts to provide individualized study opportunities during the 1950s, 1960s, and 1970s (Dressel and Thompson, 1973; Vermilye, 1976). Such programs were characterized by the following: (a) active rather than passive learners; (b) explicit learning goals; (c) a preference for small lesson units, each dealing with a single concept; (d) adequate feedback and evaluation; and (e) learner control over the pace of the presentation (Cross, 1977). A variety of teaching and learning approaches were used, including programmed learning, computer-assisted instruction, computer-managed instruction, self-paced modules, audiovisual tutorial kits, community internships, independent study, and many other forms of self-directed learning (Dressel and Thompson, 1973).

Community colleges, too, have long attempted to meet the needs of self-directed learners, as well as provide college transfer programs (Kerwin, 1984). Gleazer suggests that the aim of the community college is "to develop a community of learners. The qualities sought are independence, self-reliance, and cooperation, not a condition of dependency upon an educational monopoly" (Gleazer, 1980: 88). Hunter (1971) examined community college students and determined that they benefited from an experimental program of self-directed learning.

Finally, what Apps (1981: 11) calls a "quiet revolution" is taking place throughout the United States and in most other parts of the world, too. As Knowles (1984: 59) notes: "We have shifted from a youth-centered to an adult-centered society with drastic implications for our whole educational enterprise." This change is reflected by the return of thousands of older adults to college campuses. A recent National Center for Education Statistics (1989) report revealed that a 2.5 percent increase in college enrollments in 1988 over 1987 was driven mainly by sharp increases in the number of adult students 25 years and older.

Such people are enrolling in undergraduate programs, graduate programs, and various non-traditional programs (Coe, *et al.*, 1984). The result has been changes in traditional programs and the development of new programs (Bloch, 1984; Boud and Prosser, 1984; Eldred, 1984; Farquharson, 1984; Kilpatrick, *et al.*, 1984; Loacker and Doherty, 1984; Schuttenberg, 1984). Hesburgh *et al.*, (1973) describe some of the necessary changes, such as new admission and registration procedures, new orientation programs, and special support services for adult students. New ways of determining educational achievement, such as credit for past experience, credit granting through examination, and bachelor- or masters-level general-studies degrees have developed.

Unfortunately, the response of higher education to this revolution has not been rapid: "It is perhaps a sad commentary that, of all our social institutions, colleges and universities have been among the slowest to respond to adult learners" (Knowles, 1984: 100). Hopefully, the types of changes begun recently will multiply in scope and number.

External degree programs

External degree programs for college credit utilize a multitude of resources or settings to enhance individualized programs of study (Houle, 1973). Much of this learning does not take place in any traditional form of a classroom or university setting. As Wedemeyer (1981), in a discussion of non-traditional degree programs, noted: "more learning and teaching go on throughout life outside the classroom than in" (p. 30). Below, we describe various non-traditional or external degree activities, most of which happen to be associated with universities.

Perhaps the most widely known of all such efforts has been the concept of the Open University (OU) which originally started in 1970 in Britain and has now spread to several other countries. Harrington describes the learning approach of the British OU as follows:

> The heart of the work is in correspondence study, which explains the change of name from the originally planned University of the Air. Regularly scheduled radio and television lectures, outside reading, and home experiments round out the program .... Even though emphasis is on individual study, students are brought together on occasion, usually during the summer, for residential seminars. In addition, there are regional centers where students can consult reference books, obtain tutorial and counseling help, and study.
>
> (Harrington, 1977: 60)

A variety of similar efforts have developed in the United States, as well as in other countries, for example: (a) The University of Mid-America centered at the University of Nebraska, a home study effort involving television, lesson material printed in newspapers, learning centers staffed with tutors, and correspondence courses; (b) The New York State Regents External Degree Program, or the Thomas Edison College in New Jersey, which permit learners to earn degrees through credit by examination, credit for life experiences, and formal college credit (Apps, 1981; Darkenwald and Merriam, 1982).

One of the more widely known credit granting organizations based on self-directed study is the Empire State College of New York. Founded in 1971 by the State University's Board of Trustees, the organization is headquartered in Saratoga Springs with learning centers located around the state. As Knowles (1986) notes, it awards associate, bachelor's, and master's degrees based on learning that can occur in a variety of ways: (a) formal courses offered by a variety of cooperating institutions; (b) cooperative study involving several students working collaboratively; (c) tutorials; (d) self-instructional programs; (e) direct experience involving self-examination and reflection; and (f) independent study by reading, writing, travel, or other means. A learning contract developed by the learner and a resulting portfolio of achievements serves as the evaluation and validation of course work completed toward the degree.

Finally, the newest efforts at nontraditional degree or study programs involve the development of distance learning through various technologically-assisted delivery modes. Television and satellite transmissions, electronic networks, and teleconferencing are some of the forms being developed through experimentation. It is not yet clear how such efforts will assist the self-directed learner, but, as Garrison notes:

> Adult educators must recognize the ability of telecommunications and microprocessor technology to assist adult educators to reach out to adult learners in a variety of settings, and we must bridge the gap between formal institutional education and activities of self-directed learning in the natural societal setting.
>
> (Garrison, 1987: 316)

Non-traditional approaches to graduate education

The idea of nontraditional degree programming has not been limited to undergraduate areas. Indeed, it has been our experience that graduate education presents an ideal context for putting into practice the concepts of self-direction in learning. Graduate students, particularly in professional fields, are frequently mature adults who bring an array of experiences to the graduate classroom. Furthermore, a great many graduate students choose to pursue their degrees on a part-time basis, balancing study with employment and family responsibilities. For many such individuals, these responsibilities preclude pursuing a degree in a traditional format with such requirements as a period of residency. In order to illustrate the potential of nontraditional approaches to graduate study, we would like to present examples of two programs in the field of adult education. These programs are models of innovative, high-quality alternatives that reflect the application of self-directed learning concepts. One is the AEGIS program at Teachers College, Columbia University, and the other is the Weekend Scholar program at Syracuse University.

AEGIS

The Adult Education Guided Independent Study Program (AEGIS) is an alternative doctoral program offered by the Department of Higher and Adult Education at Teachers College, Columbia University. Established in 1981, the program is designed for:

> senior professionals with substantial experience in program development,

administration of continuing education, staff development, or training who wish to earn a doctorate in two or three years ... without having to relinquish their full-time employment or change locations in order to attend.

(Bauer, 1985: 41)

The program consists of 2 academic years of course work, comprised of monthly day-long meetings, independent work on course requirements between sessions, and advising with faculty members (most frequently by telephone or mail). In addition, participants are expected to complete a 3-week intensive session during two consecutive summers. Through such aspects as the accelerated format, the use of learning contracts within each course, and a pass/fail grading format that emphasizes revision until a learning activity has been "successfully" completed, the program offers opportunities for learners to assume a high level of responsibility for their programs.

Some of the challenges that arise in the operation of the AEGIS program include dealing with different levels of self-directedness among learners, recognizing various institutional and program constraints that place limits on the extent of self-directedness truly possible in the program, and considering the impact of this format on the professional (and personal) lives of faculty members. With regard to the last concern, Bauer (1986), based on a 3-year case study of the AEGIS program, concluded:

Because of the intensity of the personal professional commitment necessary in innovative program development, institutions must provide stronger support to faculty in substantive areas of tenure criteria, monetary reward for involvement of this kind, and adjustment of teaching and administrative load.

(Bauer, 1985: 2518-A)

In spite of such concerns, the AEGIS program has been a success, as measured by its longevity as well as by the number and accomplishments of its graduates.

Weekend scholar

A second illustration of nontraditional graduate study in adult education can be found in the Weekend Scholar program, which has been in operation at Syracuse University since September, 1982. While the AEGIS program is limited to doctoral study and stresses independent study, Weekend Scholar emphasizes master's degree study (though doctoral or other advanced students are able to complete a sizable portion of their course requirements in this format) and is essentially an adaptation of the existing curriculum to a weekend format, thus making graduate study possible for students who are unable to attend late afternoon and evening courses on campus. As described elsewhere:

> The program involves the completion of 30 semester credits comprised of 10, three-credit courses. Each course meets four times, roughly every other weekend, with class sessions running from Friday evening until late Saturday afternoon. Two courses are offered back-to-back in a semester, giving students a 'typical' part-time load of six credits per semester. In addition, each student is required to write a comprehensive examination upon completion of all coursework. Quality is stressed in that all teaching and advising is done by regular members of the Syracuse University faculty and students are expected to fulfill all university, school, and department-wide requirements. An ongoing evaluation process helps to ensure that the program is effectively serving the needs of the target audiences while maintaining high quality.

> (Brockett, 1988a: 289)

The program has been offered in several locations throughout the northern portion of New York State. Students come from New York State and Ontario, Canada. Although students typically meet in group settings throughout most of the course, the use of learning contracts and individualized study promotes considerable self-directed learning. Currently, a distance education component is being developed that will use computer-mediated instruction to supplement group meetings. Overall, the program has been an effective vehicle for providing educational opportunities to people not able to participate in campus-based offerings.

Other institutional applications of self-directed learning

The use of self-directed learning approaches and concepts in a wide variety of agencies and organizations has been increasing in recent years. For example, several authors describe how self-directed learning principles have been used throughout the health professions to affect basic training, graduate training, continuing education, and staff development efforts (American Nurses' Association, 1984; Arms *et al.*, 1984; Ash, 1985; Dare, 1984; Neufeld and Barrows, 1984; University of Southern California, 1984). As Ash notes:

> The very nature of the way in which professionals, such as physicians and nurses, function and the lives they affect as a result of their practice require them to possess a high degree of competence. Self-directed or autonomous

learning must often be relied on in the development of such competence because of the differences in the needs of individual practitioners for information and in the time frame in which such information must be obtained.

(Ash, 1985: 63)

Ash goes on to describe how self-directed learning strategies have been applied at the Sloan-Kettering Cancer Center in New York City. Nurses are encouraged to use self-directed learning strategies and resources in their job orientation efforts. Most formal lecture presentations used in the past have been replaced by self-instructional modules, a variety of reference materials, performance checklists, selected resources, and individuals as resources:

The learner's time is divided between acquiring information and applying that information in the clinical area. Blocks of self-directed learning time included in the program schedule allow learners to select one of the content areas to complete; learners may also choose to spend the time in some other way.

(Ash, 1985: 68)

Self-directed learning techniques also are being introduced in business and industry (Green, 1984; Lloyds Bank, 1984; Margolis, 1984; Sinclair and Skerman, 1984; Sullivan, 1984). One study (Rymell and Newsom, 1981) involved an examination of the learning projects of a group of engineers in an aerospace industry. Using Tough's (1979) learning-project procedure, the authors determined that, in at least this setting, the employees engaged in significant job-related self-directed learning. In another study of managers and non-managers from a large utility company who had worked independently on learning activities, Guglielmino and Guglielmino (1983) used the Self-Directed Learning Readiness Scale (SDLRS) and found that the subjects scored considerably higher on the scale than other adult populations previously tested.

Some organizations have also begun to implement self-directed learning approaches in their training efforts:

IBM's Santa Teresa Laboratory has included an Information/Library/Learning Center since 1975. The center is designed to serve 2,000 computer programmers involved in developmental and design work. It includes all of the self-educational resources of all divisions of the company as well as commercially produced self-study materials relevant to its users.

(Guglielmino and Guglielmino, 1988: 145)

A similar center exists at the SUNOCO headquarters in Radner, Pennsylvania, suggesting that business and industry will use self-directed learning increasingly in their future training endeavors.

Technology and self-direction

The number and type of resources available to educators of adults are growing at an astounding rate, primarily because technological developments have speeded the process of accumulating and disseminating information. Such technological developments can be used for self-directed learning purposes if creatively designed. One such effort is being made by the Kellogg Project at Syracuse University.

This multi-million dollar project, funded by the W. K. Kellogg Foundation (Battle Creek, Michigan), has been designed to create a system of adult education knowledge-dissemination through advanced computer technology. The world's largest repository of English-language adult education materials, housed in the university library, serves as the foundation for the dissemination effort.

The project has both technological and intellectual components. The technological component features a computerized system for storing and retrieving archival documents. It also has a computer-mediated electronic network, referred to as AEDNET – Adult Education Network. AEDNET has enabled adult educators from all over the world to communicate with each other electronically. It operates on BITNET, an international computer network currently joining universities and other research institutions on five continents. AEDNET features electronic messaging, electronic conferencing, electronic forums, and an electronic journal entitled *New Horizons in Adult Education*.

There are also a number of intellectual components. For example, the project sponsors research on the historically-rich adult education collection at Syracuse University and periodically holds conferences on campus. In addition, a distance education program is being developed that operates through computer conferencing software. Through this program, it is possible for learners to work individually or to interact with the instructor and students as needed.

Having access to such a system can add immensely to the power an educator has in meeting the needs of adult learners. Self-directed learners may, in fact, benefit the most from access to increased information and improved retrieval systems, assuming that they have access to the systems and know how to use them.

The notion of being able to retrieve lots of information by oneself has implications for self-directed learning approaches and resources. Adult educators who work with self-directed learners need to find ways to help such learners access and utilize appropriate information more effectively.

BARRIERS TO IMPLEMENTING SELF-DIRECTED LEARNING IN INSTITUTIONS

Are there barriers that can hinder the implementation of self-directed learning approaches and programs? Cross suggests there are at least three types of barriers that inhibit adult learning, and that each of these types has relevance for self-direction in learning:

> *Situational barriers* are those arising from one's situation in life at a given time. Lack of time due to job and home responsibilities, for example ... *Institutional barriers* consist of all those practices and procedures that exclude or discourage working adults from participating in educational activities – inconvenient schedules or locations, full-time fees for part-time study, inappropriate courses of study, and so forth. *Dispositional barriers* are those related to attitudes and self-perceptions about oneself as a learner.
>
> (Cross, 1981: 98)

For example, an inadequate place to study in the home setting, a situational barrier may prevent a person from taking on an independent learning project. Some learners will have had past negative experiences in educational settings and will believe they are incapable of independent study – a dispositional barrier. In addition, many administrators have traditional views about education and how courses must be taught, an institutional barrier, that prevents them from understanding the potential value for learners of opportunities for self- direction. Sometimes such views are compounded by a desire to "do it the old way" or a feeling that regular, credit courses are the only means of programming that are permissible. In addition, there may even exist a variety of policies or procedures that prevent independent decision-making on the part of the learner regarding such issues as needs, goals, content, and evaluation aproaches. Facilitators, program designers, and administrators need to work constantly in attempting to remove or lessen such barriers.

CONCLUSION

Throughout this chapter we have decribed how institutions have become more responsive to the idea of self-direction in learning as a way of life. While it would be naive to suggest that all of the strategies described will be accepted overnight throughout the educational world, we *do* believe that it is important for institutions to recognize the potential of self-direction as a way of enhancing adult learning experiences. We conclude this chapter with four recommendations that summarize key ideas developed throughout the previous pages.

1 It is important that administrators who can affect decisions regarding education be helped to understand the theory, research, and teaching-learning approaches related to self-direction in learning.

A related institutional problem centers on the many administrative policies and procedures that may inhibit or even prevent implementation of approaches designed to foster self-direction in learning. For instance, many formal organizations have fairly rigid policies regarding registration, attendance, and the format for classes. Similarly, a number of grading traditions may be in place that penalize adult learners who wish to set their own pace or level of achievement, such as limitations to the use of learning contracts, pass/fail grades, and incomplete grades. In addition, budgetary limitations or standardized approaches to the use of supportive materials in the classroom may make it difficult for teachers to provide a variety of resources for the self-directed learner.

2 It is often necessary that the teacher of adult learners must spend considerable time and energy fostering change in those institutional policies and procedures that inhibit self-direction in learning. At times this will require courage, persistence, and fortitude in the light of heavy institutional pressure to resist such change.

A larger problem sometimes exists within educational institutions or even organizations like businesses which sponsor a variety of training programs. The problem is that negative attitudes of inadequately trained educators frequently become a barrier in the decision-making process. For example, some trainers in an organization may employ only traditional approaches to teaching where the instructor is used primarily as an authority who passes on certain information to trainees. Then, when another trainer attempts to use self-directed learning approaches that call for involving the trainee in the educational process, this becomes threatening to the normal way. As another example, some elementary school teachers hired to teach evening literacy classes may be unwilling to permit the flexibility necessary for an adult learner to use individualized study materials in the program's learning center.

3 It is important that all educators of adults receive adequate preparation in adult education principles, beliefs, and instructional approaches. It may be necessary for some beginning adult education teachers to undertake considerable graduate or in-service training, so that personal philoso-

phies, teaching approaches, and beliefs regarding adults as learners can be re-examined.

The wide range of dispositional barriers described by Cross (1981) can actually be more problematic in promoting self-direction in learning, at least initially. For example, many adults approaching a learning situation bring to it a variety of negative ideas about education. Some of the institutional obstacles described above have helped to create many of these, but so have the variety of situational barriers that each adult must face from day to day. Thus, a fear of something unknown or different, suspicions about what that so-called facilitator really is trying to do, and a general lack of understanding about personal potential as a learner are factors with which most adult education teachers will have to deal. In our view, the individualized approach we have described in previous chapters can be used with people who have widely varying degrees of preparedness for self-direction in learning activities, but some learners will resist such an approach initially because of low self-concepts or past negative learning experiences.

4 It is usually necessary that the adult education instructor prepare for a wide variety of attitudes about and willingness to participate in self-directed learning. This will require patience, the ability to communicate clearly to learners about the teaching approach being used, and a recognition that the rate of acceptance of self-directed approaches will vary from learner to learner.

Perhaps the biggest weapon a teacher or trainer has in overcoming the many barriers that inhibit self-direction in learning is the constant striving to ensure that a high quality learning experience exists. This will require hard work, continual efforts at securing good learning resources, and the flexibility necessary to deal with varied learning needs and abilities. However, we believe that the results will be well worth those efforts.

9   Policy issues

In this book we have presented our views regarding the value of self-direction in learning as a means for helping people cope with the many demands of living characterized by constant and rapid change. But how widespread is the acceptance of views like ours? There is considerable evidence that an increasing acceptance is taking place. Much of the research reported in Chapters 3, 4, and 5 included discussion on the growing involvement of adults in learning, and many formal institutions involved with education are increasing their attention to the adult learner. In Chapter 10 we also discuss the implementation of self-directed learning activities from a global perspective. Chapter 12 offers a scenario illustrating such acceptance, which we anticipate could be present by the turn of the century.

However, we think an appropriate question to ask is: "Are we at present a self-directed learning society? " We believe the answer is no, and think that much more attention must be given to understanding the societal implications of learning as a crucial component of successful lifelong living. We are concerned, too, that educational and political leaders at national levels have not yet fully understood the importance of learners taking responsibility for their own education. Indeed, at least in North America, it appears that many higher education administrators and, increasingly, private entrepreneurs seem to be embracing the adult learner primarily as a clientele base of dollars waiting to be spent on educational resources and opportunities.

Obviously, there are some such administrators and private organizations dedicated to serving the adult learner, as was pointed out in Chapter 8, but Cross sums up our discomfort nicely:

> I am becoming increasingly concerned about the overeagerness of some colleges to attract adult learners into college classrooms; their goal would appear to be institutional survival rather than social good .... I believe that *all* education, especially post-secondary education, should be directed toward making people more self-directed learners, and colleges can

contribute very constructively to that goal if they are encouraged to think beyond institutional survival to providing for the real needs of adult learners.

(Cross, 1980: 629)

This concern closely parallels some of the ethical concerns we have related to self-directed learning. These are discussed in Chapter 11.

Still other educators or entrepreneurs working with adult programs are either discounting self-directed adult-learning research or viewing the attempts to serve self-directed learners as threatening to their own head counts. Unfortunately, in our view, there have been far too few reports in the literature of efforts to think through the implications, policy needs, and programming changes related to self-direction in learning, as well as the appropriate roles for educators and educational institutions.

Jarvis (1985) is one of few authors to discuss policy issues related to the adult learner. He applies various social policy models to adult and continuing education, but concludes that much more public debate is needed. Hilton (1982) and Ziegler (1982) also urge more discussion and a comprehensive human policy related to the education of adults. Tough (1978) suggests we need to explore the various steps learners take in their learning to better understand the implications for public policy. One of us has noted that some policies are needed so that self-directed learners are not exploited by institutions (Hiemstra, 1980). Rivera calls for more systematic study of policy needs and concludes that "the subject of adult education policy, and particularly public policy, demands greater attention as a discipline for research" (Rivera, 1982: viii).

Caffarella and O'Donnell (1988: 55) ask several policy-related questions: "What is the role of the adult educator? What are the involvement parameters for educational institutions? What does the concept of self-directed learning mean to society as a whole? ". After presenting some policy statements that have been gleaned from the literature, they conclude that we must carry out research to answer such questions, and derive policy to guide people and institutions as they seek to utilize education in meeting life's challenges (Caffarella and O'Donnell, 1987, 1988).

A POLICY-BUILDING WORKSHOP

In anticipation of the need for such guiding policy, one of us conducted a workshop several years ago aimed at the derivation of policy related to self-directed learning (Hiemstra, 1980). Many of the policy statements derived then are still relevant, while others have been updated for presentation in this chapter to reflect societal changes and the growing understanding of self-direction in learning during the past several years. In addition, some implementation recommendations are presented to help guide readers of this book as they consider how various policy statements might be applied to their personal or professional situations, or as they advocate policy development within various levels of government.

The derivation of policy

The development of policy applicable for learners, educators, and educational institutions is a difficult and complicated activity. It requires a willingness to consider the knowledge within various other disciplines as well as in the adult education field itself. It also necessitates recognition of the complex nature of most human or societal problems and requires integration of knowledge, beliefs, and practice. The application of personal and institutional philosophies to the policy-building process can also be a crucial step (Hiemstra, 1988b). Finally, incorporating policy recommendations into daily practice requires much care, dedication, and patience.

When a policy statement or recommendation is described, it can be used in various ways, – as an organizational directive, societal rule or norms, institutional procedures, bureaucratic necessity, and even personal tradition. This complex situation can lead to considerable confusion in trying to communicate about or implement policies. Thus, for purposes of this discussion, the following definitions are presented:

1 Rule – an inflexible regulation or statement of action or inaction that does not permit any deviation or allow for any individual judgment. In general, the fewer the rules the better in facilitating smooth operation or in promoting individual initiative.
2 Directive – a specific order describing an *ad hoc* or one-time course of action.
3 Procedure – a specific, step-by-step description of how to perform some task. This might apply to individual or to routine organizational activities.
4 Policy – a recommended course of action for achieving some goal or for meeting some need. In general, policies are used at an organizational level, but they can be used even at individual or societal levels in guiding activities.

For purposes of this chapter, the key word in the above definition of policy is "recommended", as we believe that policies should be used as a framework for decision-making, not as rules or directives. In other words, the purpose of a policy is to provide for the integration of institutional or personal philosophies with such elements as needs, objectives, and available resources. This integration should provide for operational guidelines at both individual and organizational levels.

The writing of policies requires clear, concise language that communicates easily to others. Policy statements should be comprehensive in terms of demonstrating linkages to societal issues. If possible, they should have long- as well as short-term consequences. In addition, such statements usually need to address potential political ramifications, although there will be times when, to reflect an individual's philosophy, a policy will counter prevailing organizational or societal norms. Priorities are another consideration, in that certain policies may need to take precedence over others. Finally, the comprehensiveness of a policy usually must be examined in light of available institutional resources if a realistic expectation that it will be implemented is to be made.

Impediments to implementing policy

We hope that people reading this book will think about how self-direction in learning applies to their personal practice as educators or as representatives of institutions involved in various forms of education or training. The policies presented in this chapter are aimed at guiding implementation efforts. However, as Gross (1977) noted, there are a variety of impediments to the implementation of policies, and most policies need to be filtered through ethical, bureaucratic, and personal concerns.

For example, problems for which some policies seem to be relevant may actually have been diagnosed incorrectly or improperly. The accurate identification of problems requires some care, or at least careful interpretation, of various points of view. At the organizational level, we recommend that problems be reexamined by a team of individuals to determine their cause, those affected, and the importance of their solution to the organization. A change in procedure or a one-time directive may be more appropriate than implementing some policy. At the individual level, careful reexamination of a policy may result in new insights that, in turn, lead to seeking new guiding policies.

There also will be instances where administrators who set policy or implement policy changes do not identify and deal effectively with various related obstacles. For instance, potential staff opposition, skills required to meet some new requirement, conflicts with existing policy, and resources required for implementation all need to be examined. There also may be times when policies will not even be compatible with the existing educational programs. In some cases the obstacles, opposition, or incompatibility will be severe enough that a policy cannot be implemented or it will need to be phased in over a long period of time.

It is also true that a policy appropriate in one place may not always be transportable to a different place. Widely publicized, interesting, or "trendy" innovations at the national level may drain some organizations' resources or may run so counter to local traditions or educational philosophies that employees and even program participants resent them. A successful individualized learning center that uses learning kits or on-line conferencing may be appropriate in an urban center, but the same approaches can fail miserably in a rural setting where daily contact with mentors or fellow learners is used to meet social as well as learning needs.

Within some organizations it is also important to consider various administrative details that affect the derivation and implementation of policy statements. In other words, thinking through the procedures and leadership responsible for introducing and implementing policy is very important. For example, good evaluation, monitoring, and feedback mechanisms should be in place so that assessment and the use of assessment information is a normal procedure. We believe, too, that it is crucial to involve staff, teachers, and even learners, if possible, in determining and introducing policy, so that they can feel ownership very early in the process and not feel that policy has been dictated from the top.

There also are many questions that can be asked prior to beginning the derivation of policies. These are detailed in Table 9.1. Such questions should be helpful in stimulating dialogue and action among those concerned with the policies.

The workshop process

The workshop from which many of the policy statements presented later in this chapter were derived was held at Iowa State University in 1980 and involved sixteen people representing a variety of professional backgrounds and walks of life (Hiemstra, 1980). Workshop participants who contributed to the development of the policy statements discussed later in the chapter are listed in Appendix B.

In addition, eight people served as staff members or consultants in some capacity, all of whom have carried out research related to self-directed or lifelong learning, including Hassan (1982), Hiemstra (1976b), Judd (1980), Kurland (1980), Leean and Sisco (1981) Tough (1979), Umoren (1978), and Zangari (1978). Participants met 3 hours daily in a classroom setting, Monday through Friday, for 2 weeks. In addition, they met together for several hours outside of class for small group work, individual study, and final policy development efforts.

The workshop used a process that maximized participant involvement, input, and feedback. The process included needs diagnosis, small and large

Table 9.1 Questions to guide the derivation of policies

Who will be affected?	What kind of changes will take place?	What are the costs?	Is it worth it?	How should the policy be implemented?
Colleagues?	Temporary?	Financial?	Commitments needed by various people?	People to be involved?
Clients or students?	Permanent?	Human resources?	Long-term implications?	Time required?
Community officials and leaders?	Short-term?	Space allocations?	Changes necessary within the organization?	Sequencing requirements?
"Innocent bystanders"?	Long-term?	Others?	Changes required by various people?	Dissemination needs?
Others?	Others?		Others?	Resources required to implement?
				Others?

group discussions, agenda building, clarifying procedures, and deriving formats for policy. In addition, individual commitments for work to be produced throughout the experience were made through interactive feedback activities, individual discussions with the workshop leader, and various evaluation processes.

Perhaps the most difficult task of the entire workshop was developing a format for describing policy statements and corresponding implementation recommendations. The literature provides a variety of suggestions for developing policy; often a suggestion in one source will conflict with or have no relationship to those found in other sources. For example, Gilder (1979, 1980) writes about a policy framework primarily in terms of providing guidelines for decision-making. One specialist urged that policy specify exactly which learners are to be served and which content areas are to be stressed (Gross, 1980). Ziegler and Healy (1979) advocated the formation of policy teams and the use of various futures-invention activities to develop policy recommendations, where participants forecast future events and design actions or policies related to the predictions.

Another difficult task for workshop participants was synthesizing a procedure for developing and writing policy statements. Several sources providing ideas on what should be included in a policy statement were considered. For example, the Croft Educational Services provided information on how to develop policies for public school boards. Weichenthal (1980) described policy making needs for continuing higher education institutions. Ziegler (1970) suggested several criteria to be used in policy formation. Such information helped participants select a format for stating needs, purposes, policy statements, and implementation recommendations. These last two elements will be represented in the remainder of the material for this chapter.

POLICY STATEMENTS

The process utilized during the workshop described above resulted in three small groups developing around mutual interests and backgrounds. Group members' preferences and suggestions evolved into three categories for discussion and policy formulation:

1 Adults as learners – the student perspective
2 Adult educators – the teacher/facilitator perspective
3 Adult education agencies – the institutional perspective

Each group, therefore, assumed responsibility for developing policy for only one of these three categories so that the efforts could be concentrated. Thus, the policy statements and implementation recommendations presented in this chapter address these three perspectives, adapted from the 1980 workshop. Their use as policies and action guides by any organization or person will need to take into account these specific audience focuses. However, it is our hope that they will serve as a beginning point for individual facilitators, agency administrators, and organizational employees to analyze their involvement with self-directed learning activities.

Adults as learners

Policy recommendation I

Each adult learner should be acknowledged as having unlimited learning potential and given respect as a self-directed learner.

Implementation strategies:

1 Utilize small discussion groups or create learning networks to assist learners in discovering through trial and error, their own gifts and talents.
2 Offer opportunities for learners to focus on their own individual strengths.
3 Broaden the availability of educational resources that teach about personal potential, learning skills, and using learning materials.
4 Help individuals in adult teaching roles to understand their role in promoting self-direction in learning.

Policy recommendation II

Learners should be encouraged to objectively examine their personal strengths and weaknesses as a means for gaining self acceptance, capitalizing on individual assets, and setting goals.

Implementation strategies:

1 Provide opportunities for learners to carry out self-inventories or to complete self-concept measures.
2 Provide facilitators, learning consultants, or counselors who have skill in discussing self-inventory results as information for planning.

Policy recommendation III

Learners should be helped to develop and strengthen internal-reinforcement mechanisms to ensure continuous growth in their learning efforts.

Implementation strategies

1 Provide access to and skill in using a variety of reinforcement resources such as meditation techniques, personal-journal or diary-writing processes, and critical-thinking techniques.
2 Train teachers and learning facilitators to help learners strengthen personal-growth skills.
3 Seek learning resources and techniques that help learners with internal reinforcement.

Policy recommendation IV

Learners need to be helped to understand their own learning or cognitive style, and utilize such information in shaping their educational efforts.

Implementation strategies

1 Provide opportunities for learners to complete measures of learning and cognitive styles as an informational basis for future planning.
2 Train teachers, counselors, and learning facilitators to interpret and use information on styles in assisting learners with their planning.

Policy recommendation V

Learners should be encouraged to form autonomous learning and support groups as a means of capitalizing on synergistic learning efforts.

Implementation strategies

1 Develop learner hotlines using such agencies as libraries, learning brokers, and universities to provide support or coordination.
2 Promote the concept of learner advocacy at various adult learning centers and within various adult education professional associations.
3 Establish learning exchange networks in local communities as suggested by Draves (1980), Illich (1971), and Peterson and Associates (1979).
4 Establish study circles patterned after the Scandinavian system of both topical and open-topic types (Kurland, 1982; Oliver, 1987).
5 Foster peer support groups or systems revolving around a variety of content areas.

Policy recommendation VI

Learners need to be supported and provided with opportunities to take individual responsibility for their own learning.

Implementation strategies

1 Provide appropriate administrative support necessary to foster individual adult initiative, such as convenient scheduling, adequate resources, childcare services, and adult-counseling programs.
2 Foster time management and good planning through related workshops or learning materials.

Adult educators

Policy recommmendation VII

Continuing research is needed to explore and understand various aspects related to self-direction in learning.

Implementation strategies

1 Examine learning techniques and skills necessary both for learners and for facilitators.
2 Identify means for enhancing learners' problem-solving, resource-utilization, and evaluation skills.
3 Explore the applicability of self-directed learning techniques to various subject-matter areas as an expansion of the work reported by Knowles and Associates (1984).
4 Identify those adults who are reluctant to utilize self-directed approaches, and determine if such approaches would be beneficial in their learning endeavors.
5 Study the relationship between developmental life stages and various self-direction approaches to determine their appropriateness to a person's stage in life.

Policy recommendation VIII

Adult educators need to receive training in utilizing theories and practices related to self-direction in learning.

Implementation strategies

1 Provide students in formal adult education training programs with an understanding of self-directed learning concepts and approaches.
2 Provide in-service training in self-directed learning approaches for the many teachers of adults who have not received any formal training related to the topic.

Adult education agencies

Policy recommendation IX

Adult educators need to help agencies serving adults to incorporate the concepts of self-directed learning into their normal operating procedures.

Implementation strategies

1 Promote the use of self-direction approaches through the development of individualized resources, creation of self-study materials, and establishment of appropriate learning settings or mechanisms.
2 Conduct needs assessments of learners to determine possibilities for self-directed learning and provide such information to agency administrators and other personnel.
3 Assist agencies in their utilization of self-directed learning approaches and help to coordinate the implementation of related resources and services.

Policy recommendation X

Agencies, organizations, and institutions working in some way with adult learners need to provide opportunities for administrators, faculty, and staff to become knowledgeable about self-directed approaches.

Implementation strategies

1 Provide employees with an awareness of the research and related literature pertaining to self-direction in learning.
2 Provide employees workshops, in-service training, and resource material related to self-direction in learning.

Policy recommendation XI

Agencies, organizations, and institutions working in some way with adult learners need to develop and maintain various measures or criteria for accountability and evaluation, so that the effectiveness and value of self-directed learning can be ascertained.

Implementation strategies

1 Develop reporting systems that will include and facilitate the use of various non-traditional data-collection and reporting mechanisms, such as learning contracts, mentoring or internship reports, and credit for work experiences.
2 Experiment with new and innovative evaluation methods – such as interviewing, networking assessments, and validation through electronic means.

Policy recommendation XII

Agencies, organizations, and institutions working in some way with adult learners need to seek legislation and funding to promote and facilitate self-direction in learning at local, state, and national levels.

Implementation strategies

1 Secure learning resources and other kinds of study opportunities, such as internship assignments, agency visitations, and sharing of library materials, from a multitude of community agencies.
2 Influence legislation by working with professional associations, contacting legislators, and seeking various kinds of public support for individualized learning efforts.

Policy recommendation XIII

Agencies, organizations, and institutions working in some way with adult learners need to provide support services that help those desiring to be self-directed as they adjust to various individualized activities and any related changes in self-concept or approaches to learning.

Implementation strategies

1 Establish centers or special locations within agency settings where such learners can gather, obtain necessary resources, and support each other.
2 Provide support personnel with appropriate expertise to counsel with and help adults make effective use of their newly acquired skills and knowledge.

Policy recommendation XIV

Agencies, organizations, and institutions working in some way with adult learners need to provide physical environments that accommodate and facilitate self-direction in learning.

Implementation strategies:

1 Examine the various physical environments in which learning takes place, and make changes consistent with many of those recommended in this book, and elsewhere (Hiemstra, 1988a; Hiemstra and Sisco, 1990; Vosko, 1984, 1985; Vosko and Hiemstra, 1988).

2 Provide an on-site specialist on physical learning environments who can work with facilitators and learners in designing appropriate physical conditions.

CONCLUSION

Policy is a concern that is frequently overlooked by educators of adults. Yet each of us is, in one way or another, involved in the development or implementation of policy. Our intent in this chapter has been to present a series of recommendations with the hope that these might serve as some basic goals toward which the adult education field can strive. Further, we hope to encourage readers to become proactive regarding the creation of a future in which the self-directed learner can thrive. Other recommendations outside the area of policy are made in the final chapter.

Many of the policies and implementation recommendations presented actually may appear impossible to achieve, impractical to manage, or even too visionary in nature at first reading. Some obviously require considerable change in philosophies, new administrative mechanisms, and the expenditure of new monies. In addition, what may seem practical or appropriate in one locale will not be possible or feasible in another.

However, it is our belief that what may seem visionary or impossible today will become commonplace procedures if the learning approaches to life that we project throughout this book come to full fruition. In fact, many experimental programs and creative means for reaching self-directed adult learners are already in place, as noted in earlier chapters.

It also is obvious that refinement of the policies suggested above must take place as we learn more about self-direction in learning and as various facilitators or agencies attempt to utilize them. Many new policies will be required, too, as research and experience pushes forward the knowledge about learning preferences, approaches, and needs. We believe that the increasing interest in serving adult-learning needs and in helping adults cope with the ever-increasing pace of change will facilitate the meeting of such requirements.

10 The global context

Profound changes of various types throughout the world have caused profound thinking regarding the role that education must play in helping people enhance the quality of their lives. Compton and Parish suggest that at least three concerns must be addressed in some way through educational efforts:

1 The increasing gap between the rich and the poor; the gap between rich nations and developing nations.
2 The disproportionate share of the world's resources now allotted to the dominant world.
3 The increasing awareness in the Third World of the double standard of living.

(Compton and Parish, 1978: 31)

Such concerns as these plus the constancy and rapidity of change, suggest to us a need to help people make the most of their individual potential. Boucouvalas describes a standing regulation in Greece that captures this notion of promoting individual ability: "The view of ... [each person] as a self-sufficient and independent personality and as the agent of ... [personal] development" (Boucouvalas, 1982: 30). It seems that learner self-direction and self-directed learning skills are crucial to the achievement of this human potential.

The study of self-directed learning appears to be primarily western in orientation and interest, with little relationship to many parts of the world. In fact, the majority of recent research, writings, and language related to self-direction in learning have emanated from North America. According to Brookfield: "the majority of studies in this field have been conducted with samples of advantaged, white, middle-class Americans." (Brookfield, 1986: 51). He was referring here primarily to research related to learning projects (Tough, 1979) or the Self-directed Learning Readiness Scale (Guglielmino, 1977); indeed, there does not yet exist a large volume of related literature outside of North America although it is developing.

We thus believe that it is important to our success with adults as learners to take a more global approach in our understandings about self-direction in learning. We realize that not all our assumptions about learners and their abilities to accept personal responsibility will translate entirely from one setting or culture to another. However, this chapter's purpose is to present some reflections and understandings regarding the universality of self-directed learning principles and approaches.

SOME INTERNATIONAL PERSPECTIVES ON SELF-DIRECTION

We will present some background information before launching into discussions about self-directed learning in selected countries. Both of us have had many international students in our courses. Observing the successes and difficulties involved with facilitating their independent learning have provided us with some understanding of requirements across cultures in applying self-directed learning principles. We also have examined some of the international literature related to self-directed learning and have interviewed and talked informally with several people from other countries to obtain their views regarding such topics as autonomy, learner control, and instructor roles. Thus, what will follow is a summary of the literature we have studied regarding self-direction in selected settings outside of North America. In addition, for two countries (Indonesia and Tanzania), we present a description of how indigenous adult educators believe that self-direction in learning would be possible in their respective countries.

We also need to say something about the nature of self-direction in learning in various cultures. Based on our reading and conversations with people from various countries, there seem to be many different ideas about what it means to study or plan individually. One country will have as an avowed policy the promotion of individual learning ability, while at the same time advocating participation in governmental sponsored programs to achieve such a goal. Another country will talk about self-education as a primary means for adults to learn, but the nature of the programs described would indicate to a North American observer that few opportunities exist for individualized decision-making regarding the learning process.

Another problem stems from the structural design of certain approaches intended to promote independent study. For example, a correspondence course that requires strict adherence to a planned route of readings and testing procedures may offer little freedom to the learner other than pacing or sequencing of micro-learning components. Ljosa and Sandvold (1983), on the other hand, make a case for the various ways by which learners can exercise freedom of choice within the didactical structure of correspondence education.

Moore (1983: 24–5) describes how he thought about learner freedom in designing an Open University course. The course was based on: (a) a psychological climate that emphasized learner decision-making and experience; (b) an emphasis on self-diagnosis; (c) a personally planned route of study; (d) a tutor seen as a resource person; (e) some learner-designed evaluation criteria; and (f) an emphasis on each student's personal learning experiences.

A wide range exists in interpreting and permitting freedoms such as these within the learning setting. As noted earlier in the chapter, some suggest that self-direction is primarily a middle-class, white phenomenon by its emphasis on the individual. Even though some research has demonstrated that certain self-directed learning concepts hold across racial, economic, and social groupings, the concepts may not always directly apply in other cultural contexts. However, we firmly believe that as long as cultural context is recognized and respected, it is possible to apply many of the instructional and learning tips described in this book in any setting.

There are many countries that should be examined in terms of their self-directed practices, activities, or philosophies. However, that needs to be the subject of another book as we work toward a better understanding of various implications for the way in which adults are helped in their efforts to maximize their potential. In this section, we touch on just a few countries in order to highlight interesting aspects of self-direction in different cultural contexts.

Scandinavia

Scandinavian countries have a long history of adult education. Grundtvig's pioneering work in Denmark with the folk high school movement began in 1844 (Andresen, 1985; Engberg-Pedersen, 1970; Kulich, 1984). Grundtvig, in developing the folk high school movement (high school in Danish means a university-like setting), wanted an educational experience for adults that was residential in nature but small in scope. He also wanted a mixture of practical and theoretical work, supported by lots of discussion (Himmelstrup, 1988). These institutions therefore stress work in the group setting, and are aimed at the individual development of each person. In fact, their methods and environment are designed to encourage individuals of all social classes to broaden their personal horizons (Andresen, 1985: 20). Folk schools have spread to many other countries in the past century and a half.

Sweden has made several efforts to promote education for adults that is self-directed in nature. One stated adult education aim of the Swedish government, for example, is to cater "to individual preferences and needs" (Hall, 1981: 7). A 1977 governmental ordinance called for learning opportunities to increase awareness of personal capacity, to develop independence, to promote creativity, and to foster critical reflectivity (Svensson, 1988).

One of the most innovative approaches to adult education has been the study circle. These have been used to provide many citizens in Sweden (and elsewhere) with an opportunity to develop self-study skills. As Kurland (1982) has stated:

various religious and political groups found in the study circle a kind of self-help arrangement that enabled an essentially uneducated populace to understand the issues of the day and learn the practical skills necessary to improve their lot in life. Using their own homes as places of study, with no formally trained teachers and limited study materials, people had to rely on their own experience and their ability to share it with others. Studies had to be immediately practical, related to their own needs, or firmly rooted in the particular popular movement in whose cause they were enrolled.

(Kurland, 1982: 24)

While the group emphasis of the study circle at first glance may seem inconsistent with notions of self-direction, Oliver (1987: 5) states that, historically in Sweden: "study circles encouraged self-directed learning and full participation, blending the intensive small group format with traditional Swedish culture – particularly small-town life and the face-to-face conversations of friends and neighbors". Svensson (1988) notes that more than 2.5 million people are involved in Swedish study circles each year, with 1.5 million of these women.

While not quite as popular, another important Swedish form of individualized learning is correspondence study. The country has three such organizations: "one that is authorized to hold examinations for formal educational institutions, one that provides study materials that do not lead to any formal qualifications, and one that provides agricultural correspondence materials" (Darkenwald and Merriam, 1982: 197). Nearly 20,000 people each year enroll in correspondence study (Svensson, 1988).

In Norway, correspondence schools have long played a very important role in educating adults (Pardoen, 1977). In fact, Norway's Adult Education Act of 1976 was intended to influence learning throughout life and "should give the core ingredient for ... self-managed learning throughout the rest of life" (Pardoen, 1977: 14–15). Finland, too, has several correspondence institutes that offer expert aid through study centers to assist individual students in their educational efforts (Royce, 1970).

United Kingdom

The United Kingdom is perhaps most well-known in the area of self-directed education for its pioneering work with the open university concept described in Chapter 8. There are also many other opportunities for the learner interested in independent study. For example, the number of adults studying by correspondence in the UK is estimated to "range from 500,000 to 750,000 a year" (Darkenwald and Merriam, 1982: 197).

Another imaginative attempt to foster independent learning took place at Malvern Hills College, the center for adult education in the rural English counties of Hereford and Worcester. Several adult students were having difficulty attending a regular college class. Thus, a Correspondence Tuition Service was established, to "provide individually oriented programmes of home study supported by personal tutorials" (Brookfield, 1978: 19). An initial diagnostic interview between a tutor and the student, tutorial assistance with learning projects, and home study correspondence courses are some of the available resources.

Brookfield (1981b) also describes his research, which examined the self-directed efforts of individuals not associated with any formal organization or institution. He chose twenty-five working-class individuals whose formal education had ended at age 16, and whose expertise stemmed from extensive study of, or involvement with, a hobby or personal-interest area. His research helped to advance earlier work, primarily in North America, related to learning projects. It also demonstrated that independent efforts to obtain mastery over some area of study can take place across a wide range of cultural and educational backgrounds. He concluded that many adult learners will look to other learners for information and support rather than to societies, organizations, and professional educators. He noted: "subjects would mention influential books and magazines but would preface these comments by declaring their 'real' source of information was their fellow enthusiasts" (Brookfield, 1981b: 21).

Japan

Japan's progress in industrialization since the Second World War, coupled with its more recent emergence as a world leader in various ways, has prompted a variety of changes within the country. These range from a growth of pizza parlors and fast-food restaurants, to increasing disposable income for most people, and a constant contact with other nations. Such changes have also affected education in many ways, including the education of adults. As one example, open-university-type programs reach adults throughout the society (Darkenwald and Merriam, 1982).

The pressure to be part of a societal group remains, but subtle changes are taking place in education. A Japanese professor, Seiichiro Miura, who works with adult education activities, was interviewed about adult education in his country. He describes the change as follows:

> One thing I might mention is the use of groups in adult education practice. I recognize the heavy emphasis in the United States on the self-directed learner. But from looking at human nature I suggest it is not easy for some to be self-directed. In Japan, we would organize a self-directed group, kind of a mixture between group study [*sic*]. Subtle group pressure and a Japanese sensitivity to groups promote a kind of invisible network forcing you to be there, to participate even when you may be reluctant to attend.
>
> Thus, you sacrifice your individual desire to the group. I call this interdependent learning rather than independent learning.
>
> (Hiemstra, 1981c: 30)

Professor Miura was also asked how he would introduce learning contracts, frequently used in self-directed learning efforts, into the Japanese culture: "I will introduce the idea of the learning contract but it will be utilized within a group setting. I will need to introduce it slowly and find the ways it can work" (Hiemstra, 1981c: 30).

Thus, Japan appears to be in a transitional state where the sanctity of the group is being reevaluated in terms of individual needs and wishes. This may be most clear in adult education efforts with older Japanese. Sekiguchi (1985) describes a 1981 Recommendation Paper by the Central Committee on Education. Among the Paper's recommendations is a call for the older person's self-education. As a method of study, "learning in a large group or in a classroom will not be adequate since there is a great difference between individual learners. Instead, individual learning methods are recommended as a more suitable way" (Sekiguchi, 1985: 290). Facilities such as libraries, museums, and similar institutions are suggested as organizations which need to play a more active role in meeting older adults' needs. Study courses on radio and television and correspondence courses are recommended as effective methods for the older person.

China

The changes that have taken place in China during late 1989 and on into the 1990s make it difficult to comprehend fully what the future holds. However, the last several years have been marked by some important changes relative to adult learning: "Since 1977, when the expansion and restructuring of adult education began after the Cultural Revolution, important changes have taken place in many sectors of adult education" (Sidel, 1982: 38). For example, current radio and television delivery methods are patterned after Great Britain's Open University. The Chinese Television University (TVU) opened in 1979 and provides several degree opportunities. In fact, TVUs operate at the national and municipal levels. Televised instruction is also used at factory colleges, spare-time colleges, and regular universities (Long, 1982). Municipal television universities and corresponding study centers in a variety of settings cooperate with centralized programming efforts. They serve some 800,000 registered students and many more casual viewers who do not enroll for credit.

There are other forms of adult education in China that offer some opportunities for individualized learning. Correspondence courses are available, and individual tutoring is sometimes available. In 1980 factory universities set up correspondence courses that enrolled 240,000 students (Sidel, 1982). Zhou (1988) reports that there are some 32,000 people enrolled in independent correspondence colleges, and another 150,000 students enrolled in 148 evening college correspondence divisions.

The "visiting teacher" program also offers opportunities for a learner to work individually after the teacher provides some initial assistance: "In this program, literacy is taught by a teacher who visits the peasant's home and labels common household objects with the appropriate Chinese characters. The learner thus learns the characters as the items are used" (Long, 1982: 13).

Soviet Union

The concept of self-direction in learning is referred to in the Soviet Union as self-education. The country's beliefs regarding why a person should develop self-directed study skills sound very much like what an advocate in North America would say:

> The role of self-education naturally increases in adults, for the potential possibilities of the personality are extremely great, and the formed world outlook, self-awareness and will make it possible to develop one's abilities more successfully, systematically and comprehensively. This is especially true since life does not stand still and society is developing scientifically and technically. Anyone who does not engage in self-education, voluntarily or not, lags behind the demands of the times.

> (Ruvinsky, 1986: 31)

Several examples of Soviets engaged in self-education illustrate how the concept is employed:

> The well-known Soviet test-pilot Mikhail Gromov (1899–1984) said, for

example, that, by means of self-education, a high degree of perfection may be achieved in one's personal qualities and the new habits and skills required for the chosen profession may be acquired.

(Ruvinsky, 1986: 32).

The Soviet scientist Aksel Berg's idea was that real character cannot be formed without effort: "moreover, constant self-observation and self-accountability are required, and there may even be temporary falls, trips and other fluctuations, which, in fact, reveals the dialectical character of the process of self-education" (Ruvinsky, 1986: 32). The examples are not confined just to the most famous people in the society: "workers ... not only acquire professional knowledge in the process of self-teaching, but also develop their creative abilities and raise their cultural level" (Ruvinsky, 1986: 96).

Ruvinsky also suggests there are some techniques that can be used to facilitate independent study efforts: (a) write what is being learned in a diary or special notebook; (b) organize and classify the information in terms of some goals; (c) learn to separate primary concepts from secondary concepts (Ruvinsky, 1986: 94–5). Correspondence study also is a widely used adult-learning method, and "evening and correspondence studies last a year longer than regular studies. Studies at evening and correspondence faculties are regarded as a matter of enormous social interest and significance" (Savicevic, 1981: 77).

Indonesia

Traditional beliefs and expectations in Indonesia regarding learning have placed the instructor in a role as authority figure. In fact, learners have not been given many opportunities to assess personal needs as a basis for learning. These learners also usually expect the teacher to be an authority on whatever subject matter is being discussed. Furthermore, they view experiential learning activities, such as using various community resources outside the classroom, as a waste of time. They would believe that such time could more appropriately be spent in the classroom listening to an instructor. However, increasing levels of education among the population and a better understanding of teaching approaches outside of Indonesia among educators are indicators that self-direction in learning is possible with appropriate modifications.

For example, one Indonesian educator studying adult education in the United States told one of the authors how he would apply various self-directed learning techniques in introducing family planning to community leaders when he returned home (M. M. Maudz, personal communication with R. Hiemstra, January 11, 1988). During his initial contact with the leaders he would discuss the importance for the country of the content to be covered. He would also discuss with them their learning needs, based on their roles, tasks, and functions as community leaders. Because he would be viewed as the authority, he would come well prepared and make the initial presentation with the use of various audio-visual aids.

The participants would then complete a pre-designed, needs-assessment form, and come to some initial conclusions regarding personal needs. This educator would then lead a general discussion to determine needs, strengths, and weaknesses among the group. He would begin by listing learning needs on a chalk board or on poster paper, and ask participants to help him rank them. He would conclude with a summary of the needs, strengths, and weaknesses. Then a description sheet of the content areas that could be covered during subsequent sessions would be distributed and discussed. He would make every effort to accommodate the uncovered needs, but would be very specific in describing those content areas that he believed must be covered because of official requirements or his own personal convictions, even if they did not match well with the rankings.

After that initial session, he would spend time putting together the plans for remaining sessions. This would include determining who would be responsible for various content areas, what learning aids would be needed, what teaching and learning techniques would be used, and what arrangements were needed for outside resources or resource leaders. Passive learning activities would be expected, although small group discussion could be designed for occasional use. If any individualized or experiential learning activities were desired or necessary, special efforts would be needed to make clear the importance of such experiences. As evaluation in the form of testing would be the normal expectation, some efforts would also be needed to design the procedures and instruments.

Thus, some of the self-direction procedures described in this book would be possible, but the instructor or trainer would need to explain such procedures very carefully and help participants understand how they would enhance the learning. Cultural traditions and expectations regarding the role of the instructor do not rule out more individualized approaches, but adaptations based on an understanding of prior expectations of student and teacher roles would be required.

Tanzania

In Tanzania a general respect for elders and people in authority permeates the culture. Thus, most Tanzanian students have certain expectations regarding their roles and the roles of instructors. For example, frequently small group discussion will take place only after the teacher has spent considerable time lecturing about a subject. Even the small group discussion typically will center on questions posed by the instructor, although students feel they have some latitude in discussing areas beyond the instructor's questions.

Experiential learning activities will be looked at by most learners and instructors as a waste of time. They fear that such activities will take time away from the instructor's lecturing. Although a few learners would thrive on experiential or self-directed learning approaches, many learners would probably believe that an instructor using such approaches did not know the subject matter and was employing them to cover up for inadequacies. One Tanzanian adult educator studying in the United States felt that back home his biggest hurdle would be the unwillingness of his university administrators and fellow teachers to accept teaching approaches that placed considerable responsibility on the learner (A. C. Mgulambwa, personal communication with R. Hiemstra, January 11, 1988).

Another problem area revolves around evaluation and grading. Many of the current traditions of grading were inherited from the British, and the result is usually a highly structured process. For example, many teachers are expected or even required to give a certain number of lower grades. The Tanzanian adult educator mentioned above, who by the time of the interview had considerable experiences with self-directed learning in the classroom from his United States graduate training, felt that the use of a learning contract in his country would be problematic.

The above points suggest that the employment of self-directed learning principles in Tanzania would be difficult, at least initially, because of traditional expectations about education. However, one of the authors spent some time in Tanzania and observed some self-directed adult learning taking place at the village level (Hiemstra, 1987a). In fact, the country supports a national policy of "self-reliance," in which elected village leaders take on primary responsibility for local development.

The policy has worked only moderately well in some parts of the nation and not well at all in others. However, it may have begun a process of self-determination in some parts of the country that is translatable to other villages:

> I had the opportunity to visit three villages where male and female leaders had been trained at the regional sites and observed what appeared to be high levels of excitement by villagers at their ability to diagnose and work on their problems. My interviews with village chiefs, council members, and district officials substantiated such observations. I also had the opportunity to observe village leaders conduct training courses with villagers and viewed what I believe to be real (and I suspect newly learned) efforts

to diagnose needs, involve villagers in planning, and encourage self-planned efforts.

(Hiemstra, 1987a: 8–9)

This special effort to promote personal responsibility can perhaps best be summarized with a statement from an evaluation report:

[the project] demonstrates the power of adult education methods centered on experiential, problem-solving techniques to evoke change. It shows that these methods are applicable to working with highly educated people as well as villagers ... the trainee is actively involved in the learning process.

(Training for Rural Development, 1984: 16)

Thus, in Tanzania (and in other countries as well), there is an apparent need to overcome some traditions and cultural expectations in using self-direction approaches to learning. However, appropriate adaptations are possible:

I believe that most adults appreciate the opportunity to explore their needs, especially if they can turn such needs into real programs ... I was perhaps most surprised at the apparent willingness of village chiefs and other top leaders (almost always older males) to incorporate women and younger men in the various processes of diagnosing needs, collaborative planning, and even evaluation.

(Hiemstra, 1987a: 13)

Eastern Europe

In most Eastern European countries, a variety of independent study opportunities exist. Correspondence study seems to be quite popular for the learner who, out of preference or necessity, selects individualized approaches. Albanian workers are encouraged to educate themselves through various forms of education, including correspondence study (Savicevic, 1981). Correspondence is also one of the favored delivery methods for adult learning in Bulgaria and Poland (Savicevic, 1981).

In Germany, correspondence education is recognized as equal in value to other forms of adult study: "Those who acquire education in this manner are offered special facilities and encouragement, such as leave from work amounting to seventy-seven days per year while retaining the right to a full income" (Savicevic, 1981: 59). In Hungary, combining both correspondence study and evening courses, according to a 1975 study, "those who acquired a degree in this manner were 45.2% of the total number of people who received a university degree" (Savicevic, 1981: 63). In Rumania nearly 30 percent of all adult students study either at evening schools or through correspondence.

Yugoslavia is perhaps the most progressive of these countries. It has schools of self-guided learners, developed through federal legislation, and other institutions through which the individual learner uses various educational resources, such as cultural centers, museums, and libraries. The country also was among the first nations to provide special study on the conception of andragogy, including both graduate and undergraduate study (Savicevic, 1981).

Obviously, the events that have taken place throughout eastern Europe in the dawn of the 1990s will have an impact on the education of adults. While it is too early to speculate with any high degree of confidence, we believe that these changes signal potential for positive developments on the self-direction front. Only time will tell, though, what specific impact may take place.

Saudi Arabia

In Saudi Arabia adult education has become a social imperative as the country attempts various modernization efforts:

> Saudi Arabia needs the characteristics of modern man who is ready for new experiences, accepts change, and looks toward the future more than to the past or present. He should believe in education and technology and his own ability to improve himself.

> (Hamidi, 1979: 30).

Many of the initial educational efforts in this modernization movement have been related to literacy. Much of the recent success can be attributed to the heavy use of television as an individualized means of reaching people at home, especially women (Hamidi, 1979).

CONCLUSION

Perhaps the most obvious conclusion that can be drawn is that considerable variance exists across various cultures and geographic settings. We believe that the promotion of self-directedness can be considered a phenomenon transferrable to most cultural settings. For example, in a study of 1,000 people in Czechoslovakia, Hungary, Poland, France, Soviet Union, Yugoslavia, United States, and Canada, nearly half used some form of self-instruction to acquire some basic information (Savicevic, 1985). It also was found that the higher the level of education, the more people are engaged in self-education.

How do we make sense out of such research? Is this finding something that can be applied universally across all cultures? It probably is not, but we simply do not yet have a clear enough understanding of differences and similarities. What then are some obvious needs and conclusions as we think about self-direction in learning from a global context?

In making comparisons across various countries we also need to ask if group processes can be used for individual or self-directed development. Himmelstrup (1988), for example, noted that Denmark has few opportunities for self-directed study because the emphasis has long been on the social aspect of organizations like the folk high school. This obviously can be said about many other countries. Thus, can self-direction in learning be successful within countries or cultural settings where group or social processes have been stressed?

We believe that many of the principles and practices associated with self-direction in learning can have relevance within the context of most cultures; however, we are quick to acknowledge that our perspective is primarily a North American one. Thus, we offer the following as needs for further work on gaining a more global perspective relative to self-direction.

1 There is a need to carry out more cross-cultural research on the many implications for training adult educators, developing learning resources, and helping learners to make the best choices regarding their learning. Similarly, we need to begin developing research agendas that will consider self-direction more directly from specific cultural contexts.

2 There are cultural differences that must be understood in working with learners who may prefer to be self-directed. Expectations regarding the role of the teacher, the student, and the group will differ, so teaching techniques will need to be adjusted accordingly. Societal differences regarding the value of the group over the individual also need to be better understood.

3 The willingness and readiness to employ self-directed learning approaches within various countries is constantly changing and evolving. Thus it is important that the exchange of ideas across geographic borders takes place on a regular basis through cross-cultural research, international conferences, and visiting scholar programs.

11 Ethical dilemmas in self-direction

The late Harry Chapin once wrote a song telling the story of Mr. Tanner, a fictitious dry-cleaning store owner who found great pleasure in singing as he worked. As the story goes, friends and customers were so impressed with Mr. Tanner's avocational abilities that they encouraged him to consider a professional singing career. Eventually he agreed and, after spending most of his life savings, made his public singing debut. The critics were less than kind, suggesting that 'full-time consideration of another endeavor might be in order'. Mr. Tanner returned home to his business, saying nothing about his demise. But he never sang again, except alone late at night after the shop had closed.

There is an important message in the story of Mr. Tanner for those of us committed to promoting self-direction in learning as a way of life. This message has to do with the potential consequences of our intervention with learners. We must be careful that in our zeal to promote opportunities for self-directed learning and to enhance learner self-direction, we do not inadvertently help set such learners up for failure. We need to recognize that ideals such as "efficiency" and "success" are value-laden and relative and, for many people, are much less important than the enjoyment of the learning process itself. In the case of Mr. Tanner, it was the urging, or intervention, of others that led him to seek wider recognition for his success. In turn, this intervention led Mr. Tanner to false expectations that helped set him up for failure. And while it can be argued that had Mr. Tanner not taken the risk, he never would have known what could have been, the point is that, without outside intervention, Mr. Tanner might have gone on deriving pleasure from his self-defined personal success as a singer.

The above illustration points out potential risks of jumping too quickly on to the self-direction "bandwagon," where the joys of self-direction are uncritically extolled. The previous chapters offered a look at numerous trends and issues relative to the importance of self-direction as a way of life for many adults. It is our belief that self-direction needs to be viewed as a major element of adult education practice. At the same time, however, we are not suggesting that self-direction is *the* purpose of adult education or that self-direction is ideal in *all* adult learning endeavors. The ten myths that were presented and discussed in Chapter 1 help to illustrate many of the junctures at which ethical dilemmas can arise in self-direction.

In this chapter, we will explore some of the potential ethical conflicts that can arise in promoting self-direction among adult learners. Included will be a brief overview of adult education ethics. From this, we will shift the focus toward an application of ethics to self-direction in adult learning. This will include a discussion based on ideas from a workshop on ethics in self-direction that helped to lay the groundwork for some of our current thinking. The chapter will conclude with a look at several ethical dilemmas relative to self-direction in learning.

ETHICS IN ADULT EDUCATION

Few would argue the relevance of ethics as an element of adult education practice. Yet, as has been the case with the area of self-direction, this topic has been largely ignored in the literature of adult education. A recent book, however, has offered perspectives from several writers in the adult education field who take a look at ethics in such areas as program planning, marketing, administration, evaluation, teaching, advising, and research (Brockett, 1988c). The book also addresses such issues as social responsibility and ethics, the code-of-ethics question, ethical development in adulthood, and development of a personal philosophy.

What do we mean by "ethics"? Ethics is an elusive term that can be discussed on at least two levels. First, ethics refers to a branch of inquiry within the discipline of philosophy. Here, emphasis is on the formal study of "*right* and *wrong*, of *good* and *evil*, in human conduct" (Fagothey, 1972: 2). This study is sometimes referred to as "metaethics" (e.g., Reamer, 1982).

On another level, ethics involves the application of values in order to determine the "rightness" or "wrongness" of specific behaviors in specific situations. It is this applied view of ethics, often referred to as "normative ethics" (e.g., Reamer, 1982), that is of particular relevance to professions or professionalizing fields, such as adult education. Bayles (1981: 3) has suggested that professional ethics "encompasses all issues involving ethics and values in the roles of the professions and the conduct of professionals in society".

Although there is considerable controversy over the question of whether adult education is, indeed, a profession, it is nonetheless clear that situations abound in the education of adults where the potential for inappropriate behavior exists. As a way of understanding the different kinds of ethical questions that can arise in adult education practice, a model has been proposed where three dimensions, or levels, of ethical practice can be identified and differentiated. The "Dimensions of Ethical Practice" model (Brockett, 1988b) suggests that ethical dilemmas can be identified along the following three dimensions:

1 The personal value system of the adult educator;
2 A consideration of multiple audiences to whom the educator of adults is responsible; and
3 The ways in which values are put into practice, or operationalized.

The starting point for ethical decision making, according to this model, can be found within the *personal value system*. This dimension stresses the importance of individual values and is reflected in ethical dilemmas that can arise due to conflicts that a person holds within his or her own value system. The importance of a given dilemma is compounded by the strength with which one holds such values. For example, an educator who believes that adult learning should be a voluntary activity will face conflict in a situation where learners are required to attend a particular activity. If this belief is a strong conviction, the degree of conflict will be much greater than if the person merely states a "preference" for voluntary learning.

The next dimension of ethical practice centers on the recognition that as educators, our responsibilities extend in many directions. In any given situation, we have responsibilities to the learners, the institution, our colleagues, the profession, society, and ourselves. Meeting one set of responsibilities often creates a conflict with another set of responsibilities. This is exemplified by the educator who feels he or she is "compromising" personal values through any number of activities, such as: advising learners to enroll in a particular course in order to increase enrollments, regardless of whether the course will meet learner needs; attempting to discredit the programs of competing agencies; or not fully informing learners of what to expect from the learning experience. As another example, take the case of someone conducting an internal evaluation of an agency. In finding that the agency may be overstaffed, the evaluator is placed in an emotional tug-of-war between (a) creating a potential threat to the livelihood of colleagues and (b) failing to report findings that could lead to more effective resource utilization by the institution. At this level of ethical practice, it is crucial for the adult educator to strive toward a balance in meeting these multiple responsibilities. It is necessary to set priorities "based on the anticipated consequences of one's actions and *accepting responsibility for those actions*" (Brockett, 1988b: 12).

In the third dimension of ethical practice, which involves the *operation-*

alization of values, the emphasis shifts to an identification of strategies that will help put values into practice. Taken to an extreme, this is where a code of ethics can become relevant. However, the real concern here is that the educator should be able to reflect critically on his or her values relative to the education of adults. The development of a personal philosophy can be a valuable tool in helping educators become better able to identify potential ethical conflicts (Hiemstra, 1988b).

The Dimensions of Ethical Practice model is not a formal theory. Nor is it a prescriptive model offering solutions to specific situations. Rather, it is a process model designed to help educators of adults identify and recognize some of the points at which ethical conflict can arise in their practice. In this way, the model is viewed as a consciousness-raising tool. As Bayles (1981: 3) has stated, the "study of professional ethics will hopefully sensitize one to the ethical dimensions of professional practice and help one think clearly about ethical problems". The Dimensions of Ethical Practice model can be viewed as a tool that adult educators can use in order to facilitate this study.

A WORKSHOP ON ETHICS AND SELF-DIRECTED ADULT LEARNING

As the idea of self-direction came to take an increasingly greater hold on the adult education field, particularly during the late 1970s, a number of questions began to emerge relative to potential misuses or abuses of principles growing out of the self-direction notion. Yet, as of the early 1980s, there had been no serious effort to address what might be viewed as "ethical issues" in self-directed learning. In order to begin considering some of these concerns, the first author of this book decided to conduct a workshop entitled "Ethical Issues in Self-Directed Learning" as a major element of a three-credit graduate course on self-directed learning held at Syracuse University during the Summer 1983 term. Drawing in part from the process used by Hiemstra in his two workshops (policy and institutional issues), discussed in other chapters, each participant was asked to develop a position paper on a topic relative to ethics and self-directed learning. These papers were distributed to all participants and presented toward the end of the workshop. The names of workshop participants are listed in Appendix B. The six position papers were as follows:

1 "Self-directed learning: Appropriate for all?" (Reynolds, 1983);
2 "The rights and responsibilities of institutions promoting self-directed learning." (Henry, 1983)
3 "Rights and responsibilities of the self-directed learner." (Alegria, 1983)
4 "The ethics of promoting self-directed learning." (Creighton, 1983)

5 "Love of learning and lived experience: Necessary ingredients for the self-directed adult learner." (Kaluzny, 1983)

6 "Philosophy and facilitation of self-directed learning." (Bentti, 1983)

Upon presentation of these papers, each author was asked to glean two or more principles that could be included in a "manifesto/bill of rights" statement. More than twenty-five principles were presented. The entire list was discussed extensively among the group and a final list of sixteen principles was derived. These principles are presented in Table 11.1.

The recommendations listed in Table 11.1 were not intended to serve as a "code of ethics" for working with self-directed learners. Rather, they were viewed as principles or ideas deemed by workshop participants as being worthy of further consideration. We would suggest that there is a need for the field to move toward a greater awareness of ethical concerns if we are to help prevent future abuses or misuses. This may or may not eventually involve the development of a "formalized" set of standards or a "code of ethics." It would, however, serve to bring such concerns to the forefront of our consciousness as adult educators.

In reflecting on these points, it is clear that in many ways, we *have* begun to make progress relative to ethics in adult education and, more specifically, in self-direction. We hope this chapter, in conjunction with the book described above (Brockett, 1988c) and other periodical literature on the topic (e.g., Singarella and Sork, 1983) will stimulate even more thinking on ethical issues.

SELF-DIRECTION AND ETHICS: SOME DILEMMAS

It should be apparent that the potential for ethical conflict clearly exists within the realm of self-direction in adult learning. The questions that follow represent four illustrations of how ethical conflict can arise. The first two questions relate to the learner–facilitator relationship while the latter two questions pertain to institutional issues.

Are there situations where intervention can actually be detrimental to the learning process?

It is clear from previous research (e.g., Tough, 1979) that a key reason for the appeal of self-direction is that many adults feel it is the most *efficient* way for them to learn. By being able to select their own objectives, set schedules according to personal preferences, identify preferred strategies, and evaluate when objectives have been met, many adults believe that they are able to learn in a more efficient way. For such individuals, self-direction is viewed

Table 11.1 Ethics seminar recommendations

1 Self-directedness exists in varying degrees within different individuals. It is not an "all or nothing" notion.
2 Self-directeness is more appropriate for some adults than for others.
3 One's level of readiness for self-directed learning depends on development and cognitive growth.
4 It is possible to assess or determine an individual's degree of self-directedness.
5 Self-directed learning offers numerous emerging roles for the educator of adults.
6 An individual's level of self-directedness can be strengthened or weakened by love of learning and/or lived (i.e., life) experience.
7 Self-directed learning can be viewed as a method for supporting the voluntary nature of adult education.
8 Existing mandatory continuing education programs should recognize, respect, and accommodate the needs and learning styles of the self-directed learner.
9 Educators of adults need to be able to help learners realize their potential for self-directedness.
10 Institutions that wish to serve self-directed adult learners need to possess goals, objectives, and underlying values that are compatible with this approach. At the same time, institutions have a right to offer programs that are not necessarily in harmony with self-directedness.
11 Institutions need to provide a wide range of resources and services to assist the self-directed learner. These can include direct services such as facilitating the learning process as well as support services such as counseling and referral.
12 The learner has a right to services that will support his or her efforts as a self-directed learner.
13 Institutions that support self-directed learning need to provide a climate conducive to this kind of learning. This climate includes both the physical facilities and a positive emotional and intellectual atmosphere.
14 The self-directed learner must be willing to assume primary responsibility for his or her learning.
15 The freedom to choose self-directed learning is a highly personal issue and involves a great degree of initiative, perseverance, and self-discipline.
16 The self-directed learner should possess a number of basic rights, but must also be willing to accept responsibility for utilizing these rights.

as less costly, both in terms of time and money, than other approaches to learning. However, an ethical dilemma arises when we assume that efficiency and self-direction need *necessarily* be linked.

Consider the example of two friends who each have an interest in railroading. One of the friends pursues this interest by enrolling in courses on the history of railroading and by regular visits to the library to read books and articles on railroading. The other friend chooses to spend summers visiting old railroading sites and talking with local people who can share stories about railroading. When the two friends get together to "trade notes" on their endeavors, they find that they have uncovered much the same information. The main difference is that the friend who took courses and read about the topic spent considerably less time and money than the other friend. What might happen if the first person sought to intervene and "help" the other person become "more efficient" as a learner. From the viewpoint of an adult educator, it would be easy to conclude that since the former approach was more efficient, it is likely to also be more successful. To take this view, however, would be very shortsighted, since it fails to take into consideration the different motives of each person for undertaking the learning project.

In looking at this situation from an "outside" perspective we may be inclined to conclude that the person who chose the more "formal" route was more "successful" than the individual who chose to visit sites and talk informally with people about railroading. And, indeed, if success is defined as efficiency, such an assessment would be accurate.

However, it is important to bear in mind that adults engage in learning for a variety of reasons. For some, success is measured in terms of outcomes derived from the experience. On the other hand, there are many individuals who find joy in the *process* of learning. The person who visited railroading sites built family vacations around such travel so that everyone could find some joy in the "process" being used. For these individuals, the joy comes not so much from *what* is learned as from *how* it is learned.

The dilemma for us as adult educators, in such cases, arises from our zeal to help learners become more effective in the learning process. By stressing the importance of efficiency to the exclusion of other possible motives for learning, we run the risk of turning off learners who were already doing quite well without our "assistance," regardless of how well-intentioned that assistance was. Sometimes, we need to tread lightly when working with self-directed learners and recognize that, at times, we can do more harm than good in our educational intervention, despite our best intentions.

Are there situations where facilitators can compromise quality of a learning experience through inappropriate use of self-directed learning strategies?

With the increasing emphasis on self-direction in adult learning, it is crucial that practitioners understand what the concept means. We have tried to clarify some of the confusion surrounding the idea in previous chapters; yet this is only a beginning. Another ethical issue can arise when an educator who misunderstands the complexity of self-direction attempts to jump on the bandwagon without first reflecting on the consequences of such actions.

Among the myths presented in Chapter 1 is the idea that self-direction is an "easy way out" for instructors. This can be illustrated by the instructor who walks into class with little or no advanced planning and asks students "OK, now, what do you want to do in this class?" In our view, this is *not* a case of facilitating self-direction; in fact, we are inclined to call this approach "non-directed learning. "

In reality, as was stressed in Chapter 6, facilitating self-directed learning is a very demanding and active role. We are convinced, in fact, that it is even more demanding than the more traditional adult teaching role. Why? Because, in addition to having an understanding of the content area, a facilitator of self-directed learning must get to know each learner and be able to help them to develop and explore personal interest areas. So instead of working with ten people who are all doing the same activities at the same pace, the facilitator of self-directed learning may end up working with ten people each with very different needs and interests and only a minimal level of common interest.

It should be clear that there is a very fine line between promoting self-direction and non-direction. We believe that the successful facilitator of self-directed learning needs to assume a proactive role in working with learners. There is, too, much to be lost if this is not done.

To what extent can institutions realistically promote self-direction in learning?

One of the most pervasive problems encountered when implementing opportunities for self-direction can arise when institutions are faced with the often delicate balance between encouraging individual autonomy and learner options while maintaining adherence to existing policies and procedures. For both of us, as faculty members in graduate programs of adult education, this dilemma has been particularly thorny. On the one hand, we are deeply committed to implementing the values and practices described throughout the previous chapters of this book. At the same time, however, we are fully aware of the roles and responsibilities we have undertaken by accepting positions within our particular institutions of higher education. Such policies as assigning grades for coursework, adhering to an academic calendar, and setting and maintaining requirements for admission to and completion of the graduate program would seem to run contrary to the more "free spirited" ideals that seem a part of self-direction in learning.

For us, the resolution of this dilemma comes through understanding the first myth presented in Chapter 1. By viewing self-direction as a continuum, one could argue that all learning activities and institutional settings more or less promote, encourage, or allow a certain degree of self-direction. In this view, the question is not, "Can self-direction in learning exist within an institutional setting?" but, rather, "To what *extent* can self-direction exist within the institution? ".

The ethical dilemma arises when instructors/facilitators fail to acknowledge this question of degree. It is misleading to say that a course will be a "self-directed learning experience" and then spell out specific course requirements and grading policies. Indeed, we believe that much of the skepticism that exists about self-direction in adult learning is due more to the ways in which it is sometimes misused than to the underlying principles of self-direction themselves. Thus, the ethical concern arises when the learning experience is not what individuals were led to believe it would be.

One way to minimize this potential dilemma is for an instructor to be open with learners from the outset. We typically do this by telling learners in our classes that it is our goal to provide an environment that will foster "greater" opportunities for self-direction, and that we will support a wide range of options that will allow individuals to pursue personally identified goals and objectives. At the same time, we openly acknowledge the parameters within which we are operating (and, in fact, have agreed to operate within as employees and students of our particular institution). By taking this approach, we can ethically state that we are helping learners work toward *greater* self-direction while not misleading them by claiming the course to be entirely self-directed.

To what extent is self-direction in learning a panacea?

The current wave of interest in the idea of self-direction in learning is an outgrowth of the 1970s, which carried over to the 1980s and promises to continue into the 1990s. The concept seems to coincide with notions associated with the "me generation" and to an obsession with "finding oneself" and "being all one can be." Thus, one might criticize the entire self-direction movement as merely a way of popularizing hedonism. However, as we have stressed throughout the book, self-direction is not just another adult education fad; it is a way of life that fits very naturally with how people go about the task of learning new things in order to deal with the challenges of adult life, including the improvement of society, as well as personal growth and enrichment.

Nonetheless, the idea of self-direction remains very seductive and marketable. Of course, there is nothing wrong with marketing the idea of self-direction in and of itself. Indeed, marketing can be viewed as responding to the identified needs of adult learners. At the same time, when self-direction is viewed as a "quick fix" or a "cure all" merely because it "sells," then we should become concerned. We need to bear in mind a very basic principle: our priority as educators of adults is to serve the learner. Where self-direction best serves the learner (and we would stress that this is the case more often than not), the approach should be utilized and promoted actively. But it should not be used merely because it sells.

CONCLUSION

Self-direction holds virtually unlimited potential as a strategy for enhancing the success of adult learners. As such, it also holds unlimited potential for expanding the growth of the adult education field. As will be discussed in Chapter 13, it is up to us, as educators of adults, to create the kind of future we desire for our field. In working to promote self-directed learning and learner self-direction, the future can be bright indeed. But it is crucial that we make a deliberate effort to ask questions about the ways in which this enthusiasm has the potential to be displaced. To not address potential ethical issues relative to self-direction in adult learning would be short-sighted and, ultimately, could have serious consequences for our potential, as educators, for success with adult learners.

Part V

A glance at the future

The final part consists of two chapters designed to facilitate some thinking about the future for self-direction in learning. Chapter 12, A Way of Life Revisited, describes the activities in one day for members of a fictional family in the year 2005. In many ways, we may have been even conservative in thinking about all the ways our lives will be affected during the next 15 years. Certainly technology will play a part in promoting many changes, but the point of the chapter is to describe how we believe learning, most of it self-directed in nature, will become built into most fabrics of our daily living. The final chapter, 13, presents some conclusions and recommendations derived from the previous chapters. For example, we believe an important role for adult educators must become that of promoting self-direction in learning among all adults. We also present several recommendations related to theory, research, and practice.

12 A way of life revisited

Mary, Neal, and Alice in Chapter 1 represented real people in today's world who have learned to utilize self-direction in learning as a means to cope with life and its many challenges. However, we think the future holds even more challenges and anticipate that increasing numbers of people will find self-directed learning activities crucial for survival in a world of ever-increasing change. Thus we would like to introduce the Hammond family, five people who find themselves, in the year 2005, employing self-direction in many of their daily learning efforts. Join us in observing a day in the life of the Hammonds.

George Hammond-Treska is 45 years of age with a doctoral degree in educational psychology. He is an adjunct professor at the local university, operates a consulting service that concentrates on middle-management recruiting, training, and counseling, and is an avid electronics hobbyist. He generally operates the consulting service alone, although he has several colleagues he can call on for specific needs. George has been a computer technology enthusiast since the late 1980s and owns two personal computers, an optical scanning system, and a laser transmitter for long-distance communication.

Greta Treska-Hammond is 43, has a masters degree in social work, and since 1999 has been the director of the local educational brokering service. She has taken special courses in small-group therapy for the past 3 years, belongs to two national learning networks, and tries to keeps her hand in the local peace network, an organization devoted to maintaining the world-wide nuclear freeze achieved in 1998 after the Euro-Baltic missile scare. She does not regret the 12 years of her life devoted to being the major care-giver for the two children, but continues to be surprised at the difficulties she now confronts in meshing a full-time career with supporting two older teens.

Julie is a vivacious 19-year-old who has just started her second year at the New Jersey Open University. She spent the summer in Spain in a United Nations Study and Volunteer Program where she studied advanced Spanish, helped tutor Chilean refugees, and enhanced her weaving skills. She had commented in August to her parents that the Westville Alternative High School had prepared her well for both tutoring and weaving, although sitting in a weaving class with several others was quite different from her tri-video instructional kits in that she received quicker feedback on her skills.

Stan is a muscular young man of 17 who is in his junior year of high school at the First Westville Preparatory School. Taller than his father by a full 6 inches, Stan just found out he made the varsity on the robo-ball team, a new sport that has taken the country by storm in the past few years. He will be playing halfwing on offense and robo-tech on defense. Stan was worried that he might not make the team because he spent his interim year apprenticing on the moon's Star-III colony, but steady work with the anti-grav equipment apparently paid off. In addition, he only had to spend one week in the SEAT center (Star/Earth Adjustment and Training) upon his return so the extra workouts he did during July and August helped as well.

Bill Hammond, George's father, is a healthy 73 years of age. George had been Bill and Wilma's last child. Wilma's death in 1969 of cancer resulted in Bill and George having a closer relationship than many fathers and sons, so when Bill retired in 1996, George and Greta had another bedroom built and would not hear of Bill moving anywhere else but into their Trenton home. The symbiosis had been fruitful in many ways. Bill, who loves to tinker, has left everything around the house in tip top condition; George and Greta's culinary skills have provided Bill with many wonderful meals. Fortunately, the anti-weight-gain and cholesterol-reducing drugs of the past few years have helped him control his weight.

So here we have a fairly normal family of the year 2005. As a matter of fact, an annual census would find the Hammond household just about mid-center in terms of American statistics in this time of dependency on electronic technology: one registered Republican, one registered Democrat, and three declared independents; four automobiles and one commuter helicopter; an average family income from two wage earners of $300,000 per year; a house of 3,300 square feet containing 4.5 bathrooms, an intercom system with speakers in every room, six radios, one large screen video receiver and playback system, one 3-D videx receiver, one fax machine, six video-phones, one optical scanning system with both audio and digital readers, five mini-computer systems, two laser printers, one dot-matrix multi-font printer and a print spooler, one laser transmitter, two electronic-mail and data-retrieval systems, two robo-cleaners, and one combination upload and download satellite transmitter system. Now that we have a picture of this middle-America family, let us follow them on a particular Monday.

6.00 a.m. George, Greta, and Stan rise. George does his stretching exercises, grabs a glass of water, gets in the car and heads for the Sunup Club for 80 minutes of exercising. Greta does her stretching exercises and starts out the door for her typical 6-mile run with a group of neighbors. Stan ambles over to the newly acquired home exo-arobo machine and programs in the 20-minute physio-total sequence.

6.45 a.m. Stan finishes his shower, grabs a frozen breakfast for the car's microwave, and starts off for his 30-minute commute to First Westville Prep.

7.00 a.m. Bill wakes, contemplates resetting the alarm for another hour, but remembers his important 9.00 appointment at the senior center. So he gets up, does his normal 12 minutes on the McKenzie plan, and heads out the door for his 45-minute walk.

7.15 a.m. Greta returns, showers, gets dressed and sits down to a breakfast of amni-biotic flakes, milk, and fruit-bits. She turns on the Neuter-Rotandnews and begins to read the articles scrolling on the screen in front of her. A piece on the revival of the old National Training Laboratory catches her eye, she requests a hard copy, checks the spooler menu to make sure there is an open slot on one of the laser printers, and hears with quiet satisfaction the humming of the machine as the downloading begins. She walks over to the scanner's audio reader, puts in the audio tape she dictated yesterday on her way home, and begins to read the material as it pops up on the screen.

7.30 a.m. Stan arrives at First Prep and ambles into the daily assignment center. He punches in his ID and password and receives some suggestions from his psychology mentor for some readings he might try. There also is a request from the microbiology study group leader that all members convene for a seminar at 10.00 a.m. He audio-inputs his affirmative response and heads for the library to do some reading before the meeting.

7.40 a.m. George returns, wolfs down an applo-fiber, a glass of lacto-milk, and a cup of that new mufti herb tea Stan brought back from the moon colony. He then fires up the BIS internet and reads his electronic mail accumulated since last night. He responds to three important messages, uploads a file on management counseling to one of his consultants living in California, and downloads a copy of the latest issue of *Socio-Psych News* for reading later in the day. He picks up his new clipboard mini-computer, presses the corner latch, and lifts up the lipto-laser display panel to reveal the touchpad keyboard. After a check to see how much memory is left in the Datamold Field Mini-computer's three-megabyte bubble field, he thinks about how he will pursue mastery of the new on-line conferencing techniques for one-on-one counseling developed by his professional association.

8.00 a.m. Bill finishes his shower, gets dressed, and ambles over to his mini-fridge for a usual breakfast of old-fashioned corn flakes and 2 percent milk. After rinsing his dishes, he walks out to the car for the 30-minute drive to the senior center. As he drives he considers what his answer will be to the center director's request that he teach a woodworking course to center members. He never taught before, but has often thought about it.

8.05 a.m.   Greta picks up her briefcase, pops into George's study and gives him a kiss goodbye, checks the electronic sensor to see if Bill is still in his room and then says goodbye to him through the intercom, types out a quick message to both Stan and Julie, and uploads the messages to their electronic mailboxes. She then ambles out to the helicopter, HELEN (Helo-ELectronic-Energy Network), hears its quiet hum as she turns on the network system, and lifts off for the quick commute to her office.

8.30 a.m.   Meanwhile, in that exciting new community under the dome, West Brunswick, Julie wakes and goes through her normal routine of aerobics, jacuzzi-spray showering, and breakfasting on egg whites, juice, and cellulose with high-iron toast (what Stan always laughingly calls that "sawdust and rust" bread). She also gives Annie, her friend in Miami, a call on the video-phone and they critique each other's new haircuts for a while.

9.15 a.m.   George connects to the laser transmission satellite, uploads the graphics needed for today's class, and checks his mini-lecture notes. As soon as he receives the class-connect signal, he begins to talk about learning contracts with his class of graduate students in psychology. He describes the various kinds of learning contracts, holds up examples for students to see, and tells them how to download copies of any of those they choose. He answers an important question from Thabo Bolatto in Capetown and another one from Hilda Correro in Mexico City. He then announces the on-line study group assignments, asks the groups to work on the model-building assignment and to discuss their preferences for either group or individual learning contracts, and reminds students how to contact him on-line for both interactive and delayed communications. Assuring himself that all questions have been answered and the assignment made clear, he signs off the satellite, sends a report to the central administration data bank, and begins checking his electronic mail for any new messages.

9.45 a.m.   Greta finishes a meeting with a client, dictates a quick note via the Newfair Lipto-neutron network her organization time-shares, and heads out to catch the subway across town for the weekly tele-conference meeting of the Africa-to-America learning exchange network on small group techniques. She checks her briefcase to make sure her notes are there, as well as the micro-diskette on which she has stored the three files to be uploaded to all participants at the beginning of the meeting.

10.00 a.m. Julie heads to the West Brunswick Interactive Museum to work with a family of low-grav monkeys being groomed for life on the Star colonies. Her Open University course on anthropology requires this hands-on experience plus a term paper she has been painfully dictating into the laser steno each evening.

11.15 a.m. Bill pulls into the central library parking lot. He walks into the lobby and up to the on-line catalogue that he has used so much in the past few years. He keys in a few boolean-based commands centered on the subject of teaching adults and watches the resulting "hits" scroll on the screen. He selects several possibilities and requests a hard-copy printout. As he heads for the stacks to look at whatever he can find on his list, he muses again about George's suggestion that he learn to use the electro-library software on one of the home computer systems. However, he recognizes that he would miss searching for real books on his own.

11.30 a.m. As soon as the study group session is over, Stan heads for the student center to have a lunch of syntho-burgers and real fries with Cindy. He remembers to drop off his chemistry assignment that he had completed last night. He finds Cindy at the front of the building and they head for the cafeteria's food line.

12.30 p.m. Greta heads to the conservatory two blocks from the tele-conference site to take her weekly lesson on the electro-organ. Her lifelong love for music has not dampened from her early days of piano and trumpet lessons and she finds the discipline of nightly practice to be quite rewarding. As she walks, she reaches in her purse for a laser-dry lunch wafer, reminding herself to grab a non-caffeine soda from the vendor in front of the conservatory.

12.45 p.m. George pops a frozen dinner in the laser-wave, pours a glass of milk, and pulls out the steaming dish. As he eats the synthetic meat dish, getting used to the taste now that real meat is almost impossible to get, he puts on a headset and lets the theta wave stabilizer clear out the cobwebs. He remembers that he needs to use the SCALE (Super Computer Analog Library Educer) to research and extract some new management conclusions before tomorrow's training session with those clinical psychologists from Asia and Africa.

1.00 p.m. Meanwhile, Julie finishes her lunch of sprouts and fruit and heads for her study group on the cultural history of the Aztecs during the late 1400s. On Friday, they had observed some construction activity during their retrogressive scanning probe and were nearing an ability to record some supporting data for their hypothesis that the Aztecs had actually invented a form of electrical transmission. Today she hoped they could refine the picture, at least on the small scope, so that it could be recorded and translated by the Newfair 4792 lipto-neutron parallel architecture-based computer on which they had leased space.

2.15 p.m. After a lunch of synthetic pork chops, carrots, green beans, and coffee, Bill checks the pneumatic mail tube to see if any information has arrived on the elderhostel in Denmark he will be participating in next month. Finding only a copy of his *Self-Directed Learners Guide*, he heads for his room carrying the dozen books he checked out on teaching adults. Having decided to teach a woodworking class, he follows his customary plan of attack in learning about a subject, knowing that he will be as prepared as possible when the class starts next month. Whoever said that retirement would be boring!

4.00 p.m. Greta finishes training her new triad leaders and provides each with a list of their lifelong learning case groups. She then fires up the desktop computer in her office and contacts the LID (Learning Information Database) system in San Jose, California, to see if any new learning exchange groups or free university organizations have been started in her area.

4.15 p.m. Stan heads for the locker room to get dressed for robo-ball practice. He is still thinking about the French class he has just completed and the earlier discussion that emanated from his debriefing group regarding the Star-III experience. The mentors had urged each member to consider astro-physics as a career, but he is not sure. He still thinks a lot about a career as a professional robo-ball player, but has not discussed it with Mom and Dad recently. Perhaps he should take up that offer from Pete Marley of the New York Titans and spend a few weeks working with the team during their spring training.

4.30 p.m. George and Bill head for the basement shop to continue work on their experimental motor. George's skill in computers and Bill's experience with piston-driven motors have convinced them that they can build a better motor for the old rider-mower Bill had brought with him when he sold the house. Bill would like to adapt one of the robo-cleaners for mowing the lawn and George has accepted the challenge of redesigning the computer networks to operate the system. The video version of the *Electronics Encyclopedia* is already scrolling on the screen in front of them.

5.00 p.m. Although the study group had not been able to find the same construction site because the satellite position had changed and they did not have the new site coordinates, Julie thought they had made nice progress in the refinement scan. The etched lines on the face of the woman carrying the water were so powerfully shown that Julie had decided to use the hard copy printout as the basis for her next art project. As she entered the studio of her water-colors mentor, she began to think about how to convince him that she could combine her electronic pictures with his somewhat archaic approach: using hand brush strokes.

6.30 p.m. Greta finishes her last report for the day, files a copy electronically, and requests the software to archive a hard copy in the Trenton central office. She walks to the "chopper" as Bill fondly calls it, heads for home wondering what George has prepared for the evening meal, and looks forward to some conversation with the men in her life and, later, relaxation with the electro-organ. Fortunately, tonight she has no office work to catch up on. She might even have an opportunity to do some reading for pleasure.

6.45 p.m. George heads to the kitchen and pulls out several containers from the proto-freezer. He decided that they will eat Mexican food that evening, and he busies himself with setting the table, chilling the wine, programming the robo-cleaner for a quick run-through of the dining room, and checking the electronic mail while the food cooks in the standard oven and laser-wave. He then decides to give his brother, Charley, a call on the video-phone to see if he would like a game of astro-golf on the weekend.

7.30 p.m. Stan rushes in, says a quick "hi" to everyone, gobbles down an enchilada and taco, still warm on the dining room table. He punches in a ticket request for himself and Cindy at the downtown holograph-movie, gets a confirm signal, and waves goodbye to everyone. He announces that he will be in by his midnight curfew. As the dust settles, Greta sighs and says, "Was that a tornado or what that just went through here? "

8.00 p.m. Having read her Mom's plea for a phone call, Julie gives the folks a ring on the video-phone and chats with Mom, Dad, and Gramps. Mom liked her hair, Dad did not comment, and Gramps wondered if it was perhaps too short. She asks Mom to send her that file on minority groups and color preferences that the Euro-Americas Learning Network pulled together, noting that it would be useful for the paper she was writing for her socio-ethno course. Julie then gets ready for a fun evening at the laso-disco with Betty, Pablo, and Rhyne.

11.30 p.m. George, Greta, and Bill finish watching the TBS evening news. George mentions that Jane Edwards looks better than ever, especially since their holographic fine-tuner was repaired, and that he appreciated the network's decision to run a half hour of national news prior to the late show. Greta and George decide to head off to bed and Bill says he will indulge his addiction to Jake Burrows and the New Night show. "Tonight Jake is interviewing Helen Weaver regarding her sponsorship of the Lifelong Learning Bill and I want to see how he turns that into something humorous," Bill exclaims.

We are going to leave Greta, George, Bill, Julie, and Stan to their almost frantic rush into the future. They do appear to have things under control, though. Is the story of their lives only fiction or is it possible? Obviously, it comes out of our imagination, but we believe the future will be something like this for us, for our children, and for our grandchildren if we want it to be. It is only necessary to do a little extrapolation from today's technology and thinking to come up with what we have forecasted. In many ways, we have even been conservative about what is possible and even probable.

There is no question in our minds, assuming we can avoid worldwide calamities such as nuclear war and ozone layer depletion, that technological innovations will continue to amaze us and make life easier or at least very interesting. Obviously, we will have to continuously learn to cope with the changes. Lifelong, self-directed learning skills will be even more necessary than today.

The Hammond family used many technological gadgets for their ongoing learning endeavors, as well as for their day-to-day activities. Reading and accessing information in their world took on a much different flavor than what we may be used to, but our current world of microform readers, electronic messaging, fax machines, and interactive video seem natural precursors to what the Hammonds took for granted each day. We, for example, were in constant, almost daily, communication via email (electronic mail) throughout the writing of this book. Collectively, we communicate weekly with dozens of adult education colleagues throughout North America as well as in many other parts of the world. This "instant" communication has enlarged our worlds and facilitated learning in a way neither of us could have predicted only a decade ago when we first became colleagues.

Many technological innovations also are evolving as devices for facilitating self-direction in learning. Just as the Hammonds were involved in various forms of computer-mediated learning or electronic networking, many of us working today with the education of adults use similar, although comparatively primitive, resources. Just think how exciting it will be when that retrogressive scanning probe system is developed. We can go back and view Lindeman first writing the word "andragogy" (Brookfield, 1984b) or perhaps even Benjamin Franklin's first Junto meeting.

The Hammonds also employed a variety of learning techniques each day. Independent study, contract learning, learning-exchange networks, study groups, traditional classes, internships, and just plain old reading a book all appeared to be part of each family member's attempts to cope with the requirements of daily living. One of the messages we hope we have conveyed in this book is that all such techniques are viable for people of all ages if employed in caring, facilitative ways. In fact, for the Hammonds, lifelong and self-directed learning skills were integral to their daily lives.

One of the messages we also want to portray using the Hammond family is that lifelong physical exercise, good eating habits, and obvious medical advances – the precursors of which are in place today – are likely to produce healthy people with good minds who normally will live long and fruitful lives. As a matter of fact, we could easily have introduced great grandmother or grandfather Hammond into the story and described a healthy, vibrant person. Bill's learning throughout life will become increasingly more viable, we believe, and will continually produce challenges for those of us desiring to promote effective experiences and resources for the self-directed learner.

The story of the Hammonds also revealed that a variety of "communities" can be expected in the future. From Julie's West Brunswick to Greta's learning exchange groups to George's worldwide electronic classroom, the concept of interrelationships with corresponding impacts on learning must be addressed by us as we move toward the future. No doubt, most of us have already experienced a widening of our community bases and can recognize the implications for learning, information exchange, and forming new relationships.

As we move toward the type of future described in this chapter – and we are optimistic that this will happen – important decisions must be made by leaders at various levels of society. Political leaders must find ways of solving crucial problems, such as growing numbers of homeless, environmental hazards, and drug abuse. Educational leaders must solve problems of illiteracy, inadequate learning resources, and constantly rising costs. Those of us in the trenches must find means to meet ever-increasing learning needs, continue to carry out research on educational issues, and keep ourselves up to date with ever-growing knowledge. We hope that this book will contribute some encouragement to the efforts by many concerned educators of adults who strive every day to help solve local, national, and international problems. In the concluding chapter we will provide some ideas and recommendations that we hope will lead to some solutions.

13 Conclusions and recommendations

As we have stressed throughout the previous chapters, self-direction in learning is not merely a current fad. Rather, it is an idea that is clearly rooted in history. In our view, the idea of self-direction, where individuals assume personal responsibility for their learning, will continue to thrive as we move toward the year 2000 and beyond. As adult educators, each of us needs to take an active role in creating this future. This can be viewed in the following way:

> Regardless of the roles assumed in subsequent years, skill in projecting the future should be helpful, because then it is possible to work toward that future and even create the situations we desire. However, ongoing study to understand both the changes we experience and those we create will always be necessary.
>
> (Hiemstra, 1987b: 11–12)

The intent of this book has thus been to stimulate readers' thinking relative to self-direction, with the hope and expectation of helping to create a future where individual initiative by learners is not only rewarded, but is also expected as a means for personal growth. We also anticipate that our thoughts will stimulate some of the ongoing study, reflection, and action necessary for the promotion of self-direction in adult learning.

The Personal Responsibility Orientation (PRO) model, which was presented in Chapter 2, was designed not as a "theory" of self-direction *per se*, but rather to demonstrate some of our own reflections on the growing body of related knowledge. We view the model as a paradigm that may assist both practitioners and scholars in efforts to create greater understanding of, and activity related to, self-direction in adult learning. In subsequent chapters, we demonstrated various aspects of the PRO model, and from these chapters we can identify at least eight key ideas that should help promote better understanding of the concept:

1 The research base on self-direction has grown steadily over the years. We are confident that researchers will continue to build on this base to advance knowledge of self-direction even further;
2 Essential to success in facilitating self-directed learning is the need to help learners assume greater responsibility for the process. We believe that learners are capable of assuming increasing degrees of responsibility for their learning;
3 Self-direction is rooted in the belief that human potential is unlimited. We are convinced that educators of adults can play a role in helping learners more fully realize this potential;
4 The community provides an array of resources that self-directed learners can utilize. Our view is that an understanding of the community is important because it is the social context for self-direction in learning;
5 Educators of adults can use what is known about self-direction to encourage the development of relevant policies at institutional, local, state, and national levels;
6 Those who wish to work with self-directed learners need to understand the learning environment and the many kinds of resources that can be used to facilitate self-direction;
7 We know that self-direction in learning is not exclusive to a single culture or class of people. At the same time, we recognize the need to understand and respect cross-cultural differences that may impact upon the desirability of self-direction in certain contexts; and
8 Because of the highly personal nature of self-direction, the potential for ethical conflict clearly exists whenever intervention takes place. In our view, it is crucial for educators of adults to recognize the potential for this conflict and be diligent in minimizing any negative results.

We believe the PRO model offers some ideas that can assist educators in various ways related to these themes.

CREATING GREATER AWARENESS OF SELF-DIRECTION

In looking to the future of self-direction in adult learning, perhaps one of the most important considerations for educators will be how to create greater awareness of, and support for, the idea of self-direction within society. In Chapter 8, for example, we addressed some of the barriers within the institutional context that often limit opportunities for self-direction. It is our belief that if self-direction is truly to be recognized as a way of life, there are at least two key roles for educators of adults. One role will be to provide advocacy for learners who wish to assume responsibility for their own learning. A second role is to promote the concept of self-direction in learning throughout society as a strategy for successful human development.

Further, we believe that self-direction is very much in tune with the natural way that people live and learn. Yet institutions often lose this perspective, becoming set in their traditional policies, procedures, and philosophies, which in turn lead to a "this is the way we've always done it" or "if it ain't broke, don't fix it" way of thinking. However, we believe self-direction options need not necessarily compromise quality within the institution (Brockett, 1988a).

As we noted in Chapter 2, the assumptions underlying self-direction derive from a variety of philosophical perspectives. Educators who work with self-directed learners need to understand these assumptions and how their own philosophies are similar to, or different from, these assumptions. This is where the importance of developing and articulating one's personal philosophy becomes so important (Hiemstra, 1988b). There is no single "theory" of self-direction in learning; yet, there *are* some key assumptions that are essential to the support and promotion of the idea.

From our perspective, there is a need to carry out the advocacy function both within and outside of the adult education field. Within the field, courses and workshops provide a good arena in which to advocate for self-direction. In recent years, we have conducted a combined total of six credit-bearing graduate courses and numerous non-credit workshops and conference presentations directly related to self-directed learning. For us, the ideas exchanged in such activities have played an important role in advancing knowledge about self-directed learning concepts, approaches, and problems. Several publications have resulted from these efforts (Hiemstra, 1980, 1982b, 1985c) and we believe that we have a much clearer understanding of this area than would have been possible in any other manner. Thus, these efforts have served us well in our role as advocates for self-direction.

In the classroom we have experimented with various means of employing self-directed approaches with adult learners. Although this has been an evolutionary development of our own personal teaching styles, the feedback we constantly receive from learners indicates that we have developed the means for learners to maximize their abilities to take responsibility for their learning. We also have shared our accumulating knowledge about applying self-directed concepts with colleagues through loaning course materials, supporting advanced doctoral students in co-teaching activities, and engaging in oral discussions of the approaches with colleagues interested in making changes.

As another example of our own advocacy effort, we have attempted to contribute to the literature of self-direction in numerous ways. Between us, we have published separately or jointly over twenty-five journal articles, monographs, book chapters, and conference papers on the subject. These publications, combined with chairing a large number of related dissertations and theses, and numerous discussions with informal networks of colleagues throughout the field who share an interest in this area, have led us toward a growing knowledge of the ideas discussed in this book and have served to reinforce our own commitment to the study and practice of self-direction in adult learning. We hope, too, that the ideas presented here can stimulate others in the field to share our continued enthusiasm.

Outside the field of adult education there is a constant need to demonstrate to professional colleagues in education, higher education administrators, and, indeed, society in general, that self-direction in learning has tremendous importance for helping adult learners realize their potential. For example, some critics from outside the field of adult education suggest that the quality of the learning experience will be compromised if educators, content specialists, or institutions do not retain major control of teaching and learning decisions.

There is thus a heavy demand on adult educators to demonstrate that quality can be maintained. We have discussed this issue to some extent in Chapter 1 but it is useful to refer once again to the work of Knowles and Associates (1984). They have shown the wide applicability of self-directed learning principles in an array of settings, including business and industry, government, higher education, public schools, religious institutions, and health-related settings. These illustrations consistently show that when efforts are made carefully to monitor quality issues, self-direction proves to be an effective approach to learning within various institutional contexts.

As we have stressed throughout the book, we are convinced that further understanding of, and commitment to, the ideals of self-direction in learning are vital to the adult education field if we are to facilitate development of the human potential more fully. In the following section, we offer a number of recommendations, gleaned from ideas presented in the previous chapters, that we believe are important in the future development of theory, research, and practice relative to self-direction in adult learning.

RECOMMENDATIONS FOR THE FUTURE

How might adult educators work toward further development and refinement in the area of self-direction? The previous chapters have offered perspectives on the development and current status of self-direction relative to theory, research, and practice. In this section, we would like to offer a number of recommendations relative to each of these areas in the hope that they may stimulate questions and experimentation with new ideas designed to ensure that the phenomenon of self-direction in learning will continue to be a way of life for years to come.

Recommendations for theory

The PRO model should be subjected to critical scrutiny by the adult education field

Our intent in developing the PRO model was not to offer a formal theory of self-direction in adult learning. Rather, the model was designed to clarify what we believe to be some of the conceptual confusion about self-directed learning and related terms. It is also our way of helping to make distinctions between characteristics of the teaching/learning transaction and individual learner characteristics. However, we recognize that this is at a basic conceptual level, so we welcome critical scrutiny of the concept. In this way, we envision the PRO model evolving over time, much in the way that Knowles has refined his ideas about andragogy and pedagogy.

There is a need for further understanding of the social context in which self-direction exists

Because self-directed learning rarely takes place in total isolation, understanding of the social setting becomes especially important. Discussion of the various factors that can limit participation and success in self-directed learning efforts is only one way of approaching an understanding of social settings. We believe there is room for considerable theoretical work on other social aspects such as those introduced in Chapter Ten on the global dimension of self-direction.

The political dimension of self-direction continues to be largely overlooked by adult educators and this needs to be remedied

One of the major criticisms of the work in self-directed learning identified by authors such as Brookfield (1984c, 1988) is that it has largely ignored the political contexts in which learning occurs. While the PRO model begins to address some of these concerns, we recognize that much theoretical development is still needed. For instance, we believe that the notion of empowerment, as reflected in the work of such educators as Freire (1970) and institutions such as Highlander (Adams, 1975), are closely tied to the ideas of self-direction. While we recognize that the PRO model may be at odds with those who view society rather than the individual as the point of departure for adult education, we also recognize that this dimension needs to be considered in much greater depth than has been the case to date.

Recommendations for research

Self-direction in learning should continue to evolve as one of the major research directions in the field of adult education

While some would suggest that self-direction has been studied extensively, and thus it is time to move on to other areas, we believe that it is crucial for work in this area to continue and, in fact, to be expanded even further. A major limitation of adult education research to date has been a failure to develop *sustained* research agendas in key areas. Research on self-direction has laid an important foundation for our understanding of this area. Still, much work remains to be done. We are convinced of the need for such continued research because (a) we are just beginning to unlock some very important doors to knowledge and, without further progress, some doors will remain unopened, and (b) because of the work in the area to date, continued research on self-direction can add to the "credibility" and understanding of the completed studies.

Future researchers should continue to approach the study of self-direction using a variety of research methodologies

Perhaps one of the major contributions of research to date on self-direction has been the realization that what we know about this area has emerged through a variety of research methods. By looking at self-direction from several research perspectives, it has been possible to construct a picture of the landscape with much more depth than would be possible by only looking at the area through a single paradigm. We believe that there can be no single "best" way to study self-direction, and that a key for future research development will be the ability to look at research problems in innovative ways.

In addition to continued work with correlational, quasi-experimental, and qualitative designs, we recommend the development of historical and philosophical investigations to further support the conceptual base of self-direction. Also, we see potential for directing research toward a host of policy questions, such as many of those addressed in Chapter 9.

There is a continuing need for the refinement of existing measures of self-direction and the development of alternative instruments

While there have been various criticisms of the primary instruments used to measure self-direction to date (and both of us have at times been among the critics), we applaud the work of Guglielmino and Oddi, for despite limitations that have been reported relative to the Self-Directed Learning Readiness Scale (SDLRS) and the Oddi Continuing Learning Inventory (OCLI), without these instruments, and without the willingness of the developers of these measures to take on such a task, our knowledge of self-direction in adult learning would be set back at least a decade. As a future research direction, we recommend that efforts be made to refine existing measures in response to limitations as they are identified. One approach might be the development of alternate forms of the instruments, such as the new version of the SDLRS developed by Guglielmino for adults with low literacy levels.

Another possibility might be the development of new measures of self-direction, based on emerging views of the concept. For instance, it might be possible to use the PRO Model as a theoretical basis for such an instrument.

There is a need for research on the roles and functions of institutions relative to self-direction in adult learning

What kind of role can or should institutions play in support of self-direction in adult learning? How can institutions foster greater self-direction among learners? Are there ways to provide better resources and to address barriers to self-direction? Questions such as these are relevant, not only within colleges and universities, but also within non-higher education institutions such as corporate training departments, health and human service programs, adult basic education programs, and voluntary agencies.

An understanding of the role of the instructor is important

In other publications (e.g., Brockett and Hiemstra, 1985) and in earlier chapters, we have discussed the role of the instructor from a practice perspective. There is also a need to explore this role from a research perspective. Some relevant questions may include the following: What are the major responsibilities of the facilitator? How do such factors as teaching style, interpersonal trust, rational thinking, cross-cultural awareness, and personality influence one's ability to be an effective facilitator of self-direction?

Cross-cultural research could help to provide a better understanding of certain social and political aspects of self-direction

As we have tried to stress throughout the book, it is crucial to understand the interface between self-direction and the social context in which one is operating. There is ample evidence that self-direction is much more than a "middle-class, white" phenomenon. Yet it would be equally short-sighted to go to the other extreme and suggest that the ideas underlying self-direction in adult learning are universally valued by all cultures. Research that approaches self-direction from a cross-cultural perspective could provide some important insights in this regard.

It is important to build bridges from research to practice

Research, in our view, lies at the core of future developments in self-direction. Yet, the ultimate value of this research depends on how it eventually can be tied to improved practice. This is not to suggest that every research study must have immediate and direct application to practice. Rather, we would argue that what is needed are three types of researchers: (a) those who conduct *basic* research aimed at expanding the knowledge base of self-direction; (b) those who conduct *applied* research such as evaluation studies, which have direct implications for specific programs and practices; and (c) those who attempt to *synthesize* the research in such a way that it is possible to draw implications and conclusions from the "big picture" of research. In large measure, this latter emphasis has been our attempt with this book.

Recommendations for practice

There is a continuing need to promote the use of learning contracts

As we noted in Chapter 6, learning contracts make it possible to individualize the teaching-learning process. This device brings about a multitude of possibilities for meeting learners' needs, provides for a variety of outlets for evaluating learners' experiences, and aids planning by eliciting choices about scheduling, resources, learning strategies, and outcomes. It even permits a very structured route through a learning experience for those who desire such structure.

From our experience in more formal settings, it is also very important that any communication between the learner and facilitator be clear. We believe contracts are an ideal means for promoting such clarity. We would suggest, too, that contracts are useful mechanisms to aid people in planning their learning outside of the formal institutional setting. In other words, such a device becomes a personal tool for thinking about goals, identifying resources, facilitating time management, and building commitment to complete learning endeavors.

It is important to help learners identify and utilize a variety of resources

Much of the research cited in earlier chapters about adults' learning projects and learning activities has consistently shown that self-directed learners use a wide variety of resources. Thus, as facilitators aid learners in becoming comfortable and more proficient with self-directed activities, it is crucial that help in locating and using resources be provided. Facilitators can provide reading lists, locate available learning materials, and collect a variety of institutional or instructor-owned materials for loan to learners. They can also guide learners in identifying support services in the local community. Chapter 8 provided several ideas on how to find and use various learning resources, but we believe that future attempts to help learners be more efficient and effective in the actual use of resources are warranted.

The potential of networking for and among self-directed learners needs to be more fully explored, understood, and exploited

Considerable discussion of networking has taken place in the past few years. Much of this discussion has centered on networks of people built around common needs, concerns, or interests, for example, professional networks, informal hobby-related networks, and networks devoted to specialized populations such as women's support groups. However, Fingeret's (1983) impressive work with the social networking activities of illiterate adults and the various efforts to promote learning exchange networks in the United States (Draves, 1980; Lewis, 1978, Perkins, 1985a, 1985b) suggest the potential value of networks for adult learners. The future certainly needs to include practical efforts aimed at initiating various learning networks.

There is a continuing need to help educators better understand the impact they can have on learner self-direction

Schuttenberg and Tracy (1987) suggest that educators must play the following roles if they are to foster self-directed learning: leadership, direction, collaboration, coaching, modeling, and being a colleague. We can add several more roles from our experience, such as mentoring, locating resources, serving as a validator of learning, and building confidence in personal abilities. There are obvious overlaps in the above roles, and other roles have, no doubt, been overlooked. However, the point is that in situations of facilitating self-direction in learning, educators have a number of crucial roles to play.

We believe, though, that this importance and the resulting impact on learners is not very well understood. As we noted in Chapter 1, in our attempt to address some of the myths regarding self-direction in learning, facilitating such learning is not easy for most educators. It requires lots of work, considerable advance planning, and a faith in the inherent ability of learners to take charge of their own learning. It is thus imperative that adult educators who are interested in self-directed learning foster the type of training that will help teachers understand the impact they do have on learners' abilities to accept personal responsibility for their educational activities.

It is important to be cognizant of cross-cultural differences that may influence the impact and perceived value of self-direction among learners from different cultures

We have found that many international students and, sometimes, students from different cultural groups within the United States have some initial difficulties with our self-directed approaches. These difficulties often match those experienced by Alice in the first chapter. Most initial problems seem to be related to expectations that the instructor will play a very directive role or to a lack of confidence in personal abilities to assume major responsibility for the planning and evaluation of learning experiences.

Thus, there is a need to provide appropriate orientation to such individuals very early in the learning experience. This should involve such activities as special meetings outside of the classroom, pairing such people with others who have been involved in self-directed learning at prior times for in-class small group sessions, and careful communication about processes, learning expectations, available resources, and assuming individual responsibility. In our own courses and workshops, for example, we take great care in developing the written materials explaining the teaching and learning process, providing samples of devices like learning contracts, and looking for non-verbal frustration or confusion clues. Even given such measures, some initial problems are natural and will need to be dealt with on a case-by-case basis.

There is a need to help facilitators learn how to foster self-direction with large groups as well as with individuals in small groups

It has been our experience that large group size need not deter the use of self-direction in learning approaches. However, it will necessitate working with such groups in ways different from a typical lecture format. One suggestion we have is to break such large groups into smaller groups for portions of the formal sessions. This can be accomplished in several ways. We have had success with the following three techniques: (a) forming groups of two to six people who move their seats together, (b) by having some people turn their front row seats to work with people in back row seats, and (c) if the initial room has fixed seats or is an auditorium with increasing tiers of seats to the back of the room, by moving people to folding chairs in any open areas of the room or to different breakout rooms.

We also continue to use learning contracts with large groups, and we encourage students to use study groups frequently, to form learning networks or support groups, and to work together in other ways in developing and carrying out learning contract activities. Instructors will need to be available for individual meetings and consultations, but a larger group obviously means that more time will be required outside the classroom for such meetings. We have had considerable success in the past few years using electronic mail for communications outside the classroom. Large numbers of people can be accommodated this way in reasonable amounts of time.

For adult education college professors, it is important to work with faculty in and out of colleges of education who may be interested in self-directed approaches, but who have little past experience with it

Many such people, especially if they have not received professional adult education training, will experience initial doubts about the value of self-directed learning for both students and teachers. In essence, many of the myths described in Chapter 1 will be operating consciously or sub-consciously as they attempt intellectually to understand self-directed approaches, learning contracts, and the risks or benefits in giving learners increased responsibility. Modeling, testimonials from students, and in-service workshops are some of the techniques we have employed in helping colleagues learn about our approach. We have used all of these approaches in settings involving both new and experienced faculty members and have generally been pleased with the response. The task is not easy and the result will not always be successful, but we urge that the effort be made.

It is important for instructors to help administrators understand why they are employing self-directed approaches and how they can be integrated into the existing system

In previous chapters, we discussed some of the changes necessary for the self-directed learning process to be successful, such as how resources are utilized, how evaluation procedures differ from more traditional grading approaches, and how time-bound bureaucratic policies may need alterations. However, it is important to stress once again the importance of helping administrators, who impact on teaching in various ways, to understand the value and appropriateness of the facilitative processes. Often, it will be necessary to describe or defend changes that will facilitate greater opportunity for self-direction, such as alternative residency requirements, new uses of learning contracts or field placements, and increased use of independent study activities.

Promoting such an understanding generally is not an easy task because policy and procedures have been established to foster smooth administrative operations, and the educator's approaches may necessitate changes or anomalies such as a heavy use of grading incompletes, staggered registrations, and grade changes after supplemental work by learners. It is our belief, though, that the constant defending and describing is worth the effort because of the enhancements possible for learners. In addition, they discover and build on their individual learning potential.

Finally, we believe that there is a great need for adult educators to become more active in popularizing and promoting notions of self-direction in learning throughout society

We recognize that by and large in writing this book we are preaching to the converted. Certainly we hope that we can convince many people currently not aware of all aspects of working with self-directed individuals of the potential of the approaches advocated in the book. However, because we are so convinced of the value of helping people take responsibility for their own learning – not only for those involved in more formalized educational pursuits but also for those who constantly need to cope with life's many changes – we think it important to find ways of reaching the unconverted.

Thus, we urge that adult educators carry out various activities that will promote self-direction in learning throughout society. This can include such actions as writing about one's approaches for the popular literature, facilitating workshops on self-direction in institutions such as libraries, museums, and art galleries, and spreading the messages to various audiences with a missionary zeal. Efforts like these will require work outside our normal responsibilities, but we do believe the potential impact throughout society is worth it.

CONCLUSION

This book has been written for a broad audience. We have tried to present a wide range of strategies, ideas, and issues and hope that they have been useful in stimulating those who want to improve or enhance their efforts in working with self-directed learners. We also have tried to present a "state of the art" look at theory and research. We recognize that our own perspectives have limited the social context in which we have examined the self-direction in learning phenomenon. Nonetheless, we have attempted to provide as broad a perspective as possible by sharing information on such diverse areas as literature relative to the "middle class phenomenon," the global aspects of self-direction, and even some likely future scenarios for adult learners.

Ultimately, what we believe we have done is to raise a number of questions for future examination of self-direction in learning. We hope that the PRO model will serve as a conceptual device to stimulate future dialogue and investigation. And we hope that the many implications we have identified and described in the book will stimulate research by colleagues in North America and the world.

This book is actually a culmination of several years of our research, study, scholarship, and direction of graduate student colleagues' research efforts. As such, we see this not as an end of our agendas, but rather, as a new beginning. We anticipate involvement in new research directions, expect expanded concern for the global perspective of self-direction, and desire opportunities to try new practices relative to self-direction. Thus, for us the odyssey continues.

Appendix A

Annotated bibliography of sources related to andragogy*

As has been pointed out throughout the various chapters of the book, our view of self-direction in adult learning is intimately linked to the concept of andragogy. This appendix is designed to be a resource for those readers seeking a greater understanding of what has been written about andragogy. Sources are presented in alphabetical order and cover the years 1927 through 1989. A brief annotation is provided for each reference.

SOURCES

Anderson, M. L., and Lindeman, E. C. (1927). *Education through experience*. New York: Workers Education Bureau.

In this work the authors provide an interpretative translation of literature describing the folk high school system in Germany. They include a section entitled, "Andragogy, " and describe some teaching methods used by the folk high school teachers. Anderson's role was primarily that of translator because much of their source material was in German.

Beder, H., and Carrea, N. (1988). The effects of andragogical teacher training on adult students' attendance and evaluation of their teachers. *Adult Education Quarterly, 38*, 75–87.

The authors examine two hypotheses with an experimental design: (a) andragogically trained teachers of adults will have higher rates of student attendance in their classes than teachers not trained in andragogy and (b) students will evaluate more positively andragogically-trained adult education teachers than teachers not trained in andragogy. The treatment was found to have a positive effect on attendance but not on student evaluations.

Boyer, D. L. (1984). Malcolm Knowles and Carl Rogers: A comparison of andragogy and student-centered education. *Lifelong Learning: An Omnibus of Practice and Research, 7*(4), 17–20.

---

* The occasional spelling of andragogy as "androgogy" is as it was found in the source. For an explanation of the spelling variations, see Knowles (1980).

He suggests that there are commonalities between the two authors' concepts. For example, both assert that their theories are separate and distinct from traditional education. In addition, humanism is somewhat foundational to both concepts. Rogers comes at his ideas from a psychotherapy background and tends to be more individual and small-group oriented. He emphasizes interpersonal and small-group dynamics. Knowles' experience base is in informal and continuing education programs and tends to be more supportive of group and larger organizational perspectives. He emphasizes program development.

Brookfield, S. D. (1984). The contribution of Eduard Lindeman to the development of theory and philosophy in adult education. *Adult Education Quarterly, 34,* 185–196.

In tracing some of the contributions of Lindeman, Brookfield points out that Lindeman, who undertook (with Martha Anderson) an interpretative translation of the folk high school in Germany, first used the term "Andragogy" in their 1927 monograph, *Education Through Experience.*

Brookfield, S. D. (1986). *Understanding and facilitating adult learning.* San Francisco: Jossey-Bass.

Brookfield presents an entire chapter describing and analyzing andragogy, in which he delineates various authors who have in some way evaluated or critiqued andragogy. He also presents several case studies of andragogy in practice.

Brookfield, S. D. (1987). *Learning democracy: Eduard Lindeman on adult education and social change.* Wolfeboro, New Hampshire: Croom Helm.

Brookfield pulls together a number of Lindeman's writings and adds some synthesizing chapters. He includes material from the Anderson and Lindeman (1927) discussion of andragogy and speculates as to how Lindeman's interpretation of andragogy might have influenced his later writings.

Brown, H. W. (1985). Lateral thinking and andragogy: Improving problem solving in adulthood. *Lifelong learning: An Omnibus of Practice and Research, 8*(7) 22–25.

Lateral thinking, also referred to as synectics, creative thinking, and conceptualization, is defined as a restructuring of the knowledge a person already has to bring about new ideas and insights. The author suggests that lateral thinking can be incorporated into the andragogical process as a mechanism to promote problem-solving abilities.

Candy, P. C. (1981). *Mirrors of the mind: Personal construct theory in the training of adult educators.* Manchester Monographs 16. Manchester: Department of Adult and Higher Education, University of Manchester.

He places andragogy within what he calls the principle of self-direction. He compares Knowles to George Kelly, a psychologist, who suggested that interpretation of the future is what drives a person to seek knowledge.

Carlson, R. A. (1979). The time of andragogy. *Adult Education, 30,* 53–57.

He suggests that Elias' attack on andragogy does not give much credence to the notions of or possibilities for adult self-directed learning. He supports the notion of facilitating the capable adult learner. He further feels that both a philosophical and political meaning for andragogy must be developed.

Christian, A. C. (1983). A comparative study of the andragogical–pedagogical orientation of military and civilian personnel. (Doctoral dissertation, Oklahoma State University). *Dissertation Abstracts International, 44*, 0643a.

The researcher developed the scale for this study, designed to measure the purpose of education, nature of learners, characteristics of learning experience, management of learning experience, evaluation, and relationships of educator to learners and among learners. The instrument was adapted from work by Hadley and Kerwin (annotated in this bibliography). Military subjects were shown to be less pedagogical than civilians.

Conti, G. J. (1985). Assessing teaching style in adult education: How and why. *Lifelong Learning: An Omnibus of Practice and Research, 8*(8), 7–11, 28.

Although not an article dealing directly with the subject of andragogy, the author describes his development of PALS – the Principles of Adult Learning Scale – which identifies different teaching styles, including some that incorporate some of the andragogical concepts.

Courtenay, B., and Stevenson, R. (1983). Avoiding the threat of gogymania. *Lifelong Learning: The Adult Years, 6*(7), 10–11.

They talk about all the efforts to label instruction of various groups of individuals by some sort of "gogy." They suggest that the distinctions between various groups are not great enough to warrant a label and certainly not great enough to talk about there being, or the need for, a related theory. They believe that appropriate program development principles are what is important.

Cranton, P. (1989). *Planning instruction for adult learners*. Toronto: Wall and Thompson.

The author provides in Chapter One a description of what she refers to as some principles of adult learning. Andragogy and the influence of Knowles is described on pages 6–9 as a strong influence on adult education practice.

Cross, K. P. (1981). *Adults as learners*. San Francisco: Jossey-Bass.

Cross presents her views on the strengths and weaknesses of the andragogical concept. She believes it is closer to a theory of teaching than to a theory of learning.

Daloisio, T., and Firestone, M. (1983). A case study in applying adult learning theory in developing managers. *Training and Development Journal, 37*(2), 73–78.

The authors talk about andragogy as a tool for the American Management Associations' Competency Program, a non-traditional approach to graduate management education. The andragogy assumptions and process elements are used to describe the operation of the program.

Darkenwald, G. D., and Merriam, S. B. (1982). *Adult education: Foundations of practice*. New York: Harper and Row.

The authors describe andragogy in some capacity several times throughout their book. They place andragogy within a context of self-directed learning in their attempt to help the novice reader better understand the field, its terms, and its scholars.

Davenport, J., III. (1987). Is there any way out of the andragogy morass? *Lifelong Learning: An Omnibus of Practice and Research*, *11*(3), 17–20.

The author suggests that a way to deal with all the debate and discussion about andragogy is to redefine the term and base its evolving understanding on empirical research.

Davenport, J., and Davenport, J. A. (1985a). A chronology and analysis of the andragogy debate. *Adult Education Quarterly*, *35*, 152–159.

The authors describe the debate and dialogue that have developed regarding andragogy during the past several years, including some of the dissertations on the subject. Considerable space is devoted to the debate in *Adult Education* that was held over a period of several years and to the various "gogy" terms that have been developed. They suggest that it is time we move beyond debate to research.

Davenport, J., and Davenport, J. A. (1985b). Andragogical–pedagogical orientations of adult learners: Research results and practice recommendations. *Lifelong Learning: An Omnibus of Practice and Research*, *9*(1), 6–8.

The authors describe some of the recent research efforts by people studying the andragogical–pedagogical orientation of adults. A variety of practice implications for adult educators are presented.

Davenport, J., and Davenport, J. A. (1985c). Knowles or Lindeman: Would the real father of American andragogy please stand up. *Lifelong Learning: An Omnibus of Practice and Research*, *9*(3), 4–6.

In this article the authors point out that not only did Lindeman (and Anderson) first introduce the term "andragogy" in American educational literature, the work of Lindeman appears to have played an important foundational role in Knowles's development of andragogical principles and process elements. They suggest that Lindeman should be seen as the spiritual father and Knowles as the protective father who popularized the term.

Day, C., and Baskett, H. K. (1982). Discrepancies between intentions and practice: Reexamining some basic assumptions about adult and continuing education. *International Journal of Lifelong Education*, *1*, 143–155.

The authors criticize the "andragogy" notion and suggest that andragogy is not a theory of adult learning, but is an educational ideology rooted in an inquiry-based learning and teaching paradigm. They believe that Knowles's conception of pedagogy has been incorrectly conceived.

Elias, J. L. (1979). Andragogy revisited. *Adult Education*, *29*, 252–255.

Elias takes the view that the promoters and defenders of andragogy have not proven their case and that there is no sound basis for a distinction between andragogy and pedagogy. He also feels that the slogan "andragogy, not pedagogy" is a well intentioned, but inadequate, attempt to enhance the professionalization of adult education. He suggests that andragogy and pedagogy merely represent two different approaches to the education of children and adults.

Elias, J. L., and Merriam, S. (1980). *Philosophical foundations of adult education.* Huntington, NY: Robert E. Krieger Publishing Company.

They place Knowles into a grouping labeled "humanistic adult educators." They suggest that andragogy is basically a humanistic theoretical framework applied primarily to adult education.

Fisher, J. C., and Podeschi, R. L. (1989). From Lindeman to Knowles: A change in vision. *International Journal of Lifelong Education, 8,* 345–353.

The article compares Knowles and Lindeman in relationship to the primary purpose of adult education. They conclude that Knowles and Lindeman are quite different in terms of the process of learning which each espouses. They believe Knowles' focus is on the effectiveness of individual means and initiative, whereas Lindeman's stress was on social commitment and the importance of understanding learning within a social context.

Gelfand, B., and associates (1975). An andragogical application to the training of social workers. *Journal of Education for Social Work, 11*(3), 55–61.

The authors present a discussion of how andragogical principles can be used in social work training. They highlight some research findings that support various of the andragogical principles.

Godbey, G. C. (1978). *Applied andragogy: A practical manual for the continuing education of adults.* College Park: Pennsylvania State University.

Godbey developed a manual for use in training workshops where participants are shown how to apply andragogical concepts. Guidance is provided on how a variety of teaching/training methods can be utilized.

Griffin, C. (1983). *Curriculum theory in adult and lifelong education.* London: Croom Helm.

Griffin presents a section in the book describing andragogy. He also presents some views on the limitations of andragogy and laments that Knowles does not account for crucial distinctions between the individual purposes and social consequences of learning.

Grubbs, J. C. (1981). A study of faculty members and students in selected midwestern schools of theology to determine whether their educational orientation is andragogical or pedagogical. (Doctoral dissertation, Indiana University). *Dissertation Abstracts International, 42,* 0055a.

The Educational Orientation Questionnaire and Educational Orientation Scales (see Hadley) were used in this study. Female faculty, faculty in the pastoral ministries, and faculty in the religious education areas were significantly more andragogically-oriented. Female and younger students were also more andragogically-oriented.

Hadley, H. (1975). Development of an instrument to determine adult educators' orientations: Andragogical or pedagogical. (Doctoral dissertation, Boston University). *Dissertation Abstracts International, 35,* 7595a.

The "Educational Orientation Questionnaire" incorporates six attitudinal dimensions of an adult educator's role: Purposes of education, nature of learners, characteristics of learning experience, management of learning experience, evaluation, and relationships of educator to learners and among learners. A second instrument, "Educational Orientation Scales," with six bipolar measures, was designed to examine predictive validity of the first instrument. A factor analysis determined eight factors, including pedagogical orientation, andragogical orientation, and self-directed change among them.

Hartree, A. (1984). Malcolm Knowles's theory of andragogy: A critique. *International Journal of Lifelong Education, 3*, 203–210.

Hartree analyzes Knowles' work and provides both a critique and some criticism. He proposes for adult educators a critical reformulation of andragogy.

Hiemstra, R. (1976). *Lifelong learning.* Lincoln, Nebraska: Professional Educators Publications. Reprinted by HiTree Press, Baldwinsville, New York, 1984.

Hiemstra presents andragogy as an evolving theory area. He suggests that a great deal more research will be required to bring support for and a fuller understanding of the emerging area.

Hiemstra, R. (1985). [Review of *Andragogy in action; Applying modern principles of adult learning*]. *Lifelong Learning: An Omnibus of Practice and Research, 9*(3), 23–25.

In addition to reviewing the book, Hiemstra introduces the reader to some of the debate that has surrounded andragogy in North American adult education literature.

Hiemstra, R. (1987, May). *Comparing andragogy in two cultures: Tanzania and the United States.* Paper presented at Comparative Adult Education: An International Conference, Oxford, England.

Hiemstra describes a Training and Rural Development project in Tanzania sponsored by the U.S. Agency for International Development for which he served as an external evaluator. The project had been designed, in part, around andragogical concepts. He compares the project activities with a United States example and suggests several similarities.

Holmes, M. R. (1980). Interpersonal behaviors and their relationship to the andragogical and pedagogical orientation of adult educators. *Adult Education, 31*, 18–29.

A research piece in which the author demonstrates some positive relationships between andragogical orientations and perceived effective interpersonal behaviors.

Hopkins, M. A. (1983). An analysis of nurse educators' educational orientation: Andragogical or pedagogical. (Doctoral dissertation, Virginia Polytechnic Institute and State University). *Dissertation Abstracts International, 44*, 0043a.

In this study the Hadley Educational Orientation Questionnaire was utilized to measure the orientation of nurse educators. The subjects were found to be pedagogically oriented toward education.

Houle, C. O. (1972). *The design of education.* San Francisco: Jossey-Bass Publishers.

In a couple of locations in the book Houle describes how he can't accept the notion that there are real differences between youth and children warranting a science of andragogy. He also describes the European and other roots of the term.

Ingalls, J. D. (1973). *A trainer's guide to andragogy*. (Rev. ed.). Washington, DC : U.S. Department of Health, Education, and Welfare.

The author developed a workbook for use in workshops or courses designed to help staff members in social service agencies understand and apply andragogical principles. A variety of exercises, techniques, and application suggestions are included.

Jahns, I. W. (1973). [Review of *Modern practice of adult education*]. *Adult Education*, *24*, 72–74.

A fairly straightforward review, although it is a little more critical of the technical aspects of the book than was Thornton (annotated in this bibliography).

Jarvis, P. (1984). Andragogy – a sign of the times. *Studies in the Education of Adults*, *16* (October), 32–38.

Jarvis provides some sociological explanation of why andragogy became popular. He contends that andragogy emerged at a time when the structures of society were conducive to the acceptance of new ideas. He believes it is an expression of the romantic curriculum.

Jones, G. E. (1982). An analysis of the andragogical–pedagogical orientation of selected faculty at Oklahoma State University. (Doctoral dissertation, Oklahoma State University). *Dissertation Abstracts International, 43*, 2569a.

The Educational Orientation Questionnaire was utilized with selected faculty teaching at least 25 percent of the time. There was a significant difference among departments, by sex, by the time spent off-campus working on extension or service projects, and by the number of years of teaching experience in higher education.

Katz, E. A. (1976). The belief in andragogy and the development of self-actualization. (Doctoral dissertation, Boston University). *Dissertation Abstracts International, 36*, 7129a.

This study was designed to determine whether extrinsic learning (belief in andragogy) or intrinsic learning (development of self-actualization) do occur in the same learning experience. The purpose was to investigate whether a particular andragogical process of teaching was effective in the growth of participants' beliefs in andragogy and in their development of self-actualization. The Educational Orientation Questionnaire was utilized. Belief in andragogy increased throughout the learning experiences but the development of self-actualization did not increase.

Kerwin, M. A. (1979). The relationship of selected factors to the educational orientation of andragogically-and pedagogically-oriented educators teaching in four of North Carolina's two-year colleges. (Doctoral dissertation, North Carolina State University). *Dissertation Abstracts International, 40*, 0610a.

The study's purpose was to determine if students perceived differences between the teaching behavior of andragogically-and pedagogically-oriented educators. The Educational Orientation Questionnaire was adapted and used to determine the two groups of educators and to determine student types. Students of andragogically-oriented educators perceived that their instructors provided more student involvement and counseling and less control over their class than students of pedagogically-oriented educators did for theirs. Andragogically-oriented educators tended to be women and to be in general educational programs (rather than in vocational programs).

Kerwin, M. A. (1981). Andragogy in the community college. *Community College Review*, 9(3), 12–14.

Kerwin describes how andragogical techniques were used in a community college communications course. He designed a questionnaire that measures a student's perceptions of an instructor's behavior. The instrument was used before and after the educational experience in order to help students think about their own role as teachers.

Knowles, M. S. (1968a). Androgogy, not pedagogy! *Adult Leadership, 16*, 350–352, 386.

In accepting the Delbert Clark Award in 1967, Knowles laid out his androgogical (as he spelled it then) concepts. He refers to it as a technology, introduces self-concept of the adult, experience of the adult, time perspective, and problem centered education as differentiating factors, and suggests some of the technological (teaching) implications – such as climate, needs diagnosis, planning process, mutual self-directed inquiry, and evaluation.

Knowles, M. S. (1968b). How andragogy works in leadership training in the girl scouts. *Adult Leadership, 17*, 161–162, 190–194.

Knowles describes how he tested the andragogical concepts with a leader training program for the Girl Scouts program. This case study report outlines the steps used and gives an analysis of the final results.

Knowles, M. S. (1970). *Modern practice of adult education: Andragogy versus pedagogy*. Chicago: Follett Publishing Company, Association Press.

In this first version of the book, Knowles lays out the premise of andragogy as an art and science of teaching adults as opposed to what is used to teach children. The book initiated lots of debate, dialogue, and change in terms of instructional approaches.

Knowles, M. S. (1973). *The adult learner: A neglected species*. Houston: Gulf Publishing Company.

In a presentation of various learning theories and teaching approaches, Knowles slots in the andragogical model.

Knowles, M. (1975). *Self-directed learning*. New York: Association Press.

Although andragogy is mentioned only a very few times in this little book, Knowles actually is utilizing his andragogical principles and process elements as guides in developing the various inquiry projects and learning resource suggestions throughout.

Knowles, M. (1979). Andragogy revisited: Part II. *Adult Education, 30*, 52–53.

Knowles suggests that he made a mistake in subtitling *Modern Practice of Adult Education* as "Andragogy versus Pedagogy." He suggests that the title should have been "From Pedagogy to Andragogy" and that his assumptions should have been presented on a continuum. However, he feels that some service came out of the dialogue and debate that was established. A caveat is presented: That an ideological pedagogue would want to keep a learner dependent throughout the learning situation whereas a true andragogue would want to do everything possible to provide the learner with whatever foundational content was needed and then encourage a self-directed process of further inquiry.

Knowles, M. S. (1980). *Modern practice of adult education: From pedagogy to andragogy*. Revised and updated. Chicago: Follett Publishing Company, Association Press.

In this revised edition, Knowles recognizes the considerable debate that took place since the 1970 version was published and approaches andragogy as an alternative teaching and learning approach, albeit one relying on the fact that adults are capable of self-directed learning, as are many youth. He also understands that a person utilizing andragogy as an approach will attempt to move the learner to independent learning as quickly as possible.

Knowles, M. (1984). *The adult learner: A neglected species*. (3rd ed.), Houston: Gulf Publishing.

In this book Knowles discusses within two different chapters, andragogy in terms of a review of his organizing concepts, teaching, and publication, and the use of andragogy in HRD settings.

Knowles, M. S., and associates (1984). *Andragogy in action: Applying modern principles of adult learning*. San Francisco: Jossey-Bass.

This book is made up of two chapters by Knowles (introduction and conclusion) and seven other chapters (grouped according to institutional settings) containing thirty-six selections written by fifty-two authors, five organizational representatives, and some "associates". The various selections are case study reports of how andragogy (or some variations of it) has been used.

Knowles, M. S. (1989). *The making of an adult educator: An autobiographical journey*. San Francisco: Jossey-Bass.

In this autobiography, Knowles traces his career and the development of his ideas. Of particular interest to readers seeking information on andragogy is a chapter on how Knowles' ideas have evolved over the years. Here, he presents his current conceptualization of six assumptions comprising the andragogical model and includes a discussion on some of the writers who have influenced his thinking in recent years.

Knudson, R. S. (1979). Humanagogy anyone? *Adult Education*, 29, 261–264.

Knudson promotes humanagogy as a theory of learning that takes into account the differences between people of various ages as well as their similarities. It is a human theory of learning as opposed to a theory of child, adult, or elderly learning. The accumulation of experience, for example, is a lifelong process that needs to be considered in educational planning.

Knudson, R. S. (1980). An alternative approach to the andragogy/pedagogy issue. *Lifelong Learning: The Adult Years*, 3(8), 8–10.

Knudson suggests that rather than argue the strengths and weaknesses of andragogy or pedagogy based on assumptions about whether or not adults and children are different, we use a law of identity (defining what is meant by being a child independent of what is meant by being an adult) and a theory of emergence (we emerge into adulthood based on experiences we had as a child). He suggests, therefore, that "humanagogy" replace both pedagogy and andragogy. He likens this to a "holistic" approach to adult education.

Komisin, L., and Gogniat, D. (1987). Andragogy, adult expectations, and international programs. *Continuing Higher Education, 35*(1), 13–15.

The authors describe how andragogical concepts were used to develop international field-based experiences.

Kulich, J. (1975). [Review of *Erwachsenenbildung: Einfuhrung in die andragogik* (Hanbuch der Erwachsenenbildung, Band 1). (Adult Education: Introduction to Andragogy. Handbook of Adult Education, Volume 1)]. *Adult Education, 25,* 137–138.

This "international" piece is referenced here just to note that there is literature available from throughout the world related to the word or notion of andragogy.

Lebel, J. (1978). Beyond andragogy to gerogogy. *Lifelong Learning: The Adult Years, 1*(9), 16–18, 24–25.

Lebel suggests the existence of sufficient data supporting the need for gerogogy and advocated that it should be studied as a theory. He suggests, further, that the concepts imbued within andragogy may be appropriate only up to certain stages of development chronologically.

Lewis, L. H. (1987). [Review of *Modern practice of adult education: Andragogy versus pedagogy*]. *Adult Education Quarterly, 37,* 120–122.

A retrospective review of the book presented in a special book review feature of historical landmarks for the field of adult education.

Lindeman, E. C. (1926). Andragogik: The method of teaching adults. *Worker's Education, 4,* 38.

This is the first known use of the term andragogy in North American literature. Lindeman, in a one-paragraph article, described how Professor Eugen Rosenstock of the Frankfurt Academy of Labor coined a new word: Andragogik. He mentioned that andragogy is the true method by which adults keep themselves intelligent about the modern world.

London, J. (1973). Adult education for the 1970's: Promise or illusion? *Adult Education, 24,* 60–70.

In this essay review of *Modern Practice of Adult Education*, London talks about some of the roles adult educators might play in the 1970s. However, he suggests that Knowles' book is largely a technical book which conveys a kind of technicism in referring to adult educators. He describes a problem with the 1970 version in that there is not an effective way of translating the author's discussion into any kind of effective analysis of how adult educators can utilize the presentation of needs into programming which will help adults confront various critical problems facing society. He feels that we need more than just methods and techniques to really help adult educators confront some of the major issues of our time. He believes we may need more radical approaches to educating adults, rather than the "sameness" of the technology implied in Knowles' book.

McCullough, K. O. (1978). Andragogy and community problem solving. *Lifelong Learning: The Adult Years, 2*(2), 8–9, 31.

McCullough describes andragogy as a process, a science of teaching adults, and as a profession. He says that the andragogist believes that knowledge is the equalizing factor among people and that people can come to "know" enough through an andragogical process to be a part of community problem-solving.

McKenzie, L. (1977). The issue of andragogy. *Adult Education, 27*, 225–229.

Utilizing an Aristotelian approach (classical), a phenomenological approach, and two syllogies, McKenzie provides some philosophical support for andragogy.

McKenzie, L. (1979). A response to Elias. *Adult Education, 29*, 256–260.

McKenzie maintains that adults and children are cardinally different by virtue of different modes of being-in-the-world, that adults and children exhibit different modes of existing, that these modes may be identified through phenomenological analysis, and that the existential differences between adults and children require a strategic differentiation of educational practice. He maintains a notion that Knowles's contrast between andragogy and pedagogy remains a useful but initial effort to explicate an approach to education that is related specifically to adult life.

McTernan, E. J. (1974). Androgogical education in the health services. *Adult Leadership, 23*, 136, 148.

McTernan provides a description of how some principles of adult education were utilized in instituting a new master's degree program in the health services area. He concludes with the notion that their attempt might be a promising model for the reconciliation of andragogy and pedagogy.

Merriam, S. B. (1987). Adult learning and theory building: A review. *Adult Education Quarterly, 37*, 187–198.

Merriam presents an assessment and analysis of the literature related to adult learning, and describes andragogy as a "theory" based on adult characteristics. She also presents a summary of some of the criticism that andragogy as a theory area has received.

Merriam, S. B. (1988). Finding your way through the maze: A guide to the literature on adult learning. *Lifelong Learning: An Omnibus of Practice and Research, 11*(6), 4–7.

Merriam presents some guidelines and ideas for organizing the adult learning literature to aid one's selection and reading. Andragogy is presented and described in the article as one of several theories that attempts to explain the phenomenon of adult learning.

Meyer, S. (1977). Andragogy and the aging adult learner. *Educational Gerontology, 2*(2), 115–122.

This article identifies the basic concepts and structures of pedagogy and andragogy as teaching-learning strategies for aging adults. Andragogy is depicted as a relevant participatory adult education technique useful for aging adults.

Mezirow, J. (1981). A critical theory of adult learning and education. *Adult Education, 32*, 3–24.

Mezirow presents what he calls a charter for andragogy, and suggests that andragogy, "as a professional perspective of adult educators, must be defined as an organized and sustained effort to assist adults to learn in a way that enhances their capability to function as self-directed laymen." He presents 12 actions he believes adult educators must carry out.

Newton, E. S. (1970). Andragogy: Understanding the adult as learner. *Journal of Reading, 20,* 361–363.

Newton believes that the curriculum should be timed to be in step with developmental tasks as the individual encounters them, in order to make full use of the teachable moment. The requirements and demands of the present situation and aspiring roles in real life must dominate and supersede all other considerations in andragogy.

Nottingham Andragogy Group. (1983). *Toward a developmental theory of andragogy.* (Adults: Psychological and Educational Perspective No. 9). Nottingham, England: Department of Adult Education, University of Nottingham.

The Nottingham group has somewhat reinterpreted Knowles's andragogical concepts in terms of their beliefs about adults and adults' abilities to think creatively and critically in learning settings. The booklet provides descriptions of methods, several features of a teaching and learning process, and some stages of course development centered around their notions about critical thinking. The Nottingham group also report that they believe that Alexander Kapp, a German teacher, first used the word andragogy in 1833 to describe the educational theory of Plato.

Peterson, C. H., Adkins, D., Tzuk, R., and Scott, M. (1981). Adult problem solving training: An experimental investigation of andragogical counseling techniques. *Proceedings of the Twenty-second Annual Adult Education Research Conference* (pp. 159–163). DeKalb, IL.

The authors drew upon available literature to delineate a counseling procedure consistent with andragogical principles and a life span development perspective. They then examined the effects of implementing such procedures and determined that people can be helped to enhance their own problem solving abilities and self-confidence.

Peterson, D. A. (1983). *Facilitating education for older adults.* San Francisco: Jossey-Bass.

Peterson describes andragogy in context with older learners. He suggests where an understanding of older adults as learners intersects with various andragogical concepts. He also suggests ways in which andragogy can be applied with older learners.

Podeschi, R. L. (1987a). Andragogy: Proofs or premises. *Lifelong Learning: An Omnibus of Practice and Research, 11*(3), 14–17, 20.

The author explores the debate that has continued about andragogy during the past decade and urges adult educators to be concerned about the type and nature of research that is carried out about the topic.

Podeschi, R. (1987b). Lindeman, Knowles and American individualism. *Proceedings of the Twenty-eighth Annual Adult Education Research Conference* (pp. 195–200). Laramie, WY: University of Wyoming, Conferences and Institutes.

In analyzing these two individuals, Podeschi suggests that Lindeman's andragogy is related philosophically to republican individualism, whereas Knowles's andragogy is connected sociologically to utilitarian individualism.

Podeschi, R. L., and Pearson, E. M. (1986). Knowles and Maslow: Differences about freedom. *Lifelong Learning: An Omnibus of Practice and Research, 9* (7), 16–18.

The authors talk about Knowles's updated views of freedom and self-directed learning in his more recent writings about andragogy. They suggest that Knowles is perhaps overly dependent on the ability of all people to accept individual freedom in learning.

Pratt, D. D. (1984). Andragogical assumptions: Some counter intuitive logic. *Proceedings of the Twenty-fifth Annual Adult Education Research Conference* (pp. 147–153). Syracuse, NY: Printing Services, Syracuse University.

Pratt reviews the evolution of the concept of andragogy and examines some of the distortions and assumptions that have emerged. Two andragogical assumptions (adults as self-directed learners and shared authority for decision-making) are examined.

Pratt, D. D. (1988). Andragogy as a relational construct. *Adult Education Quarterly, 38*, 160–171.

The author suggests that andragogical practice should acknowledge and accept of its learners both self-directedness and its obverse, dependency. Several learner and teacher variables are described and some figures depicting relationships are provided.

Rachal, J. (1983). The andragogy-pedagogy debate: Another voice in the fray. *Lifelong Learning: The Adult Years, 6*(9), 14–15.

Rachal suggests that adult educators may have become too engrossed in the field's jargon and utilizes "andragogy" as a discussion term. He notes how concepts like "self-directed learning" have spun off from the philosophical underpinnings related to andragogy.

Savicevic, D. M. (1981). Adult education systems in European Socialist countries: Similarities and differences. In A. N. Charters and associates, *Comparing adult education worldwide.* San Francisco: Jossey-Bass.

The author introduces the reader to the term "anthropogogy" – a term that Hungary utilizes to cover both andragogy and pedagogy. He also describes how various other countries in this region use some form of andragogy.

Savicevic, D. M. (1988, May). *Conceptions of andragogy in different countries: Comparative considerations.* Paper presented at the 1988 Study Seminar: Comparative Research in Adult Education, Rome, Italy.

Savicevic traces the roots of andragogy from Greek philosophy up through the workers' movement in the last two centuries. Its growth in Eastern Europe in the early part of this century is described. He also relates andragogy to the social sciences and makes a plea for more comparative study efforts.

Savicevic, D. (1989). Conceptions of andragogy in different countries: Comparative considerations. In M. Lichtner (Ed.), *Comparative research in adult education: Present lines and perspectives* (pp. 65–72). Villa Falconieri, 00044 Frascati, Roma, Italy: Centro Europeo Dell Educazione.

Savicevic presents the roots and historical development of the concept of andragogy going back to Kapp. The present situation in terms of use of the concept is presented and he includes some discussion on the linkages between andragogy and other sciences.

Sheridan, J. (1986). Andragogy: A new concept for academic librarians. *Research Strategies*, *4*(4), 156–167.

A case is made for how andragogical concepts and procedures can be utilized by academic librarians to help meet the many needs of learners and to help them in using various information resources. Several recommendations and suggestions are provided.

Sheridan, J. (1989). Rethinking andragogy: The case for collaborative learning in continuing higher education. *Continuing Higher Education*, *37*(2), 2–6.

The author describes collaborative learning and cooperative learning efforts among students that is reported to be gaining wide acceptance in higher education today. Collaborative learning is purported to parallel andragogical procedures in many ways.

Stewart, D. W. (1986). Perspective. *Lifelong Learning: An Omnibus of Practice and Research*, *9*(5), 2.

Stewart provides some suggestions as to why Anderson and Lindeman did not use the term "andragogy" after their mention of it in 1927.

Stewart, D. W. (1987). *Adult learning in America: Eduard Lindeman and his agenda for lifelong education*. Malabar, Florida: Robert E. Krieger Publishing Company.

Stewart writes a masterful biography of Eduard Lindeman, considered by many in the United States as the father of scholarly work in adult education. Chapter 8, entitled "What Adult Education Means: Discovering and Rediscovering the Concept of Andragogy," describes the interconnectedness between Lindeman's thinking about adult education and much of what andragogy has come to represent. He traces the history of Lindeman's use of the term andragogy in 1926 and 1927.

Suanmali, C. (1982). The core concepts of andragogy. (Doctoral dissertation, Teachers College, Columbia University). *Dissertation Abstracts International*, *42*, 4471a.

Utilizing the charter for andragogy outlined by Jack Mezirow, Suanmali developed an "Andragogy in Practice Inventory" and administered it to a group of adult education professors. He believes that there is a consensus regarding the major concepts used in the andragogical process.

Tennant, M. (1986). An evaluation of Knowles's theory of adult learning. *International Journal of Lifelong Education*, *6*, 113–122.

Tennant discusses and evaluates a number of themes which persist explicitly or implicitly throughout Knowles's writings, including the concept of self-actualization, the difference between child and adult learners, and the clinical model influence of Carl Rogers and Abraham Maslow. He argues for a clearer articulation of several underlying tenets and takes issue with the notion that adult learning is different from child learning.

Terry, E. F. (1988). Using andragogy to foster moral development of adults within the institutional church. *Lifelong Learning: An Omnibus of Practice and Research, 12*(2), 4–6.

The author believes that the nature of andragogy is such that it can provide an appropriate vehicle for facilitating moral development within a church setting. She relates andragogical process elements closely with the process required for movement throughout the various stages of moral development. The importance of facilitation is described.

Thorne, E. H., and Marshall, J. L. (1985). Managerial-skills development: An experience in program design. *Personnel Journal, 55*(1), 15–17, 38.

The authors describe how andragogy can be adapted to an industrial setting. They describe how to create an environment in which a management skills development program can operate.

Thornton, J. A. (1973). [Review of *Modern practice of adult education: Andragogy versus pedagogy*]. *Adult Education, 24*, 70–72.

A fairly straightforward and positive review of the book.

Travis, A. Y. (1985). Andragogy and the disabled adult learner. *Lifelong Learning: An Omnibus of Practice and Research, 8*(8), 16–18, 20.

The author suggests how andragogical principles could be utilized with disabled adult learners. Several descriptive tables are included.

Warren, C. (1989). Andragogy and N. F. S. Grundtvig: A critical link. *Adult Education Quarterly, 39*(4), 211–223.

Warren compares the ideas of N. F. S. Grundtvig with those of various American adult education thinkers, particularly as those thinkers have addressed the concept of andragogy. Warren suggests that while Grundtvig has basically gone unread in North America, his ideas have had a major influence on adult education in this context, largely due to the legacy of Eduard Lindeman. He suggests that the basic ideas of Grundtvig essentially parallel Knowles's assumptions of andragogy.

Yeo, G. (1982). 'Eldergogy' a specialized approach to education for elders. *Lifelong Learning: The Adult Years, 5*(5), 4–7.

She recommends a new "gogy, " eldergogy, defined as a specialized approach to education for elders. She believes that eldergogy would help teachers of older adults to become more effective. She provides a number of instruction-related strategies.

Yonge, A. D. (1985). Andragogy and pedagogy: Two ways of accompaniment. *Adult Education Quarterly, 35*, 160–167.

In this article, Yonge talks about how discussions of andragogy revolving around learning and teaching are both necessary and confusing. Some important differences between a situation of andragogy and pedagogy are presented.

Vacca, R. T., and Walker, J. E. (1980). Andragogy: The missing link in college reading programs. *Lifelong Learning: The Adult Years*, *3*(6), 16, 24–25.

The authors talk about how andragogical assumptions and approaches can be used to teach reading to incoming college students.

Van Allen, G. H. (1982). Educational attitudes in a state system of community colleges. *Community College Review*, *10*(2), 44–47.

Using the Educational Orientation Questionnaire, – an instrument developed to measure attitudes along an andragogical–pedagogical continuum – attitudes of community college faculty and students were found to fit well together and to fall near the middle of the scale.

Appendix B
Self-directed learning seminar participants

Iowa State University; Summer, 1980

Roger Hiemstra, Facilitator

Peggy Allen	Jo Ann Barnes
Dennis D. Bejot	Virginia P. Bishop
Frederick L. Bungert	Barbara E. Burton
Rachel S. Christensen	Lynn Engen
Donald H. Goering	Sherril A. Harris
Robert A. Hoksch	Connie B. Ruggless
Joyce M. Samuels	Colina Megorden Stanton
David H. Swanson	Aaron L. Wheeler

Syracuse University; Spring, 1981

Roger Hiemstra, Facilitator

Mary Beth Bombardi (Hinton)	Ralph Brockett
Carol Cameron	John Champaigne
Joseph Ebiware	Sheila Green
Ken Landers	Joan Murphy
Hilda Patino	Dorothy Paynter
Candace Pearce	Phyllis Read
Julie Smith	Agnes Walbe
Nancy Ziegler (Gadbow)	

Syracuse University; Summer, 1983

Ralph G. Brockett, Facilitator

Henry Alegria	Fredy Bentti
John H. Creighton	Norbert J. Henry
Gerrie Kaluzny	Michael M. Reynolds

Syracuse University; Summer, 1985

Roger Hiemstra, Facilitator

Margaret (Peg) E. Chambers	Pat Green
Doris Holdorf	Jane M. Hugo
Barry W. Mack	Dawn P. Mullaney
Lois Needham	Gene A. Roche
Mary C. Rommel	Jack E. Six

References

Adams, F. (with Horton, M.). (1975). *Unearthing seeds of fire*. Winston-Salem, North Carolina: John F. Blair, Publisher.

Adler A. (1939). *Social interest*. New York: Putnam.

Alegria, H. (1983). *Rights and responsibilities of the self-directed learner*. Unpublished manuscript, Adult Education Program, Syracuse University, Syracuse, NY.

American Nurses' Association. (1984). American Nurses' Associations's guide for self-directed continuing education. In M. S. Knowles and associates, *Andragogy in action* (pp. 311–322). San Francisco: Jossey-Bass.

Andresen, A. (1985). *The Danish folk high school today*. Esbjerg, Denmark: International Committee of the Danish Folk High School Association.

Apps, J. W. (1981). *The adult learner on campus*. Chicago: Follett Publishing Company.

Apps, J. W. (1985). *Improving practice in continuing education*. San Francisco: Jossey-Bass.

Arms, D., Chenevey, B., Karrer, C., and Rumpler, C. H. (1984). A Baccalaureate degree program in nursing for adult students. In M. S. Knowles and associates, *Andragogy in action* (pp. 273–284). San Francisco: Jossey-Bass.

Ash, C. R. (1985). Applying principles of self-directed learning in the health professions. In S. Brookfield (Ed.), *Self-directed learning: From theory to practice* (New Directions for Continuing Education, Number 25, pp. 63–74). San Francisco: Jossey-Bass.

Aslanian, C. B., and Brickell, H. M. (1980). *Americans in transition: Life changes as reasons for adult learning*. New York: College Entrance Examination Board.

Baghi, H. (1979). The major learning efforts of participants in adult basic education classes and learning centers. (Doctoral dissertation, Iowa State University, 1979). *Dissertation Abstracts International, 40*, 2410A.

Bauer, B. A. (1985). Self-directed learning in a graduate adult education program. In S. Brookfield (Ed.), *Self-directed learning: From theory to practice* (New Directions for Continuing Education, Number 25, pp. 41–50). San Francisco: Jossey-Bass.

Bauer, B. A. (1986). The Adult Education Guided Independent Study (AEGIS) Program: An administrative case study (Doctoral dissertation, Columbia University Teachers College, 1985). *Dissertation Abstracts International, 46*, 2518A.

Bayles, M. D. (1981). *Professional ethics*. Belmont, CA: Wadsworth.

Beder, H. (1985). Defining the we. *Lifelong Learning: An Omnibus of Practice and Research, 8*(5), 2.

Bentti, F. (1983). *Toward a code of ethics in self-directed learning.* Unpublished manuscript, Adult Education Program, Syracuse University, Syracuse, NY.

Bertram, S. (1981). Use of a cultural voucher system to stimulate adult learning. In Z. W. Collins (Ed.), *Museums, adults and the humanities* (pp. 349–365). Washington, DC : American Association of Museums.

Bertram, S., and Sidford, H. (1977). *Final report on the cultural voucher program.* New York: Museums Collaborative.

Bestall, J. M. (1970). What can museums offer? *Adult Education* (London), *42*, 315–319.

Biddle, W. W., and Biddle, L. J. (1965). *The community development process: The rediscovery of local initiative.* New York: Holt, Rinehart, & Winston, Inc.

Bishop Carroll High School. (1984). Individualized education at a Catholic high school. In M. S. Knowles and associates, *Andragogy in action* (pp. 391–398). San Francisco: Jossey-Bass.

Bitterman, J. A. (1989). Relationship of adults' cognitive style and achieving style to preference for self-directed learning (Doctoral dissertation, Northern Illinois University, 1988). *Dissertation Abstracts International, 50,* 851A.

Blackwood, C. C. (1989). Self-directedness and hemisphericity over the adult life span. (Doctoral dissertation, Montana State University, 1988). *Dissertation Abstracts International, 50,* 328A.

Bloch, F. S. (1984). Clinical legal education at Vanderbilt University. In M. S. Knowles and associates, *Andragogy in action* (pp. 227–242). San Francisco: Jossey-Bass.

Bogdan, R. C., and Biklen, S. K. (1982). *Qualitative research for education: An introduction to theory and methods.* Boston: Allyn & Bacon, Inc.

Boggs, D. L. (1986). Case study of citizen education and action. *Adult Education Quarterly, 37,* 1–13.

Boshier, R. (1971). Motivational orientations of adult education participants: A factor analytic exploration of Houle's typology. *Adult Education, 21*(1), 3–26.

Boshier, R. (April, 1983). Adult learning projects research: An alchemist's fantasy? Invited address to American Educational Research Association, Montreal, Quebec.

Boshier, R., and Collins, J. B. (1985). The Houle typology after twenty-two years: A large-scale empirical test. *Adult Education Quarterly, 35*(3), 113–130.

Boshier, R., and Pickard, L. (1979). Citation patterns of articles published in *Adult Education* 1968–1977. *Adult Education, 29*(1), 34–51.

Boucouvalas, M. (1982). Adult education in modern Greece. *Convergence, 15*(3), 28–36.

Boud, D. J., and Prosser, M. T. (1984). Sharing responsibility for learning in a science course – staff-student cooperation. In M. S. Knowles and associates, *Andragogy in action* (pp. 175–188). San Francisco: Jossey-Bass.

Box, B. J. (1983). Self-directed learning readiness of students and graduates of an associate degree nursing program (Doctoral dissertation, Oklahoma State University, 1982). *Dissertation Abstracts International, 44,* 679A.

Boyd, R. D., and Apps, J. W. (1980). A conceptual model for adult education. In R. D. Boyd, J. W. Apps, and associates, *Redefining the discipline of adult education* (pp. 1–13). San Francisco: Jossey-Bass.

Brasfield, L. (1974). Educational attainment and participation in self-directed learning projects. Unpublished master's thesis, University of Tennessee, Knoxville.

Briggs, J. C. (1981). Community resource centers. In H. Stubblefield (Ed.), *Conti-*

nuing education for community leadership (New Directions for Continuing Education, Number 11, pp. 63–72). San Francisco, Jossey-Bass.

Brockett, R. G. (1983a). Facilitator roles and skills. *Lifelong Learning: The Adult Years*, 6(5), 7–9.

Brockett, R. G. (1983b). Self-directed learning and the hard-to-reach adult. *Lifelong Learning: The Adult Years*, 6(8), 16–18.

Brockett, R. G. (1983c). Self-directed learning readiness and life satisfaction among older adults. (Doctoral dissertation, Syracuse University, 1982). *Dissertation Abstracts International*, 44, 42A.

Brockett, R. G. (1985a). The relationship between self-directed learning readiness and life satisfaction among older adults. *Adult Education Quarterly*, 35(4), 210–219.

Brockett, R. G. (1985b). Methodological and substantive issues in the measurement of self-directed learning readiness. *Adult Education Quarterly*, 36(1), 15–24.

Brockett, R. G. (1985c). A response to Brookfield's critical paradigm of self-directed adult learning. *Adult Education Quarterly*, 36(1), 55–59.

Brockett, R. G. (1988a). Beyond tradition: Quality issues in nontraditional education. In R. G. Brockett, S. E. Easton, and J. O. Picton (Eds.), *Adult and continuing education* (pp. 287–290). Bloomington, IN: Phi Delta Kappa.

Brockett, R. G. (1988b). Ethics and the adult educator. In R. G. Brockett (Ed.), *Ethical issues in adult education* (pp. 1–16). New York: Teachers College Press.

Brockett, R. G. (Ed.). (1988c). *Ethical issues in adult education.* New York: Teachers College Press.

Brockett, R. G., and Hiemstra, R. (1985). Bridging the theory-practice gap in self-directed learning. In S. Brookfield (Ed.), *Self-directed learning: From theory to practice* (New Directions for Continuing Education, Number 25, pp. 31–40). San Francisco: Jossey-Bass.

Brockett, R. G., Hiemstra, R., and Penland, P. R. (1982). *Self-directed learning.* In C. Klevins (Ed.), *Materials and methods in adult and continuing education* (pp. 171–178). Los Angeles: Klevens Publications Inc.

Brookfield, S. D. (1978). Individualizing adult learning: An English experiment. *Lifelong Learning: The Adult Years*, 1(7), 18–20.

Brookfield, S. D. (1980). *Independent adult learning.* Unpublished doctoral dissertation, University of Leicester.

Brookfield, S. D. (1981a). The adult learning iceberg: A critical review of the work of Allen Tough. *Adult Education* (British), 54(2), 110–118.

Brookfield, S. D. (1981b). Independent adult learning. *Studies in Adult Education*, 13, 15–27.

Brookfield, S. D. (1984a). *Adult learners, adult education and the community.* New York: Teachers College Press.

Brookfield, S. D. (1984b). The contribution of Eduard Lindeman to the development of theory and philosophy in adult education. *Adult Education Quarterly*, 34, 185–196.

Brookfield, S. D. (1984c). Self-directed learning: A critical paradigm. *Adult Education Quarterly*, 35, 59–71.

Brookfield, S. D. (1985a). The continuing educator and self-directed learning in the community. In S. Brookfield (Ed.), *Self-directed learning: From theory to practice* (New Directions for Continuing Education. Number 25, pp. 75–85). San Francisco: Jossey-Bass.

250 *References*

Brookfield, S. D. (1985b). Analyzing a critical paradigm of self-directed learning: A response. *Adult Education Quarterly, 36*(1), 60–64.

Brookfield, S. D. (1985c). Self-directed learning: A critical review of research. In S. D. Brookfield (Ed.), *Self-directed learning: From theory to practice* (New Directions for Continuing Education. Number 25, pp. 5–16). San Francisco: Jossey-Bass.

Brookfield, S. D. (1986). *Understanding and facilitating adult learning.* San Francisco: Jossey-Bass.

Brookfield, S. D. (1987). *Developing critical thinkers.* San Francisco: Jossey-Bass.

Brookfield, S. D. (1988). Conceptual, methodological and practical ambiguities in self-directed learning. In H. B. Long and associates, *Self-directed learning: Application and theory* (pp. 11–38). Athens, Georgia: University of Georgia, Adult Education Department.

Bruner, J. S. (1966). *Toward a theory of instruction.* Cambridge, MA: The Belknap Press of Harvard University Press.

Bryson, L. (1936). *Adult education.* New York: American Book Company.

Bundy, M. L. (Ed.). (1977). *Alternatives to traditional library services.* College Park, MD: Urban Information Interpreters.

Burge, E. J. (Ed.). (1983). Adult learners, learning, and public libraries. *Library Trends, 31*(4), (entire issue).

Caffarella, R. S. (1982). The learning plan format: A technique for incorporating the concept of learning how to learn into formal courses and workshops. *Proceedings of the Lifelong Learning Research Conference* (pp. 45–49). University of Maryland, College Park, MD.

Caffarella, R. S. (1983a). [Review of *Intentional Changes*]. *Adult Education Quarterly, 33*(3), 186–188.

Caffarella, R. S. (1983b). Fostering self-directed learning in post-secondary education: The use of learning contracts. *Lifelong Learning: An Omnibus of Practice and Research, 7*(3), 7–10, 25, 26

Caffarella, R. S., and Caffarella, E. P. (1986). Self-directedness and learning contracts in adult education. *Adult Education Quarterly, 36*(4), 226–234.

Caffarella, R. S., and O'Donnell, J. M. (1987). Self-directed adult learning: A critical paradigm revisited. *Adult Education Quarterly, 37*, 199–211.

Caffarella, R., and O'Donnell, J. M. (1988). Research in self-directed learning: Past, present and future trends. In H. B. Long and associates, *Self-directed learning: Application and theory* (pp. 39–61). Athens, Georgia: University of Georgia, Adult Education Department.

Cameron, S. W. (1984). *The Perry scheme: A new perspective on adult learners.* Syracuse, NY: Syracuse University. (ERIC Document Reproduction Service No. ED 244 698).

Candy, P. C. (1981). *Mirrors of the mind: Personal construct theory in the training of adult educators* (Manchester Monographs 16). Manchester: Department of Adult and Higher Education, University of Manchester.

Candy, P. C. (1988). *Reframing research into 'self-direction' in adult education: A constructivist perspective* (Doctoral dissertation, University of British Columbia, 1987). *Dissertation Abstracts International, 49*, 1033A.

Carlson, R. A. (1979). The time of andragogy. *Adult Education, 30*(1), 53–56.

Carr, D. W. (1980). The agent and the learner: A study of critical incidents and contexts in assisted adult library learning (Doctoral dissertation, Rutgers, The State University of New Jersey, 1979). *Dissertation Abstracts International, 40*, 5230A.

Carr, D. W. (1983). Adult learning and library helping. *Library Trends, 16*(4), 569–583.

Carr, D. W. (1985). Self-directed learning in cultural institutions. In S. D. Brookfield (Ed.), *Self-directed learning: From theory to practice* (New Directions for Continuing Education, Number 25, pp. 51–62). San Francisco: Jossey-Bass.

Cavaliere, L. A. (1989). A case study of the self-directed learning processes and network patterns utilized by the Wright brothers which led to their invention of flight (Doctoral dissertation, Rutgers, The State University of New Jersey, New Brunswick, 1988). *Dissertation Abstracts International, 49*, 2894A.

Center for Museum Education. (1978). *Lifelong learning/adult audiences* (Sourcebook no. 1). Washington, DC: George Washington University, Center for Museum Education.

Chase, J. W. (1978). *Reinforcement of a Black cultural museum through the development of its library resources in the field of Black studies to provide educational and research material with a wide application.* Sullivan's Island, SC: Miriam B. Wilson Foundation. (ERIC Document Reproduction Service No. ED 163 928).

Chene, A. (1983). The concept of autonomy in adult education: A philosophical discussion. *Adult Education Quarterly, 1*, 38–47.

Christensen, R. S. (1981). Dear diary – a learning tool for adults. *Lifelong Learning: The Adult Years, 5*(2), 4–5, 23.

Coe, M., Rubenzahl, A., and Slater, V. (1984). Helping adults reenter college. In M. S. Knowles and associates, *Andragogy in action* (pp. 121–130). San Francisco: Jossey-Bass.

Collard, S., and Law, M. (1989). The limits of perspective transformation: A critique of Mezirow's theory. *Adult Education Quarterly, 39*(2), 99–107.

Collins, M. (1988). Prison education: A substantial metaphor for adult education practice. *Adult Education Quarterly, 38* (2), 101–110.

Compton, J. L., and Parish, A. H. (1978). E Pluribus Unum: Adult education for a global society. *Lifelong Learning: The Adult Years, 1*(10), 30–33.

Conroy, B. (1981). Continuing education in libraries: A challenge to change agents. In J. C. Votruba (Ed.), *Strengthening internal support for continuing education* (New Directions for Continuing Education, Number 9, pp. 81–88). San Francisco: Jossey-Bass.

Coolican, P. M. (1975). The learning styles of mothers of young children. (Doctoral dissertation, Syracuse University, 1973). *Dissertation Abstracts International, 35*, 783A–784A.

Cooper, S. S. (1980). *Self-directed learning in nursing.* Wakefield, Massachusetts: Nursing Resources.

Cotton, W. E. (1964). The challenge confronting American adult education. *Adult Education, 14*(2), 80–88.

Craik, G. L. (1840). *Pursuit of knowledge under difficulties: Its pleasures and rewards.* New York: Harper and Brothers.

Creighton, J. H. (1983). *Fostering self-directed learning in the traditional institution.* Unpublished manuscript, Adult Education Program, Syracuse University, Syracuse, NY.

Crook, J. (1985). A validation study of a self-directed learning readiness scale, *Journal of Nursing Education, 24*(7), 274–279.

Cross, K. P. (1977). *Accent on learning.* San Francisco: Jossey-Bass.

Cross, K. P. (1980, May). Our changing students and their impact on colleges: Prospects for a true learning society. *Phi Delta Kappa, 61*, 627–630.

Cross, K. P. (1981). *Adults as learners*. San Francisco: Jossey-Bass.

Cunningham, J. R. (1989). An examination of the self-directed learning readiness of selected students and graduates of masters degree programs of Southern Baptist Seminaries (Doctoral dissertation, Southwestern Baptist Theological Seminary, 1988). *Dissertation Abstracts International, 49*, 3246A.

Curry, M. A. (1983). The analysis of self-directed learning readiness characteristics in older adults engaged in formal learning activities in two settings (Doctoral dissertation, Kansas State University, 1983). *Dissertation Abstracts International, 44*, 1293A.

Dale, D. (1981). Citizen education for effective involvement. In H. Stubblefield (Ed.), *Continuing education for community leadership* (New Directions for Continuing Education, Number 11, pp. 41–52). San Francisco: Jossey-Bass.

Dale, S. M. (1979). The adult independent learning project: Work with adult self-directed learners in public libraries. *Journal of Librarianship, 11*(2), 83–106.

Dale, S. M. (1980). Another way forward for adult learners: The public library and independent study. *Studies in Adult Education, 12*, 29–38.

Daniels, J. P. (1981). The Ringling museum's medieval and renaissance fair – A community program. In Z. W. Collins (Ed.), *Museums, adults and the humanities* (pp. 338–348). Washington, DC : American Association of Museums.

Danis, C., and Tremblay, N. (1985). Critical analysis of adult learning principles from a self-directed learner's perspective. *Proceedings of the 26th Annual Adult Education Research Conference* (pp. 138–143). Arizona State University, Higher and Adult Education, Tempe, Arizona.

Dare, C. B. (1984). Teaching nurses technical skills at a metropolitan hospital. In M. S. Knowles and associates, *Andragogy in action* (pp. 323–334). San Francisco: Jossey-Bass.

Darkenwald, G. G., and Merriam, S. B. (1982). *Adult education: Foundations of practice*. New York: Harper and Row.

Darkenwald, G. G., and Valentine, T. (1985). Factor structure of deterrents to participation in adult education. *Adult Education Quarterly, 35*(4), 177–193.

Davenport, J. (1987). Is there any way out of the andragogy morass? *Lifelong Learning: An Omnibus of Practice and Research, 11*(3), 17–20.

Davenport, J., and Davenport, J. A. (1985a). A chronology and analysis of the andragogy debate. *Adult Education Quarterly, 35*, 152–159.

Davenport, J., and Davenport, J. A. (1985b). Andragogical-pedagogical orientations of adult learners: Research results and practice recommendations. *Lifelong Learning: An Omnibus of Practice and Research, 9*(1), 6–8.

Davenport, J., and Davenport, J. A. (1985c). Knowles or Lindeman: Would the real father of American andragogy please stand up. *Lifelong Learning: An Omnibus of Practice and Research, 9*(3), 4–5.

Davis, S. A. (1974). *Uplift: What people themselves can do*. Washington, DC: National Self-Help Resource Center.

Davis, S. A. (1976). *Community resource centers: The notebook*. Washington, DC: National Self-Help Resource Center.

Day, M. J. (1988). Educational advising and brokering: The ethics of choice. In R. G. Brockett (Ed.), *Ethical issues in adult education* (pp. 118–132). New York: Teachers College Press.

Day, C., and Baskett, H. K. (1982). Discrepancies between intentions and practice: Reexamining some basic assumptions about adult and continuing professional education. *International Journal of Lifelong Education, 1*(2), 143–155.

Dean, G. J., and Dowling, W. D. (1987). Community development: An adult education model. *Adult Education Quarterly, 37*, 78–89.

Della-Dora, D., and Blanchard, J. (Eds.). (1979). *Moving toward self-directed learning.* Alexandria, VA: Association for Supervision and Curriculum Development.

DeMott, R. (Ed.). (1989). *Working days: The journals of The Grapes of Wrath.* New York: Viking.

Denys, L. O. J. (1975). The major learning efforts of two groups of Accra adults. (Doctoral dissertation, University of Toronto, 1973). *Dissertation Abstracts International, 35*, 5759A.

Dickinson, G., and Rusnell, D. (1971). A content analysis of *Adult Education. Adult Education, 21*(3), 177–185.

Draves, B. (1980). *The free university.* Chicago: Follett Publishing Company.

Dressel, P. L., and Thompson, M. M. (1973). *Independent study.* San Francisco: Jossey-Bass.

East, J. M. (1987). The relationship between self-directed learning readiness and life satisfaction among the elderly (Doctoral dissertation, Florida State University, 1986). *Dissertation Abstracts International, 47*, 2848A.

Egan, G. (1975). *The skilled helper.* Monterey, CA: Brooks/Cole.

Egan, G. (1986). *The skilled helper (3rd Ed).* Monterey, CA: Brooks/Cole.

Eisenman, J. G. (1989). Self-directed learning: A correlational study of fifth grade students, their parents and teachers (Doctoral dissertation, University of Georgia, 1988). *Dissertation Abstracts International, 49*, 3587A.

Eldred, M. (1984). An external undergraduate degree program. In M. S. Knowles and associates, *Andragogy in action* (pp. 131–140). San Francisco: Jossey-Bass.

Elias, J. L. (1979). Andragogy revisited. *Adult Education, 29*(4), 252–256.

Elias, J. L., and Merriam, S. (1980). *Philosophical foundations of adult education.* Huntington, New York: Robert K. Krieger Publishing Company.

Ellis, A. (1962). *Reason and emotion in psychotherapy.* New York: Lyle Stewart.

Ellis, A. (1973). *Humanistic psychotherapy.* New York: Institute for Rational Living, Inc.

Ellis, A. (1982). Self-direction in sport and life. *Rational Living, 17*(1), 27–33.

Ellis, A., and Harper, R. A. (1975). *A new guide to rational living.* Englewood Cliffs, NJ: Prentice-Hall.

Engberg-Pedersen, H. (1970). Danish folk high schools in the new industrial state. *Convergence, 3*, 84–88.

Erikson, E. (1964). *Insight and responsibility.* New York: W. W. Norton.

Estrin, H. R. (1986). Life satisfaction and participation in learning activities among widows (Doctoral dissertation, Syracuse University, 1985). *Dissertation Abstracts International, 46*, 3852A.

Even, M. J. (1982). Adapting cognitive style theory in practice. *Lifelong Learning: The Adult Years, 5*(5), 14–17, 27.

Fagothey, A. (1972). *Right and reason: Ethics in theory and practice (5th Ed.).* St. Louis: Mosby.

Farquharson, A. (1984). Learning through teaching among undergraduate social work students. In M. S. Knowles and associates, *Andragogy in action* (pp. 265–272). San Francisco: Jossey-Bass.

Faure, E., Herrera, F., Kaddoura, A. R., Lopes, H., Petrovsky, A. V., Rahema, M., and Ward, F. C. (1972). *Learning to be.* New York: Unipub.

Fellenz, R. A. (1985). Self-direction: A clarification of terms and causes. In *Proceed-*

ings of the 26th Annual Adult Education Research Conference (pp. 164–169). Tempe, AZ.

Ferrell, B. (1978). Attitudes toward learning styles and self-direction of ADN students. *Journal of Nursing Education, 17*, 19–22.

Field, J. L. (1979). The learning efforts of Jamaican adults of low literacy attainment (Doctoral dissertation, University of Toronto, 1977). *Dissertation Abstracts International, 39*, 3979A.

Field, L. (1989). An investigation into the structure, validity, and reliability of Guglielmino's Self-Directed Learning Scale. *Adult Education Quarterly, 39*, 125–139.

Finestone, P. M. (1984). A construct validation of the Self-Directed Learning Readiness Scale with labour education participants (Doctoral dissertation, University of Toronto, 1984). *Dissertation Abstracts International, 46*, 05A.

Fingeret, A. (1982). Methodological issues and theoretical perspectives on research. In G. C. Whaples and W. M. Rivera (Eds.), *Lifelong Learning Research Conference Proceedings* (88–92). College Park, MD: Department of Agricultural and Extension Education, University of Maryland.

Fingeret, A. (1983). Social network: A new perspective on independence and illiterate adults. *Adult Education Quarterly, 33*, 133–146.

Fitts, W. H. (1965). *Manual for the Tennessee Self Concept Scale*. Nashville: Counselor Recordings and Tests.

Fitts, W. H., and Richard, W. C. (1971). The self concept, self-actualization, and rehabilitation: An overview. In W. H. Fitts, J. L. Adams, G. Radford, W. C. Richard, B. K. Thomas, M. M. Thomas, and W. Thompson (Eds). *The self concept and self-actualization* (pp. 1–10). Nashville: Dede Wallace Center.

Flexner, J. M., and Hopkins, B. C. (1941). *Readers' advisors at work*. New York: American Association for Adult Education.

Freire, P. (1970). *Pedagogy of the oppressed*. New York: Herder and Herder.

Garrison, D. R. (1987). Self-directed and distance learning: Facilitating self-directed learning beyond the institutional setting. *International Journal of Lifelong Education, 6*, 309–318.

Gerstner, L. S. (1988). On the theme and variations of self-directed learning: An exploration of the literature (Doctoral dissertation, Columbia University Teachers College, 1987). *Dissertation Abstracts International, 49*, 27A.

Gibbons, M., Bailey, A., Comeau, P., Schmuck, J., Seymour, S., and Wallace, D. (1980). Toward a theory of self-directed learning: A study of experts without formal training. *Journal of Humanistic Psychology, 20*(2), 41–56.

Gibbons, M., and Phillips, G. (1979). Teaching for self-education: Promising new professional role. *Journal of Teacher Education, 30*(5), 26–28.

Gibbons, M., and Phillips, G. (1982). Self-education: The process of life-long learning. *Canadian Journal of Education, 7*(4), 67–86.

Gibbons, M., and Phillips, G. (1984). Applications in elementary and secondary education. In M. S. Knowles and associates, *Andragogy in action* (pp. 365–378). San Francisco: Jossey-Bass.

Gilder, J. (Ed.). (1979). *Policies for lifelong education: Report of the 1979 Assembly*. Washington, DC: American Association for Community and Junior Colleges. (ERIC Document Reproduction Service No. ED 168 668).

Gilder, J. (1980). Lifelong education: The critical policy questions. In B. Heerman, C. C. Enders, and E. Wine (Eds.), *Serving lifelong learners* (New Directions for Community Colleges, Number 29, pp. 69–86). San Francisco, CA: Jossey-Bass.

Ginther, J. (1974). *Progress report to the National Heart and Lung Institute* (NHLI–72–2923). Chicago: The University of Chicago.

Gleazer, E. J. (1980). *The community college: Values, vision and vitality.* Washington, DC : American Association of Community and Junior Colleges.

Goble, F. G. (1970). *The third force.* New York: Grossman.

Gough, H. G., and Heilbrun, A. B. (1983). *The Adjective Check List manual* (3rd ed.). Paulo Alto, CA: Consulting Psychologists Press, Inc.

Gould, R. L. (1978). *Transformations.* New York: Simon & Schuster.

Grabowski, S. M. (1972). Adult education in museums. *Continuing Education for Adults, 171,* 1–5.

Graeve, E. A. (1987). Patterns of self-directed professional learning of registered nurses (Doctoral dissertation, University of Minnesota, 1987). *Dissertation Abstracts International, 48,* 820A.

Grattan, C. H. (1955). *In quest of knowledge.* New York: Association Press.

Green, G. M. (1984). Product use training for customers at Du Pont. In M. S. Knowles and associates, *Andragogy in action* (pp. 81–86). San Francisco: Jossey-Bass.

Griffin, C. (1983). *Curriculum theory in adult and lifelong education.* London: Croom Helm.

Gross, R. (1977). *The lifelong learner.* New York: Simon and Schuster.

Gross, R. (Contributing Editor). (1980). Because people matter. In University of Mid-America, *Issues for the '80s: Federal policy and the adult learner* (National symposium, Washington, DC, March 3–4, 1980, special report). Lincoln, NB: University of Mid-America, Office of Information and Publications.

Gross, R. (1982). *The independent scholar's handbook.* Reading, MA: Addison-Wesley.

Guglielmino, L. M. (1977). Development of the self-directed learning readiness scale. (Doctoral dissertation, University of Georgia, 1977). *Dissertation Abstracts International, 38,* 6467A.

Guglielmino, L. M. (1989). Guglielmino responds to Field's investigation. *Adult Education Quarterly, 39*(4), 235–240.

Guglielmino, L. M., and Guglielmino, P. J. (1988). Self-directed learning in business and industry: An information age imperative. In H. B. Long and associates, *Self-directed learning: Application and Theory* (pp. 125–148). Athens, Georgia: University of Georgia, Adult Education Department.

Guglielmino, P. J. and Guglielmino, L. M. (1983). *An examination of the relationship between self-directed learning readiness and job performance in a major utility.* Unpublished manuscript.

Guglielmino, P. J., Guglielmino, L. M., and Long, H. B. (1987). Self-directed learning readiness and performance in the workplace. *Higher Education, 16,* 303–317.

Gurian, E. (1981). Adult learning at children's museum of Boston. In Z. W. Collins (Ed.), *Museums, adults and the humanities* (pp. 271–296). Washington, DC : American Association of Museums.

Habermas, J. (1970). *Toward a rational society.* Boston: Beacon Press.

Habermas, J. (1971). *Knowledge and human interests.* Boston: Beacon Press.

Hall, G. L. (1981). Adult education means equality in Sweden. *Lifelong Learning: The Adult Years, 4*(8), 6–7.

Hall-Johnsen, K. J. (1986). The relationship between readiness for, and involvement in, self-directed learning (Doctoral dissertation, Iowa State University, 1985). *Dissertation Abstracts International, 46,* 2522A.

Hamidi, A. S. (1979). Adult education in Saudi Arabia. *Lifelong Learning: The Adult Years, 2*(5), 30–33.

Hamm, C. (1982). Critique of self-education. *Canadian Journal of Education, 7*(4), 85–106.

Harrington, F. H. (1977). *The future of adult education.* San Francisco: Jossey-Bass.

Hassan, A. M. (1982). An investigation of the learning projects among adults of high and low readiness for self-direction in learning. (Doctoral dissertation, Iowa State University, 1981). *Dissertation Abstracts International, 42,* 3838A.

Hayes, E. R. (1988). A typology of low-literate adults based on perceptions of deterrents to participation in adult education. *Adult Education Quarterly, 39*(1), 1–10.

Hayes, E. R. (Ed.) (1989). *Effective teaching styles* (New Directions for Continuing Education, Number 43). San Francisco: Jossey-Bass.

Heine, A. (1977). *Museums and the teacher* (Occasional Papers no. 3). Corpus Christi, TX: Friends of the Corpus Christi Museum. (ERIC Document Reproduction Service No. ED 146 077).

Heisel, M. A. (1985). Assessment of learning activity level in a group of Black aged. *Adult Education Quarterly, 36,* 1–14.

Henry, N. J. (1983). *The rights and responsibilities of institutions promoting self-directed learning.* Unpublished manuscript, Adult Education Program, Syracuse University, Syracuse, NY.

Hesburgh, T. M., Miller, P. A., and Wharton, C. R., Jr. (1973). *Patterns for lifelong learning.* San Francisco: Jossey-Bass.

Hiemstra, R. (1975). *The older adult and learning.* (ERIC Document Reproduction Service No. ED 117 371).

Hiemstra, R. (1976a). *Lifelong learning.* Lincoln, Nebraska: Professional Educators Publications. Reprinted in 1984 by HiTree Press, Baldwinsville, New York.

Hiemstra, R. (1976b). The older adult's learning projects. *Educational Gerontology, 1,* 331–341.

Hiemstra, R. (1980). *Policy recommendations related to self-directed adult learners* (CEP 1). Syracuse, New York: Syracuse University Printing Service. (ERIC Document Reproduction Service No. ED 193 529).

Hiemstra, R. (1981a). Adults as learners. In Z. W. Collins (Ed.), *Museums, adults and the humanities* (pp. 61–72). Washington, DC: American Association of Museums.

Hiemstra, R. (1981b). The implications of lifelong learning. In Z. W. Collins (Ed.), *Museums, adults and the humanities* (pp. 120–130). Washington, DC: American Association of Museums.

Hiemstra, R. (1981c). American and Japanese adult education: A cultural comparison. *Lifelong Learning: The Adult Years, 4*(10), 8–9, 30.

Hiemstra, R. (1982a). The elderly learner: A naturalistic inquiry. Proceedings of the 23rd Adult Education Research Conference (pp. 103–107). Lincoln, NE: University of Nebraska.

Hiemstra, R. (1982b). *Self-directed learning: Some implications for practice* (CEP 2). Syracuse, NY: Syracuse University Printing Service. (ERIC Document Reproduction Service No. ED 262 259).

Hiemstra, R. (1985a). *The educative community: Linking the community, education, and family.* Baldwinsville, NY: HiTree Press.

Hiemstra, R. (1985b). The older adult's learning projects. In D. B. Lumsden (Ed.), *The older adult as learner* (pp. 165–196). Washington, DC: Hemisphere Publishing.

Hiemstra, R. (1985c). *Self-directed adult learning: Some implications for facilitators* (CEP 3). Syracuse, New York: Syracuse University Printing Service. (ERIC Document Reproduction Service No. ED 262 260).

Hiemstra, R. (1987a, July). Comparing andragogy in two cultures: Tanzania and the United States. Paper presented at the Comparative Adult Education: An International Conference, Oxford, UK.

Hiemstra, R. (1987b). Creating the future. In R. G. Brockett (Ed.), *Continuing education in the year 2000* (New Directions for Continuing Education, Number 36, pp. 3–14). San Francisco, CA: Jossey-Bass.

Hiemstra, R. (1987c). Turning research on older persons into daily practice. *Perspectives on Aging, 16*(1), 17–19.

Hiemstra, R. (1988a). Self-directed learning: Individualizing instruction. In H. B. Long and associates, *Self-directed learning: Application and theory* (pp. 99–124). Athens, Georgia: University of Georgia, Adult Education Department.

Hiemstra, R. (1988b). Translating personal values and philosophy into practical action. In R. G. Brockett (Ed.), *Ethical issues in adult education* (pp. 178–194). New York: Teachers College Press.

Hiemstra, R., and Sisco, B. R. (1990). *Individualizing instruction: Making learning personal, empowering, and successful.* San Francisco: Jossey-Bass.

Hilton, W. J. (1982). Toward a comprehensive policy for the education of adults. In G. C. Whaples and W. M. Rivera (Eds.), *Policy issues and processes* (pp. 23–31). College Park, MD: University of Maryland, Department of Agricultural and Extension Education.

Himmelstrup, P. (1988, February). Lifelong learning: The Scandinavian perspective. Paper presented at a colloquium for the School of Education, Syracuse University, Syracuse, NY.

Horn, A. (1979). The adult tour dilemma. *Roundtable Reports, 4*(4), 1–4.

Hosmer, W. (1847). *Self-education: Or the philosophy of mental improvement.* Havana, NY: W. H. Ongley.

Houle, C. O. (1961). *The inquiring mind.* Madison, Wisconsin: The University of Wisconsin Press.

Houle, C. O. (1972). *The design of education,* (5) 2. San Francisco: Jossey-Bass.

Houle, C. O. (1973). *The external degree.* San Francisco: Jossey-Bass.

Houle, C. O. (1988). *The inquiring mind* (2nd ed). Norman, OK: Oklahoma Research Center for Continuing Professional and Higher Education, University of Oklahoma.

Hunter, W. E. (1971). *Self-directed learning at Meramec Community College.* (ERIC Document Reproduction Service No. ED 045 081).

Illich, I. (1971). *Deschooling society.* New York: Harper and Row.

Ingham, R. J. (1984, November). Self-directed learning: Looking at the concept from a different perspective. Paper presented at the annual meeting of the Commission of Professors of Adult Education, Louisville, KY.

Jarvis, P. (1984). Andragogy – a sign of the times. *Studies in the education of adults, 16*(October), 32–38.

Jarvis, P. (1985). *The sociology of adult and continuing education.* London: Croom Helm.

Jensen, G. (1960). The nature of education as a discipline. In G. Jensen (Ed.), *Readings for educational researchers.* Ann Arbor, MI: Ann Arbor Publishers.

Jensen, G., Liveright, A. A., and Hallenbeck, W. (Eds.). (1964). *Adult education:*

Outlines of an emerging field of university study. Washington, DC : Adult Education Association of the USA.

Johnson, E. (1973). Selected characteristics of learning projects pursued by adults who have earned a high school diploma and/or high school equivalency certificate (Doctoral dissertation, University of Georgia, 1973). *Dissertation Abstracts International, 34,* 2332A–2333A.

Johnson, J. A., Sample, J. A., and Jones, W. J. (1988). Self-directed learning and personality type in adult degree students. *Psychology: A Journal of Human Behavior, 25*(1), 32–36.

Johnstone, J., and Rivera, R. (1965). *Volunteers for learning, a study of the educational pursuits of American adults.* National Opinion Research Center report. Chicago: Aldine Publishing Company.

Judd, R. (1980). *The decision making processes involved in institutional and non-institutional self-directed learning.* Unpublished master's thesis, Iowa State University, Ames, IA.

Kaluzny, G. (1983). *Love of learning and lived experience: Necessary ingredients for the self-directed adult learner.* Unpublished manuscript, Adult Education Program, Syracuse University, Syracuse, NY.

Kasworm, C. E. (1982). An exploratory study of the development of self-directed learning as an instructional/curriculum strategy. *Proceedings of the Lifelong Learning Research Conference* (pp. 125–129). University of Maryland, College Park, Maryland.

Kasworm, C. E. (1983). An examination of self-directed learning contracts as an instructional strategy. *Innovative Higher Education,* 8(1), 45–54.

Kasworm, C. E. (1988a). Self-directed learning in institutional contexts: An exploratory study of adult self-directed learners in adult education. In H. B. Long and associates, *Self-directed learning: Application and theory* (pp. 65–98). Athens, Georgia: University of Georgia, Adult Education Department.

Kasworm, C. E. (1988b, November). *Part-time credit learners as full-time workers: The role of self-directed learning in their lives.* Paper presented at the annual conference of the American Association for Adult and Continuing Education, Tulsa, OK.

Kay, E. R. (1982). *Participation in adult education 1981.* Washington, DC: US Department of Education, National Center for Education Statistics.

Kerwin, M. A. (1984). Instruction in public speaking at a community college. In M. S. Knowles and associates, *Andragogy in action* (pp. 189–192). San Francisco: Jossey-Bass.

Kidd, J. R. (1973). *How adults learn.* Chicago: Association Press.

Kilpatrick, A. C., Thompson, K. H., Jarrett, Jr., H. H., and Anderson, R. J. (1984). Social work education at the University of Georgia. In M. S. Knowles and associates, *Andragogy in action* (pp. 243–264). San Francisco: Jossey-Bass.

Knowles, M. S. (1968). Androgogy, not pedagogy! *Adult Leadership, 16,* 350–352, 386.

Knowles, M. S. (1970). *The modern practice of adult education.* New York: Association Press.

Knowles, M. S. (1975). *Self-directed learning.* New York: Association Press.

Knowles, M. S. (1979). Andragogy revisited part II. *Adult Education, 30*(1), 52–53.

Knowles, M. S. (1980). *The modern practice of adult education* (revised and updated). Chicago: Association Press.

Knowles, M. S.(1984). *The adult learner: A neglected species*. Houston: Gulf Publishing.

Knowles, M. S. (1986). *Using learning contracts*. San Francisco: Jossey-Bass.

Knowles, M. S., and associates. (1984). *Andragogy in action*. San Francisco: Jossey-Bass.

Knox, A. B. (1981). Basic components of adult programming. In Z. W. Collins (Ed.), *Museums, adults and the humanities* (pp. 95–111). Washington, DC : American Association of Museums.

Knudson, R. S. (1979). Humanagogy anyone? *Adult Education, 29*(4), 261–264.

Kordalewski, J. B. (1982). *The regional learning service: An experiment in freeing up lives*. Syracuse, New York: Regional Learning Service of Central New York, Inc., 405 Oak Street.

Kulich, J. (1970). *An historical overview of the adult self-learner*. Paper presented at the Northwest Institute Conference on Independent Study: The adult as a self-learner, University of British Columbia, Vancouver.

Kulich, J. (1984). N. F. S. Grundtvig's folk high school idea and the challenge of our times. *Lifelong Learning: The Adult Years, 7*(4), 10–13.

Kurland, N. D. (1980). Alternative financing arrangements for lifelong education. In A. J. Cropley (Ed.), *Towards a system of lifelong education: Some practical considerations* (pp. 162–185).

Kurland, N. D. (1982). The Scandinavian study circle: An idea for the US. Oxford: Pergamon Press. *Lifelong Learning: The Adult Years, 5*(6), 24–27, 30.

Lacey, L. C. (1989). Readiness for self-directed learning in women during the four stages of pregnancy (Doctoral dissertation, University of Missouri-Kansas City, 1988). *Dissertation Abstracts International, 49*, 2496A.

Landers, K. (1990). *The Oddi Continuous Learning Inventory: An alternate measure of self-direction in learning*. (Doctoral disertation, Syracuse University. 1989). *Dissertation Abstracts International, 50*, 3824A.

Lawson, K. (1979). *Philosophical concepts and values in adult education*. Milton Keynes, England: Open University Press.

Leean, C., and Sisco, B. (1981). *Learning projects and self-planned learning efforts among undereducated adults in rural Vermont* (Final Report No. 99–1051). Washington, DC : National Institute of Education.

Leeb, J. G. (1985). Self-directed learning and growth toward personal responsibility: Implications for a framework for health promotion. (Doctoral dissertation, Syracuse University, 1983). *Dissertation Abstracts International, 45*, 724A.

Lewin, K. (1951). *Field theory in social science: Selected theoretical papers*. New York: Harper & Row.

Lewis, G. R. (1978). *A comparative study of learning networks in the United States*. Evanston, IL: Northwestern University. (ERIC Document Reproduction Service No. ED 007 129).

Lindeman, E. C. (1926). *The meaning of adult education*. New York: New Republic.

Litchfield, A. (1965). The nature and pattern of participation in adult education activities (Doctoral dissertation, University of Chicago, 1965). *American Doctoral Dissertations 1965–1966*, 74.

Little, D. (1979). Adult learning and education: A concept analysis. In P. M. Cunningham (Ed.), *Yearbook of adult and continuing education* (1979–1980). Chicago: Marquis Academic Media.

Little, D. J. (1985). Self-directed education: A conceptual analysis. *Proceedings of the 26th Annual Adult Education Research Conference* (pp. 189–194). Arizona State University, Higher and Adult Education, Tempe, Arizona.

Ljosa, E., and Sandvold, K. (1983). The student's freedom of choice within the didactical structure of a correspondence course. In D. Sewart, D. Keegan, and B. Holmberg (Eds.), *Distance education: International perspectives* (pp. 291–315). London: Croom Helm.

Lloyds Bank of California. (1984). Self-directed learning on the job at Lloyds Bank of California. In M. S. Knowles and associates, *Andragogy in action* (pp. 69–72). San Francisco: Jossey-Bass.

Loacker, G., and Doherty, A. (1984). Self-directed undergraduate study. In M. S. Knowles and associates, *Andragogy in action* (pp. 101–120). San Francisco: Jossey-Bass.

London, J. (1973). Adult education for the 1970s: Promise or illusion. *Adult Education, 24*(1), 60–70.

Long, H. (1976). *Continuing education of adults in Colonial America.* Syracuse, New York: Syracuse University Publications in Continuing Education.

Long, H. B. (1982). Adult education in China: AEA's 1980 China tour. *Lifelong Learning: The Adult Years, 5*(7), 12–14.

Long, H. B. (1987). Item analysis of Guglielmino's self-directed learning readiness scale. *International Journal of Lifelong Education, 6*, 331–336.

Long, H. B. (1989). Some additional criticisms of Field's investigation. *Adult Education Quarterly, 39*(4), 240–243.

Long, H. B., and Agyekum, S. K. (1983). Guglielmino's Self-Directed Learning Readiness Scale: A validation study. *Higher Education, 12*, 77–87.

Long, H. B., and Agyekum, S. K. (1984). Teacher ratings in the validation of Guglielmino's Self-Directed Learning Readiness Scale. *Higher Education, 13*, 709–715.

Long, H. B., and Agyekum, S. K. (1988). Self-directed learning readiness: Assessment and validation. In H. B. Long and associates, *Self-directed learning: Application and theory* (pp. 253–266). Athens, Georgia: University of Georgia, Adult Education Department.

Long, H. B., and Agyekum, S. K. (1990). Toward a theory of self-directed learning: An appraisal of Gibbons' principles and strategies. In H. B. Long and associates, *Advances in research and practice in self-directed learning.* Norman, OK: Oklahoma Research Center for Continuing Higher and Professional Education, University of Oklahoma.

Lundgren, P. M. (1988). Intentional change and learning: Diabetes related health changes by Type II diabetics (Unpublished doctoral dissertation, Montana State University, 1987). *Dissertation Abstracts International, 49*, 186A.

Margolis, F. H. (1984). Teaching technical skills in a national accounting firm. In M. S. Knowles and associates, *Andragogy in action* (pp. 45–54). San Francisco: Jossey-Bass.

Martin, A. B. (1972). *A strategy for public library change: Proposed public library goals – feasibility study.* Chicago: American Library Association.

Maslow, A. H. (1954). *Motivation and personality.* New York: Harper and Row.

Maslow, A. H. (1970). *Motivation and personality* (2nd ed.). New York: Harper and Row.

Mavor, A. S., Toro, J. O., and DeProspo, E. R. (1976). *Final report: The role of the public library in adult independent learning.* New York: College Entrance Examination Board.

McCarthy, W. F. (1986). The self-directedness and attitude toward mathematics of younger and older undergraduate mathematics students (Doctoral dissertation, Syracuse University, 1985). *Dissertation Abstracts International, 46,* 3279A.

McClusky, H. Y. (1960). Community development. In M. S. Knowles (Ed.), *Handbook of adult education in the United States* (pp. 416–427). Washington, DC : Adult Education Association of the USA

McCoy, C. T. (1988). Self-directed learning among clinical laboratory science professionals in different organizational settings (Doctoral dissertation, University of Oklahoma, 1987). *Dissertation Abstracts International, 49,* 187A.

McCune, S. K. (1989a). A meta-analytic study of adult self-direction in learning: A review of the research from 1977 to 1987 (Doctoral dissertation, Texas A & M University, 1988). *Dissertation Abstracts International, 49,* 3237A.

McCune, S. K. (1989b). A statistical critique of Field's investigation. *Adult Education Quarterly 39*(4), 243–245.

McGinnis, P. St. C. (1981). The focus should be on human liberation. In B. W. Kreitlow and associates, *Examining controversies in adult education.* San Francisco: Jossey-Bass.

McKenzie, L. (1977). The issue of andragogy. *Adult Education, 27*(4), 225–229.

McKenzie, L. (1979). A response to Elias. *Adult Education, 29*(4), 256–260.

Mezirow, J. (1975). *Education for perspective transformation: Women's reentry programs in community colleges.* New York: Center for Adult Development, Teachers College, Columbia University.

Mezirow, J. (1978). Perspective transformation. *Adult Education, 28*(2), 100–110.

Mezirow, J. (1981). A critical theory of adult learning and education. *Adult Education, 32*(1), 3–24.

Mezirow, J. (1985). A critical theory of self-directed learning. In S. Brookfield (Ed.), *Self-directed learning: From theory to practice* (New Directions for Continuing Education Number 25, pp. 17–30). San Francisco: Jossey-Bass.

Mezirow, J. (1989). Transformation theory and social action: A response to Collard and Law. *Adult Education Quarterly, 39*(3), 169–175.

Middlemiss, M. A. (1988). Relationship of self-directed learning readiness and job characteristics to job satisfaction for professional nurses (Doctoral dissertation, Syracuse University, 1987). *Dissertation Abstracts International, 49,* 1035A.

Miller, N., and Botsman, P. B. (1975). Continuing education for extension agents. *Human Ecology Forum, 6*(2), 14–17.

Mocker, D. W., and Spear, G. E. (1982). *Lifelong learning: Formal, nonformal, informal, and self-directed* (Information Series No. 241). Columbus, Ohio: ERIC Clearinghouse for Adult, Career, and Vocational Education, Ohio State University.

Monroe, M. E. (1963). *Library adult education: The biography of an idea.* New York: Scarecrow Press.

Moore, D. R. (1986). An investigation of self-reports of decisions to change in prison inmates. (Doctoral dissertation, Syracuse University, 1985). *Dissertation Abstracts International, 46,* 3570A.

Moore, M. G. (1973). Towards a theory of independent learning. *Journal of Higher Education, 44.*

Moore, M. G. (1980). Independent study. In R. D. Boyd, J. W. Apps, and associates, *Redefining the discipline of adult education* (pp. 16–31). San Francisco: Jossey-Bass.

Moore, M. (1983). *Self directed learning and distance education* (Ziff Papiere 48). Hagen: Zentrales Institut fur Fernstudienforschung.

Moore, R. J. (1988). Predictors of success in courses for nurses requiring a degree of self-direction (Doctoral dissertation, Florida Atlantic University, 1987). *Dissertation Abstracts International, 48,* 1670A.

Morstain, B. R., and Smart, J. C. (1974). Reasons for participation in adult education courses: A multivariate analysis of group differences. *Adult Education, 24*(2), 83–98.

Mourad, S. A. (1979). Relationship of grade level, sex, and creativity to readiness for self-directed learning among intellectually gifted students (Doctoral dissertation, University of Georgia, 1979). *Dissertation Abstracts International, 40,* 2002A.

Murray, J. A. (1988). The effect of a clinical internship on the self-directed learning readiness of baccalaureate nursing students (Doctoral dissertation, University of Iowa, 1987). *Dissertation Abstracts International, 49,* 1036A.

National Center for Educational Statistics. (1989). *National estimates of higher education: School year 1988–89* (CS89–315). Washington, DC : Information Services.

Neufeld, V. R., and Barrows, H. S. (1984). Preparing medical students for lifelong learning. In M. S. Knowles and associates, *Andragogy in action* (pp. 207–226). San Francisco: Jossey-Bass.

Newsom, R. (1977). Lifelong learning in London: 1558–1640. *Lifelong Learning: The Adult Years, 1*(4), 4–5, 19–21.

Nunnally, J. C., Jr. (1970). *Introduction to psychological measurement.* New York: McGraw-Hill.

Oddi, L. F. (1984). Development of an instrument to measure self-directed continuing learning. (Doctoral dissertation, Northern Illinois University, 1984). *Dissertation Abstracts International, 46,* 49A.

Oddi, L. F. (1985). Development and validation of an instrument to identify self-directed continuing learners. *Proceedings of the 26th Annual Adult Education Research Conference* (pp. 229–235). Arizona State University, Higher and Adult Education, Tempe, Arizona.

Oddi, L. F. (1986). Development and validation of an instrument to identify self-directed continuing learners. *Adult Education Quarterly, 36,* 97–107.

Oddi, L. F. (1987). Perspectives on self-directed learning. *Adult Education Quarterly, 38*(1), 21–31.

O'Hara, M. (1989). Person-centered approach as conscientizacão: The works of Carl Rogers and Paulo Freire. *Journal of Humanistic Psychology, 29*(1), 11–36.

Oliver, L. P. (1987). *Study circles.* Cabin John, MD: Seven Locks Press.

Palumbo, D. V. (1990). Influence of upper division education on adult nursing students as self-directed learners. (Doctoral dissertation, Syracuse University, Syracuse, NY). *Dissertation Abstracts International, 51,* 382A.

Pardoen, A. R. (1977). Lifelong learning legislation in Norway. *Lifelong Learning: The Adult Years, 1*(3), 12–15.

Parks, T. (1981). NEW learning museum programs. In Z. W. Collins (Ed.), *Museums, adults and the humanities* (pp. 203–235). Washington, DC : American Association of Museums.

Penland, P. R. (1977). *Self-planned learning in America.* Pittsburgh: Book Center, University of Pittsburgh.

Penland, P. R. (1978). *Self-planned learning in America.* (ERIC Document Reproduction Service No. ED 154 987).

Penland, P. (1979). Self-initiated learning. *Adult Education Quarterly, 29,* 170–179.

Penland, P. R. (1981). *Towards self-directed learning theory.* (ERIC Document Reproduction Service No. ED 209 457).

Perkins, A. T. (1985a). The learning exchange network: An evolutionary step in providing support for self-directed learning (Part I). *Lifelong Learning: An Omnibus of Practice and Research, 8*(4), 9–11, 28.

Perkins, A. T. (1985b). The learning exchange network: An evolutionary step in providing support for self-directed learning (Part II). *Lifelong Learning: An Omnibus of Practice and Research, 8*(5), 23–25.

Perry, W., Jr. (1970). *Forms of intellectual and ethical development in the college years: A scheme.* New York: Holt, Rinehart, & Winston.

Peters, J. M. and Gordon, R. S. (1974). *Adult learning projects: A study of adult learning in urban and rural Tennessee.* Knoxville: The University of Tennessee, Knoxville. (ERIC Document Reproduction Service No. ED 102 431).

Peterson, R. E., and associates. (1979). *Lifelong learning in America.* San Francisco: Jossey-Bass.

Podeschi, R. L. (1987). Andragogy: Proofs or premises. *Lifelong Learning: An Omnibus of Practice and Research, 11*(3), 14–16, 20.

Podeschi, R. L., and Pearson, E. M. (1986). Knowles and Maslow: Differences about freedom. *Lifelong Learning: An Omnibus of Practice and Research, 9*(7), 16–18.

Pratt, D. D. (1984). Teaching adults: A conceptual framework for the first session. *Lifelong Learning: An Omnibus of Practice and Research, 7*(6), 7–9, 28, 31.

Pratt, D. D. (1988). Andragogy as a relational construct. *Adult Education Quarterly, 38,* 160–172.

Progoff, I. (1975). *At a journal workshop.* New York: Dialogue House Library.

Rachal, J. R. (1983). The andragogy-pedagogy debate: Another voice in the fray. *Lifelong Learning: An Omnibus of Practice and Research, 6*(9), 14–15.

Ralston, P. A. (1979). The relationship of self-perceived educational needs and activities of older adults to selected senior center programs: A community study. (Doctoral dissertation, University of Illinois at Urbana-Champaign, 1978). *Dissertation Abstracts International, 39,* 7196A–7197A.

Ralston, P. A. (1981). Educational needs and activities of older adults: Their relationship to senior center programs. *Educational Gerontology, 7,* 231–244.

Reamer, F. G. (1982). *Ethical dilemmas in social service.* New York: Columbia University Press.

Reynolds, M. M. (1983). *Self-directed learning: Appropriate for all?* Unpublished manuscript, Adult Education Program, Syracuse University, Syracuse, NY.

Reynolds, M. M. (1986). The self-directedness and motivational orientations of adult part-time students at a community college (Doctoral dissertation, Syracuse University, 1984). *Dissertation Abstracts International, 46,* 571A.

Riesman, D. (1950). *The lonely crowd.* New Haven, CT: Yale University Press.

Rivera, W. M. (1982). Reflections on policy issues in adult education. In G. C. Whaples and W. M. Rivera (Eds.), *Policy issues and processes* (pp. 1–22). College Park, MD: University of Maryland, Department of Agricultural and Extension Education.

Roberts, D. G. (1986). A study of the use of the Self-Directed Learning Readiness Scale as related to selected organizational variables (Doctoral dissertation, George Washington University, 1986). *Dissertation Abstracts International, 47,* 1218A–1219A.

Rogers, C. R. (1951). *Client-centered therapy: Its current practice, implications, and theory.* Boston: Houghton Mifflin.

Rogers, C. R. (1961). *On becoming a person.* Boston: Houghton Mifflin.

Rogers, C. R. (1969). *Freedom to learn.* Columbus, OH: Charles E. Merrill.

Rogers, C. R. (1977). *Carl Rogers on personal power.* New York: Delacorte Press.

Rogers, C. R. (1983). *Freedom to learn for the eighties.* Columbus, OH: Charles E. Merrill.

Rotter, J. B. (1966). Generalized expectancies for internal versus external control of reinforcement. *Psychological Monographs, 80*(1, Whole No. 609).

Royce, M. (1970). Study circles in Finland. *Convergence, 3,* 69–73.

Russell, J. W. (1989). Learning preference for structure, self-directed learning readiness, and instructional methods (Doctoral dissertation, University of Missouri-Kansas City, 1988). *Dissertation Abstracts International, 49,* 1689A.

Rutland, A. M. (1988). Effects of a self-directed learning group experience on the self-directed learning readiness and self-concepts of adult basic education students and general educational development students (Doctoral dissertation, Florida Atlantic University, 1987). *Dissertation Abstracts International, 49,* 29A.

Ruvinsky, L. I. (1986). *Activeness and self-education* (J. Sayer, Trans.). Moscow: Progress Publishers.

Rydell, S. T. (1983). Educational materials development and use with self-directed learners. In J. P. Wilson (Ed.), *Materials for teaching adults: Selection, development and use* (New Directions for Continuing Education, Number 17, pp. 61–67). San Francisco: Jossey-Bass.

Rymell, R. G., and Newsom, R. (1981). Self-directed learning and HRD. *Training and Development Journal, August,* 50–52.

Sabbaghian, Z. S. (1980). Adult self-directedness and self-concept: An exploration of relationships (Doctoral dissertation, Iowa State University, 1979). *Dissertation Abstracts International, 40,* 3701A.

Salamon, M. J., and Conte, V. A. (1981). *The Salamon–Conte Life Satisfaction in the Elderly Scale and the eight correlates of life satisfaction.* Presented at the Annual Meeting of the Gerontological Society of America, Toronto, Ontario.

Sanda, R. (1984). Involving the community as a resource for learning. In M. S. Knowles and associates, *Andragogy in action* (pp. 379–389). San Francisco: Jossey-Bass.

Savicevic, D. M. (1981). Adult education systems in European Socialist countries: Similarities and differences. In A. N. Charters (Ed.), *Comparing adult education worldwide* (pp. 37–89). San Francisco: Jossey-Bass.

Savicevic, D. M. (1985). Self-directed education for lifelong education. *International Journal of Lifelong Education, 4,* 285–294.

Savicevic, D. M. (1988, May). *Conceptions of andragogy in different countries: Comparative considerations.* Paper presented at the 1988 Study Seminar: Comparative Research in Adult Education, Rome, Italy.

Savicevic, D. M. (1989). Conceptions of andragogy in different countries: Comparative considerations. In M. Lichtner (Ed.), *Comparative research in adult education: Present lines and perspectives* (pp. 65–72). Villa Falconieri, 00044 Frascati, Rome, Italy: Centro Europeo Dell Educazione.

Savoie, M. M. (1980). Continuing education for nurses: Predictors of success in courses requiring a degree of learner self-direction (Doctoral dissertation, University of Toronto, 1979). *Dissertation Abstracts International, 40,* 6114A.

Scanlan, C. L., and Darkenwald, G. G. (1984). Identifying deterrents to participation in continuing education. *Adult Education Quarterly, 34*(3), 155–166.

Schon, D. A. (1987). *Educating the reflective practitioner*. San Francisco: Jossey-Bass.

Schuttenberg, E. M. (1984). Teaching school administration at Cleveland State University. In M. S. Knowles and associates, *Andragogy in action* (pp. 285–295). San Francisco: Jossey-Bass.

Schuttenberg, E. M., and Tracy, S. J. (1987). The role of the adult educator in fostering self-directed learning. *Lifelong Learning: An Omnibus of Practice and Research*, *10*(5), 4–6, 9.

Sekiguchi, R. W. (1985). Education and the aged: Social and conceptual changes in Japan. *Educational Gerontology*, *11*, 277–293.

Shackelford, R. A. (1983). Self-directed learning projects among black adults in Havana, Florida. (Doctoral dissertation, The Florida State University, 1983). *Dissertation Abstracts International*, *44*, 647A.

Shaw, D. M. (1987). Self-directed learning and intellectual development: A correlation study. Unpublished master's thesis, Montana State University, Bozeman, MT.

Shipley, W. C. (1982). *Shipley Institute of Living Scale: Scoring key*. Los Angeles: Western Psychological Services.

Shostrom, E. L. (1964). An inventory for the measurement of self-actualization. *Educational and Psychological Measurement*, *24*, 207–218.

Shostrom, E. L. (1974). *Personal Orientation Inventory Manual*. San Diego: Educational and Industrial Testing Service.

Sidel, M. (1982). Adult education in the People's Republic of China. *Convergence*, *15*(3), 37–47.

Sinclair, C., and Skerman, R. (1984). Management development at a public service board. In M. S. Knowles and associates, *Andragogy in Action* (pp. 87–97). San Francisco: Jossey-Bass.

Singarella, T. A., and Sork, T. J. (1983). Questions of values and conduct: Ethical issues for adult educators. *Adult Education Quarterly*, *33*(4), 244–251.

Sisco, B. (1983). [Review of *Intentional Changes*]. *Lifelong Learning: The Adult Years*, *6*(9), 27.

Six, J. E. (1989a). *Measuring the performance properties of the Oddi continuing learning inventory*. (Doctoral dissertation, Syracuse University, 1987). *Dissertation Abstracts International*, *49*, 701A.

Six, J. E. (1989b). The generality of the underlying dimensions of the Oddi Continuing Learning Inventory. *Adult Education Quarterly*, *40*(1), 43–51.

Six, J. E., and Hiemstra, R. (1987). The classroom learning scale: A criterion measure of the Oddi continuing learning inventory. *Proceedings of the 28th Annual Adult Education Research Conference* (pp. 233–238). University of Wyoming, Laramie, Wyoming.

Skager, R. (1979). Self-directed learning and schooling: Identifying pertinent theories and illustrative research. *International Review of Education*, *25*, 517–543.

Skaggs, B. J. (1981). The relationship between involvement of professional nurses in self-directed learning activities, loci of control, and readiness for self-directed learning measures (Doctoral dissertation, The University of Texas, Austin, 1981). *Dissertation Abstracts International*, *42*, 1906A.

Smith, J. C. (1986). Librarians and self-directed learners. *Proceedings of the 27th Annual Adult Education Research Conference* (pp. 249–254). Syracuse, New York: Syracuse University Printing Service.

Smith, J. C. (1990). Public librarian perceptions of library users as self-directed learners. (Doctoral dissertation, Syracuse University, 1989). *Dissertation Abstracts International, 51,* 1087A.

Smith, R. M. (1982). *Learning how to learn.* Chicago: Follett Publishing Company.

Smith, R. M., and Cunningham, P. M. (1987). *The independent learners' sourcebook.* Chicago: American Library Association.

Snedden, D. (1930). Self-education: A needed emphasis in current proposals for adult education. *Journal of Adult Education, 2*(1), 32–37.

Spear, G. E., and Mocker, D. W. (1984). The organizing circumstance: Environmental determinants in self-directed learning. *Adult Education Quarterly, 35,* 1–10.

Steinbeck, J. (1939). *The grapes of wrath.* New York: Viking Press.

Stewart, D. (1985). Our daily newspapers – A forgotten medium for adult education. *Australian Journal of Adult Education, 25*(1), 15–22.

Stubblefield, H. W. (1981a). A learning project model for adults. *Lifelong Learning: The Adult Years, 4*(7), 24–26.

Stubblefield, H. W. (1981b). The focus should be on life fulfillment. In B. W. Kreitlow and associates, *Examining controversies in adult education.* San Francisco: Jossey-Bass.

Sullivan, R. (1984). Introducing data processing at an insurance company. In M. S. Knowles and associates, *Andragogy in action* (pp. 73–80). San Francisco: Jossey-Bass.

Svensson, A. (1988, February). Swedish folk high schools and study circles. Paper presented at a colloquium for the School of Education, Syracuse University, Syracuse, NY.

Taylor, M., and Porterfield, W. D. (1983). *Manual for the Measure of Epistemological Reflection.* Unpublished manuscript.

Tennant, M. (1986). An evaluation of Knowles' theory of adult learning. *International Journal of Lifelong Education, 5,* 113–122.

Torrance, E. P., and Mourad, S. (1978). Some creativity and style of learning and thinking correlates of Guglielmino's Self-Directed Learning Readiness Scale. *Psychological Reports, 43,* 1167–1171.

Totten, W. F. (1970). *The power of community education.* Midland, Michigan: Pendell Publishing Company.

Tough, A. M. (1966). The assistance obtained by adult self-teachers. *Adult Education, 17*(1), 30–37.

Tough, A. (1971). *The adult's learning projects.* Toronto: Ontario Institute for Studies in Education.

Tough, A. (1978). Major learning efforts: Recent research and future directions. *Adult Education, 28,* 250–263.

Tough, A. (1979). *The adult's learning projects* (2nd ed.). Austin, Texas: Learning Concepts.

Tough, A. M. (1982). *Intentional changes.* Chicago: Follett.

Training for Rural Development. (1984). *Tanzania: Project phase II, formative evaluation* (621-0161). Washington, DC : United States Agency for International Development.

Umoren, A. P. (1978). Learning projects: An exploratory study of learning activities of adults in a select socioeconomic group. (Doctoral dissertation, University of Nebraska, 1977). *Dissertation Abstracts International, 38,* 2490A.

University of Southern California. (1984). Self-directed learning for physicians at the University of Southern California. In M. S. Knowles and associates, *Andragogy in action* (pp. 297–298). San Francisco: Jossey-Bass.

Vermilye, D. W. (1976). *Individualizing the system*. San Francisco: Jossey-Bass.

Verner, C. (1964). *Adult education*. Washington, DC: The Center for Applied Research in Education.

Verner, C. (1975). Fundamental concepts in adult education. In J. Knoll (Ed.), *Internationales Jahr buch für Erwachseneubildung*. Gutersloh, Fr. Germany: Bertelsmann Universitatsverlage.

Vosko, R. S. (1984). Shaping spaces for lifelong learning. *Lifelong Learning: An Omnibus of Practice and Research, 9*(1), 4–7, 28.

Vosko, R. S. (1985). The reactions of adult learners to selected instructional environments. (Doctoral dissertation, Syracuse University, 1984). *Dissertation Abstracts International, 45*, 3519A.

Vosko, R. S., and Hiemstra, R. (1988). The adult learning environment: Importance of Physical Features. *International Journal of Lifelong Education, 7*, 185–196.

Wagner, R. F., and Wells, K. A. (1985). A refined neurobehavioral inventory of hemispheric preference. *Journal of Clinical Psychology, 41*(5), 671–676.

Warren, R. L. (1979). *The community in America*. Boston: Houghton Mifflin Company.

Watson, D. L., and Tharp, R. G. (1985). *Self-directed behavior: Self-modification for personal adjustment* (4th Ed.). Monterey, CA: Brooks/Cole.

Wedemeyer, C. A. (1981). *Learning at the back door: Reflections on nontraditional learning in the lifespan*. Madison, WI: University of Wisconsin Press.

Weichenthal, P. (1980). Impact of a shift in national public policy on continuing education administration in institutions of higher education. (Doctoral dissertation, University of Illinois at Urbana-Champaign, 1980). *Dissertation Abstracts International, 41*, 2401A.

Wexler, R. A., and Wexler, R. L. (1980). *The principles and practice of rational-emotive therapy*. San Francisco: Jossey-Bass.

White, B. A., and Brockett, R. G. (1987). Putting philosophy into practice. *Journal of Extension, 25* (Summer), 11–14.

Wiley, K. R. (1982a). Effects of a self-directed learning project and preference for structure on the self-directed learning readiness of baccalaureate nursing students (Doctoral dissertation, Northern Illinois University, 1981). *Dissertation Abstracts International, 43*, 49A–50A.

Wiley, K. R. (1982b). Effects of a self-directed learning project and preference for structure on self-directed learning readiness. In *Proceedings of the 23rd Annual Adult Education Research Conference* (pp. 227–232). Lincoln, NE.

Witkin, H. A., Oltman, P. K., Raskin, E., and Karp, S. A. (1971). *A manual for the embedded figures test*. Paulo Alto, CA: Consulting Psychologists Press.

Wriston, B. (1969). *Adult education in the art institute of Chicago*. Chicago: Art Institute of Chicago. (ERIC Document Reproduction Service No. ED. 031 670).

Yonge, G. D. (1985). Andragogy and pedagogy: Two ways of accompaniment. *Adult Education, 35*, 160–167.

Young, L. G. (1986). The relationship of race, sex, and locus of control to self-directed learning (Doctoral dissertation, University of Georgia, 1985). *Dissertation Abstracts International, 46*, 1886A.

Zabari, P. L. (1985). The role of self-directed learning in the continuing education of gerontological practitioners (Doctoral dissertation, Columbia University Teachers College, 1985). *Dissertation Abstracts International, 46*, 1060A–1061A.

Zangari, D. J. (1978). Learning projects of adult educators in Nebraska post-secondary institutions. (Doctoral dissertation, University of Nebraska, 1977). *Dissertation Abstracts International, 38,* 7086A.

Zhou, N. (1988, December). Adult education and national development: The Chinese experience. Paper presented at a Visiting Scholar Colloquium for the Kellogg Project, Syracuse University, Syracuse, NY.

Ziegler, W. L. (1970). *Essays on educational policy analysis.* Syracuse, NY: Educational Policy Research Center, Syracuse Research Corporation.

Ziegler, W. L. (1982). The quest for a fully human policy for the education of adults. In G. C. Whaples and W. M. Rivera (Eds.), *Policy issues and processes* (pp. 47–60). College Park, MD: University of Maryland, Department of Agricultural and Extension Education.

Ziegler, W. L., and Healy, G. M. (1979). Adult learning and the future of post-secondary education. In Marquis Academic Media, *Yearbook of adult and continuing education, 1979–80.* Chicago: Marquis Academic Media.

Index